Cherokee Messenger

SAMUEL AUSTIN WORCESTER

CHEROKEE MESSENGER

Althea Bass

UNIVERSITY OF OKLAHOMA PRESS : NORMAN, OKLAHOMA

TO J. H. R.

who holds no brief for piety, but
knows the proper measure of a man

AUTHOR'S PREFACE

for the Second Printing

MORE than three decades have passed since *Cherokee Messenger* first appeared in print. A much more extended knowledge of the history of the Cherokee Indians and of the State of Oklahoma, and a different material and cultural and spiritual environment will influence the readers of the new generation into whose hands this printing of the book may fall.

Extended transportation and communication, more highly mechanized processes of living and learning and entertainment, and a higher degree of material prosperity make the hardships and the economies and the diverse personal responsibilities of Samuel Worcester scarcely comprehensible to readers of today. And one of these mechanized processes, the microfilm, now makes the principal source of information for *Cherokee Messenger*, the records of the American Board of Commissioners for Foreign Missions, readily available to students of history in the library of Harvard University. But the passing of another generation has not lessened the value of Samuel Worcester's work among the Cherokees. Their full incorporation into the world in which they live, without loss of pride in their racial inheritance or of knowledge of the finest aspects of their culture, is living proof of his imperishable achievement.

A<small>LTHEA</small> B<small>ASS</small>

Norman, Oklahoma
March 8, 1968

Acknowledgments

MY greatest indebtedness for material in this book is to the American Board of Commissioners for Foreign Missions, through their librarian, Mr. Enoch F. Bell, for permission to read and copy what I chose from their valuable manuscript collection in the Andover-Harvard Library. I am likewise indebted to Dr. George B. Utley for the use of manuscripts in the Ayer Collection of the Newberry Library, and to Mrs. Mary Kathryn Armstrong, of the library of the University of Tulsa, for permission to see and copy some of the material in the Alice Robertson Collection. I have also had the use of the general library and of the Frank Phillips Collection at the University of Oklahoma, and of the library of the Oklahoma Historical Society. Mr. Elmer Adler, of the *Colophon*, has generously allowed the reprinting of an illustration from the *Colophon*, Part IX, and of material from my contributions to that quarterly.

For a more personal kind of assistance, I am indebted to the late Mrs. N. B. Moore, of Haskell, Oklahoma. She encouraged me in my undertaking, gave me her time in the narration of incidents regarding her grandfather's life and work, furnished me with an ambrotype of her grandfather, and lent me unpublished letters and manuscripts in her possession.

[7]

Several of my friends have helped me with problems of dates, footnotes, and genealogy; and all of them have endured me when the life of Samuel Worcester was my only interest and only subject of conversation.

A<small>LTHEA</small> B<small>ASS</small>

Norman, Oklahoma,
January 6, 1936.

Table of Contents

List of Illustrations

Cherokee Messenger

AUTHOR'S NOTE

Much the largest part of the quoted material in this book is from the manuscript collection owned by the American Board of Commissioners for Foreign Missions and now housed in the Andover-Harvard Library at Cambridge, Massachusetts. This material, consisting of letters to and from missionaries of the Board, journals of the various mission stations, financial accounts, and mission reports, has been temporarily assembled in large board bindings under a classification not uniform or final. Since it is not available to the general reader, and since the Board hope that funds will sometime be provided to permit a photostatic reproduction of the collection and a more systematic classification of its contents, I have thought it best not to give specific citations for quotations from this collection. It is understood, therefore, that quoted material not otherwise accounted for is from this collection; the sources of all other quoted material in the book are cited in footnotes.

Wedding Journey

BOSTON was still asleep behind closed shutters when they started on their journey. They had set the hour of dawn on Wednesday, the last of August in that year of 1825, for the time of their departure; and when two young New Englanders of the character of Samuel Austin Worcester and his wife Ann Orr Worcester appointed a time for an undertaking, there was small probability that they would fail to meet it. Now they turned their faces away from that glow in the east where the sun was soon to rise like a clear and beneficent promise of God's approval of their undertaking, and were soon on the Western Avenue turnpike, their horse trotting steadily along the road in the early morning coolness. Samuel held the lines taut, being too good a horseman to let a smooth road and a fresh beast tempt him to false progress. It was a long way to the country of the Cherokees; steady was the word for the journey. But all of the road would not be like this smooth turnpike; they must make time while they could.

For weeks they had been preparing for this journey. Whatever Ann's inclinations may have been, as a young woman bred to a certain definite standard of living, to multiply supplies of linens and blankets and silver for use in a land where such things could not be had, she was obliged to curb her desires in favor of economy of space.

[15]

Three large casks and a box, shipped by steamer from Boston, and the small amount of supplies that they might expect their horse to pull, in addition to their own weight, over roads that were to become nothing more than paths through the wilderness, were all the luggage the Worcesters might allow themselves. A feather bed, some fine woolen blankets, a small supply of linens and pewter, a minimum number of books that Samuel would need in his work as translator, a store of medicines, a wardrobe of plain shoes and wraps and other clothing chosen for service rather than for appearance—these were all the Worcesters might now call theirs. It was, indeed, a limited amount of possessions that they took with them from New England. Yet they took something larger than the bulk of these shipping casks, something compounded out of New England decorum and faith and intelligence into a way of life. That was to last, even after the feather bed and the blankets went down with an Arkansas River steamboat and the linens were worn past darning and the Worcesters themselves lay buried in the country of the Cherokees.

Samuel Worcester was yet a young man, only twenty-seven, but for years he had known that he would some day leave New England just as he was leaving it this morning to become a missionary to some nation of people that did not know his God. It was true that in the beginning he had expected his assignment to be India or Palestine or the Sandwich Islands—those destinations had a far-off and heroic sound to every ear—but he did not question the goodness of God or the wisdom of the American Board of Commissioners for Foreign Missions in sending him, instead, to the American aborigines. The vanity of human wishes had been obliterated from his personality. He had that sense of his own integrity that allowed him to submit with grace and by the very act of submission prove his superiority. With the same obedience to the authority of his church as that of a devout Roman Catholic, but by a different psychology, he was going where he was sent. His teacher of academy days, Jeremiah Evarts, now secretary of the American Board, had advised that he be assigned to the Cherokees. Their language had been rumored to be as difficult as that of the Chinese; learning it would be a task to tax even Samuel's special linguistic powers. Only a man who knew Greek and Latin and Hebrew could be expected to find the right words, in the strange, unwritten jargon of the Cherokees, for such important terms in Christian theology as *salvation* and *baptize*. Such a man, it is true, needed some additional equipment: a knowledge of printing, for books must be made for the Cherokees to read; mechanical and carpentering skill, for he might have to build his own house and his own church in the wilderness; an ability to care for himself and others under primitive circumstances, for he and his family and his horse might have uncharted journeys to make with storms and floods and lack of food to complicate their progress; an understanding of medicine and surgery, for doctors would seldom be available; some idea of how to plan a course of study for a mission school, how to keep financial accounts for an institution, how to sing and teach others to sing, how to judge and bargain for and slaughter and cure a beef for food, how in short to do everything himself that a community might need to have done. But Samuel had not spent his boyhood idly in the village of Peacham, Vermont. He had learned there all the skills that a missionary might need to know, from printing a book to curing a beef.

A boy in Vermont in those days learned all that would make him self-sufficient; there was something about the length and severity of a Vermont winter to foster self-sufficiency.

Before Samuel could remember, his father had taken the pastorate of the village church of Peacham. There, as the village parson, the Reverend Mr. Leonard Worcester had preached long sermons and ministered to his spiritual flock. He had been a printer, before he entered the ministry; from his own press he had issued an illustrated Bible. Under his father's eye Samuel had learned to cut wood and make hay and set type. At the Peacham Academy he had sat under the earnest teaching of Jeremiah Evarts, in the years before either of them had fallen under the great spell of the Foreign Missionary movement. But the influence of those young men who had met a few years earlier under the shelter of the haystack at Williams College to plan for the spread of the Gospel had been far-reaching; Peacham village and Boston city were alike under its sway. Young people came to desire education with a very earnest desire, for the salvation of the world was at hand, and the way of salvation and that of education seemed, however unexplainably, to lie in the same general direction. In the fall of 1815, then, Samuel walked seventy-one miles across the state of Vermont, stepping over the Green Mountains imperturbedly to the college at Burlington where his uncle the Reverend Doctor Samuel Austin was president. Young men took such responsibilities upon themselves, as a matter of course, in those days.

What they did not take as a matter of course was their religion. It is true that in the typical New England home children heard the Bible read daily; they were aware of an accepted theology and an accepted morality that were far-reaching and rigid; they went to church services regularly and automatically, because church-going was part of life's routine. But even the child of a minister's family did not grow in bodily and ghostly grace through the years of his childhood and so come to his confirmation in due time. He had rather to "experience religion." There was no other way to salvation for the followers of Calvin. In September, 1817, Samuel Worcester became a member of the College church, after having experienced religion during a college revival the year before. Today one suspects the power of suggestion as having something to do with Samuel's sudden awareness, after his conversion, of his call to God's ministry. The Worcester children grew up in the proud knowledge that seven generations of ministers of the Gospel had preceded them. But in his own mind and in the minds of his father the village preacher and of his uncle the president of the college at Burlington and of another uncle the great Trinitarian theologian of Salem, Dr. Samuel Worcester, the young Samuel was definitely and suddenly called. He had his vocation. The call meant Andover, for in the theological seminary there young men prepared themselves for examination and ordination. Now all this preliminary training was at an end. Samuel had been graduated from Andover Theological Seminary in 1823 and had worked, since then, in the offices of the American Board of Commissioners for Foreign Missions in Boston until he should be definitely assigned to a place in the foreign field.

In the summer just ending, things had happened rapidly. Samuel's field of foreign service, the Cherokee Nation of Indians, had been assigned to him; he had married the woman who was to go with him as assistant missionary (significant title implying no limitation of duties of wifehood, motherhood, teaching, supervision of a large mission family, nursing in the community, leadership in such minor matters of church life as fell to the women of a congregation); and he had been ordained as Missionary to the Heathen only six days before they set out to the Cherokee country where the "heathen" dwelt. His father had come from Peacham to preach the ordination sermon—a village parson so much in earnest on the occasion that he forgot to feel out of place in that Boston church among officials of the American Board, well-known theologians of the Congregational faith, professors from Andover, and a large congregation. It was a Worcester trait, indeed, not to feel out of place in any environment, to forget oneself altogether in the deep concern of the work in hand.

It had been a solemn, impressive occasion: "The services were performed in Park Street Church. The introductory prayer was made by Rev. Warren Fay, of Charlestown; the sermon was preached by Rev. Leonard Worcester, of Peacham, Vt. (the father of one of the missionaries); the ordaining prayer was offered by the Rev. Samuel Dana, of Marblehead; the charge, by Rev. Dr. Woods, of the Theological Seminary, Andover; the fellowship of the churches, by Rev. Horatio Bardwell, of Holden; and the concluding prayer, by Rev. Samuel Green, of Boston."[1] Relatives and friends and classmates of the two candidates had crowded the Park Street Church. These worshippers who studiously avoided all outward symbols of God in their church and its services had, that day, no need of any sign of His presence. God was there at the ordination of his servants.

Now, as their horse went steadily forward while the sun rose and the day advanced, Samuel and Ann Worces-

---

1 *Missionary Herald*, XXI (1825), p. 302.

ter were leaving such scenes behind. They were putting a long road between them and Boston, New England, the associations of friends and family and community that they had known all the years of their lives. But they were young; their faith in their calling was implicit; they had no fear of the strangeness that lay ahead of them. Ann Orr had been well reared in Bedford, New Hampshire; she had been a classmate of Mary Lyon and a pupil of "that excellent educator of women, Mr. Joseph Emerson, of Byfield."[2] She was, we are told, "a woman of common sense, vivacity, and wit"; certainly these were valuable characteristics to set out with, on the way to the wilderness. Perhaps this was why she was able, when her husband asserted that he had married "an indefinite article and a disjunctive conjunction," to understand that this was a philologist's way of saying that he loved her very dearly. Ann asked nothing more of life than to believe unquestioningly in God, and to love and be loved by Samuel Worcester and be by his side while they both lived. She scarcely knew in what order she put her desires; they were all one and not separable into their component parts. If she could have known what lay ahead of her in the land that she had never seen and was never afterward to leave except as she went farther into its wilderness, she could not have chosen discreetly to stay behind: childbearing and fever and suffering, candle-dipping and soap-making and knitting, cooking and washing and mending in an endless round—these things had no terror for her because they were what God and Samuel desired of her.

Outside Boston on the toll road Samuel made the first entry in his expense account: "Aug 31. Toll (Western

2 Nevada Couch, *Pages from Cherokee Indian History* (3d. ed., rev.; St. Louis: R. P. Studley & Co., [1884] p. 2.

Avenue from Boston), $0.06." He had a double steward-
ship, to God and to the American Board. They required
of him an account of every item of expense during his
journey. It was the hardest of all the duties expected of
him,—harder to make a simple account balance than to
translate the most difficult passage in the Bible into Cherokee. But it was never to occur to the Board, for the sake
of his progress in his beloved work of translating the
Scriptures, to relieve him of his burden of account-keep-
ing; neither did it ever occur to Samuel to ask for relief.
If God required accounts of him, he would render accounts.
This one, by great good fortune and effort, balanced to
the quarter-cent:

"The American Board of Commissioners for Foreign
Missions to S. A. Worcester,   Dr.
"Oct. 25, For money expended on my late journey from
Boston to Brainerd, viz.

"Aug. 31. Toll (Western Avenue from Boston) $0.06
"Sept.   1. Toll (Worcester turnpike), 18, Dinner,
              horse, greasing wheels, repairs, 91;   1.09
"   2. Supper & horse, (at Spencer)   .33
"   3. Horse 8, Toll (Cont. River) 10;   .18
"   6. Halter (purchased at Northampton)
              72¼, horse-shoeing, 37½;   1.09¾
"   7. Supper (at Southwick) and horse;   .72
"   8. Lodging & horse (at Granby) 50,
              Breakfast 37½, Supper 50, horse
              18¾, toll (turnpike) 6¼   1.61½
"   9. Lodging, horse, greasing wheels (in
              Torringford) 53, Breakfast (at Litch-
              field) 75, horse 22, toll (turnpike)
              31¼;   1.81¼

"Sept. 10. Supper, lodging, horse, wheels, (Dover, N. Y.) 62½, Breakfast 50; Supper 62½, horse 34, Toll, (Hudson River) 50; 2.59
" 12. Toll (turnpike) .11½
" 13. Dinner 50, horse 25, shoeing 6¼; .81¼
" 14. Dinner, biscuit, horse; .87½
" 15. Lodging & horse 46½, Breakfast and Supper 1.00, Toll (Delaware & Lehigh Rivers) 37½, Horse 30¾; 1.68¾
" 17. Lodging, horse, breakfast (at Revesburh), 1.12½, horse-shoeing 20, Gingerbread 12½, Supper 37½, horse 25; 2.07½
" 20. Toll (Susquehannah River & turnpike) 28¼, horse 18¾; .47
" 21. Horsekeeping 47½, Breakfast 50, toll (turnpike) 14½, horse 12½, meal 12½; 1.37½
" 22. Toll (Potomac River) 37½, Dinner 50, Horse 17¾, Hat 3.00;* 4.06¼
" 23. Lodging, horse, wheels, 75, Breakfast 50, Supper (at Winchester) 75, horse 25; 2.25
" 24. Lodging & horse 62½, Breakfast 50, Gingerbread 12½, horse 12½ 1.37½
" 26. Breakfast 50, horse 12½ .62½
" 27. Supper, lodging, horse, 1.12½, Breakfast 50, Supper 50, horse 41¼ 2.53¾
" 28. Lodging & horse 62½, Breakfast 50, horse 12½; 1.25

* "I lost my hat, which I valued at $2.00, purchased a new one, and charged the difference."

"Sept. 29. Supper, lodging, horsekeeping, Break-
        fast   2.12½

"   30. Supper, lodging, horse   1.00

Oct.   1. Supper, lodging, horse 1.00, Break-
        fast (Lexington) 50, horse 18¾   1.68¾

"   4. Supper, lodging, horse, 1.00, Break-
        fast & horse 50, toll (James River) 25 1.75

"   5. Supper, lodging, horse, wheels, 1.37½,
        Breakfast 50, horse 12½;   2.00

"   6. Supper, lodging, horse, 1.12½, Break-
        fast 50, horse 25, Toll, (turnpike, 37½,
        New River 37½) 75;   2.62½

"   7. Supper, lodging, horse, 1.12½, Break-
        fast 50, horse 25;   1.87½

"   8. Supper, lodging, horse, 1.12½, Break-
        fast & Supper 1.00, horse 25;   2.37½

"   11. Entertainment over Sabbath, 2.25,
        Breakfast 50, horse 25;   3.00

"   12. Supper, lodging, horse, 1.12½, Break-
        fast 50, Luncheon 12½; Toll, (North
        Fork of Holston R.) 50, horse 25;   2.50

"   13. Supper, lodging, horse, 1.00 Breakfast
        & Supper 1.00, horse 25;   2.25

"   14. Lodging and horse 50, Breakfast 50,
        luncheon 6¼, horse 25;   1.31¼

"   15. Supper, lodging, horse   .87½

"   17. Toll (Holston River)   .50

"   18. Toll (Little Tennessee River)   .25

"   19. Toll (Hiwassee River) 62½, Horse
        18¾   .81¼

Whole amount of expenses on the way,   59.60
For cash deposited in the hands of William Hol-
  land, Oct, 20, 1825, to be forwarded to the

Treasurer of the Board,	12.00
	————
	$71.60

Deduct — Cash received of the Treasur-
er Aug. 30, as by receipt— $50.00
Collection taken at Woodstock
Va. as before acknowledged—   10.60
Cash received of M. Houston,
Rockbridge Co, Va. as before
acknd.—   3.00 —63.60
                                      ————

                         Remains due   8.00"

There were other responsibilities besides the one of
keeping a strict account of expenses on the way to the
Cherokees. The Worcesters must make the cause of missions known along the way, and win patronage for it in
the communities through which they passed. Sometimes
meetings were arranged at which Samuel preached; sometimes collections were taken; sometimes, when plans had
been made, they must defer to representatives from some
other missionary organization. Always they must use a
nice discrimination, to gain a just hearing for their cause
and yet to avoid an appearance of begging, to waste no
time on the journey and yet never to travel between the
set of the sun on Saturday night and the dawn of Monday
morning, to avoid travel expenses and yet not to thrust
themselves too obviously upon brother clergymen along
the way. And they must also keep the American Board
informed, at intervals, of their progress, without incur-
ring the expense of postage too frequently. From Harrisburg, on the nineteenth of September, Samuel wrote his
first letter to Jeremiah Evarts.

"Very Dear Sir,

"You requested me to write from three places on my way; I did not make a memorandum, and am not certain what were the three, but believe Harrisburg was the first.

"Brother Anderson may or not have received a line from Northampton, in which I mentioned our intention to leave that place on Wednesday, the 7th inst. We did so, and arrived at Newburgh, N. Y. the next Saturday. Route by way of Litchfield, Conn. Distance from Northampton about 120 miles. We intended to spend Thursday night with Dr. Beecher at Litchfield, but were hindered by rain. When arrived in the morning at the village, we found that his house was half a mile out of our way, and did not call. At Newburgh we spent the Sabbath with the Rev. John Johnston (so he writes his name) by whom we were very cordially received, and recommended to other clergymen on the way.

"From Newburgh to Harrisburg the route is through Newton, N. Y. and Easton, Pa.—not through Wilkesbarre. We have made the distance about 194 miles. Perhaps we should have come more easily from Allentown (18 miles this side of Easton) through Reading to Harrisburg, instead of through Hamburgh, as we did, though the distance would have been eight miles greater, for we should doubtless have had much better road. Indeed I have no doubt that the road through Reading is to be preferred unless it be on account of the expense of 60 miles of turnpike, none of which we had on the Hamburgh route. Clergymen on whom we called were Rev. Mr. Arbuckle of Blooming Grove, 14 miles from Newburgh, with whom we dined on Monday,

Mr. Christie of the Dutch Church, at Warwick, 28 from Newburgh, with whom we spent Monday night, and Mr. Shafer of Newton, 28 from Warwick, with whom we spent Tuesday night. We are here with Rev. W. R. Witte, with whom we have spent the Sabbath, and are tarrying today. He is a true Gaius.

"My health is perfect, and Mrs. Worcester's nearly so. Our horse is likely to hold out very well, though I have driven too hard the last three days—106 miles—considering that the road on Friday was extremely rough, and on Saturday hilly.

"I have found no opportunity to do anything as an agent of the Board as yet. At Newburgh the Seceding Synod were in session, and Mr. Johnston had hired help for the Sabbath. In the evening was a sermon and collection for the Dom. Mis. So. of the Synod. Collections there are very frequent—Mr. Johnston said he should think 26 within a year, and he is glad to have it so. Reputed the most liberal town in the county. In this place I preached in the forenoon of yesterday. Mr. DeWitte thought it not best to give a missionary sermon. Something is done here for missions. Mr. Sessions obtained $60 a short time since for the U. F. M. S. Mr. Holmes is about to obtain what he can for the Chickasaw mission.

"The weather is very comfortable for travelling, and we think we are on our way at exactly the right time.

"Much love to yourself and Mr. Hill & families, Brother Anderson and all. Mrs. W. unites.

Very respectfully,

S. A. WORCESTER."

On October 21 the Worcesters reached Brainerd Mission, in East Tennessee, where they were to live temporarily while they learned the language of the Cherokees, made friends among the tribe, and became acquainted with their ways of living. Four days later Samuel sent in his account of the expenses of their journey to the treasurer of the Board. He had explained, in a more detailed letter to Mr. Evarts the day before, some incidents of their journey where dignity and economy had apparently conflicted and where, being New England gentlefolk, they had chosen in favor of dignity.

"I shall forward to Mr. Hill a precise account of our expenses. You will perceive that they fall short by a few cents only of your estimate, ($60.00). We might have made them considerably less by calling more on friends of missions. Perhaps we called less than we ought, but I cannot say that we think so. We thought it best not to call, where calling would much hinder our progress. Generally we did not think it best to call for a meal simply, unless we could call at meal time. We saw, or fancied we saw, some indications, that injury had been done by too much begging in that way, and therefore called less than we might otherwise have done. . . At Knoxville, after calling at Mr. Sherman's boarding house, and finding him absent, and declining an invitation to stay where it would not have been convenient for the family, and being mortified by some circumstances which wore the aspect of begging, we put up at the hotel. The next morning, however, we accepted an invitation from Mr. James Park, and on Monday morning my tavern bill was paid by Mr. Craighead. But enough of these things." Yet, favored by weather and circumstance, or by the hand of Providence,

Samuel and Ann Worcester had traveled from Boston to the Cherokee Nation in six weeks, at an expense to the Board of $59.60.

Brainerd, which had been founded in 1817, had grown into something like a pioneer New England settlement transplanted to the outskirts of the Cherokee Nation. Here were houses for the mission families, a church and a school, with a farm and a garden and a flourishing young orchard to provide food. The newcomers felt no sense of strangeness here; it was related to what they had known, and was what they had come to participate in and to help extend to the Cherokees. Indeed, when the American Board set out to carry salvation to the world, it had in mind the particular type of salvation that New England knew; and when missionaries went from the Missionary Rooms to the heathen, the salvation they took with them was inseparably bound up with that definite New England culture of which they were a product. And the Worcesters had a special kinship with this mission station to which they had come, for Samuel's uncle, Dr. Samuel Worcester of Salem, was buried in its churchyard. His monument of stone stood there, among humbler markers, to tell all passers-by that he had been one of the founders of the American Board and its first corresponding secretary, and that—on a visit to the Indian missions of the Board in 1821—he had died and been buried at Brainerd. A tie of blood relationship, as well as that of purpose, bound Samuel and Ann in advance to the place. Ann unpacked the boxes of clothing and books that they had brought with them, washed and mended the clothing which they had worn on the journey, and fell into the routine that occupied the missionary wives from dawn till night.

For the rest of their lives, neither of them was to know any other home than that of a mission family. Their wedding journey was ended; they had reached the household of faith that was their destination.

Heathen Tongues

"TO MAKE the whole tribe English in their language, civilized in their habits, and Christian in their religion," was the declared aim of the American Board for the Cherokees in its Annual Report for 1816. When the Board was founded in 1810 it had taken for its ambitious goal the evangelization of the whole world within a generation. That had not seemed too vast an undertaking, since all things were possible to God with the aid of the invincible men and women of New England. Since the men who comprised the Board did not yet know in any practical way the depths of African heathenism, the antiquity of non-Christian belief in India, the heat of religious conflict in Palestine, the complexity of interests involved in the problems of the American Indian, the undertaking seemed feasible.

But with the first of the missionaries actually in the field, it began to look as if God or his delegates might have to decide to allow a longer period of time for their evangelization project. The saving doctrines of Calvinistic theology had to be pushed temporarily into the background before the immediate problems of food, clothing, disease, commercial exploitation, and communication with the outside world. The missionaries found their flocks unprepared to learn the exact nature of the Trinity until they had learned to dig wells for a water supply, or counteract fever epidemics, or drive bargains with white traders. They were not even in command of a language in which they could be told plainly about the Trinity or free will or original sin. They had not yet learned that they were lost; how then could they know they must be saved?

That swift evangelization which the American Board, and a few other organizations of less extent and permanence, had undertaken changed from a vague and lofty ideal into a practical and complicated problem. Salvation, for the Africans or the American aborigines or the Sandwich Islanders, began to take on a decidedly New England tinge. Human saviors had to bring their own particular variety of salvation, for that was all they could command; they brought it now in terms of the English language, the household and farm management that had been developed in Massachusetts or Connecticut or Vermont, the theology of the Calvinistic churches. What had been a conception aimed at universality had descended to the local and the particular. The spread of the Gospel had resolved itself from a flourish of spiritual trumpets into a slower and more tangible thing—a way of living according to New England standards. Farming and clearing roads and organizing local governments and cooking and weaving and candle-dipping seemed to be essential elements in it, along with such other considerations as the right form of baptism and the doctrine of election.

Yet even in presenting the local and the particular there was a barrier—that of language. In the beginning it had been supposed that non-Christian nations, given the opportunity to learn English, would embrace it promptly; it would be used in the schools and in the church services and in the dealings between missionaries and natives. But no intellectual curiosity drove the heathen; they were content with whatever tongues they knew before the missionaries came. Only a few of the most advanced natives promised any aptness in the acquisition of English. It was decided, perforce, that native languages must be used; the Bible and hymns and texts on geography and arithmetic must be translated; sermons must be preached in the native tongues; by this means, eventually, natives would be brought to learn English. "The conviction was increasing," the Board concluded in 1825,[1] "that the native languages must receive attention. Preaching through an interpreter was found to answer the purposes of preaching but imperfectly, even if good interpreters could be had, which was seldom possible. Mr. Byington maintained that to teach the Choctaw children to read English, the easiest and quickest way was, to teach them to read their own language first." Men must be found, then, who were prepared to deal with linguistic problems among the pagans. Most of all this was important for the American aborigines. Cyrus Byington and Alfred Wright had gone out to the Choctaws and had sent back their conclusion that they must learn Choctaw and translate into it; the Cherokees, most advanced of all the Indian tribes in their adoption of the white man's culture, must be provided now with a capable linguist. Samuel Worcester had been sent.

He was not slow in setting about his efforts to learn Cherokee. Three days after he reached Brainerd he wrote, "I have been attending to Guyst's alphabet, with an hour's assistance from Mr. Reece. It seems to be the united

1 Joseph Tracy, *A History of the American Board of Commissioners for Foreign Missions* (Worcester: Spooner and Howland, 1840), p. 147.

opinion of all who have formed an opinion, that his mode of writing the language must prevail, though alterations may be made. The number of natives who have already learned it is very great." This hour of work with Charles Reece, the Cherokee half-breed who did whatever he undertook with deep seriousness, whether it was fighting the Battle of the Horseshoe or interpreting for white missionaries, was the beginning of Samuel Worcester's life work. At his death, the Cherokees among whom he had worked for nearly thirty-four years were to say of him, "To his work they owe their Bible and their hymn book." But now he was at the foot of that mountain of achievement that he was to climb step by step—syllable by syllable—to its height.

"Guyst's alphabet" had been one of the stumbling blocks in the ideal course of evangelization planned by the American Board. Its members had conceived a simplification of the whole scheme, a short cut, as it were, to world evangelization. It was not to be too short, for salvation meant a remaking of the whole man, but it was to do away with the complications that a variety of languages and dialects added to the missonaries' efforts. They would have a system of orthography that would be uniform for all the Indians and, if possible, for other peoples as well; if it could be extended as they hoped it might, any tongue could be represented through its symbols. It would be tried in the beginning only with the American Indian languages. John Pickering of Boston was set to work on an orthographic scheme, starting with the Cherokee language. David Brown, a young Cherokee who had recently been a student at Andover, had worked with Pickering before returning to the Indian country; they had constructed an alphabet and had begun the compilation of a grammar. The Prudential Committee of the American Board had appropriated $500 toward the publication of the Cherokee grammar when word reached Boston that the Cherokees had a system of writing of their own that was transforming the whole nation. They had burst into literacy, while the Board was perfecting a scheme to make them literate.

"Among the Cherokees," thus the History of the American Board relates its account of this literary outburst,[2] "the question of a native literature was taken out of the control of the mission, by one of the most remarkable events in the history of mind; the invention of an alphabet, by George Guess, an uneducated native. Hearing some of his young countrymen speak of the superiority of the whites, and especially of the 'talking leaf,' on which they could put down a 'talk' and 'it would stay there,' the thought struck him that he could do the same. He took up a flat stone, and attempted to write a sentence, by making a mark for every word; but his companions only laughed, and he was silent. From this time, he continued to meditate on this subject. He made a mark for each word that he could recollect, till the number amounted to several thousands. His memory was overburdened with them, and he became convinced that there must be a better way. He began to consider how words could be divided into parts, and soon found that the same character would answer for a part of many words. Every syllable in the Cherokee language is either a simple vowel sound, or a vowel preceded by a consonant. The vowel sounds are six; the consonants, simple and compound, twelve; therefore, the syllables resulting from their combination, seventy-two; by certain modifications of a few of these sylla-

2 Tracy, *op. cit.*, pp. 147-8.

bles, seven others are formed; so that the whole number is eighty-five. For each of these, a character was invented. His next labor was, to adapt his alphabet to the pen, by devising characters easily made. In this, he derived some assistance from an English spelling book; though he knew not the name of a single letter in it. With such an alphabet, the Cherokee learns to read more easily than any other people. He has only to learn the names of eighty-five characters; for reading is only naming them, one after another as they stand on the paper to be read; just as, by naming the letters F I K C, the word efficacy is pronounced. To learn these characters, two or three days were usually found sufficient.

"When Guess first announced his discovery, his countrymen were incredulous; but repeated and careful experiments soon convinced them of its reliability. Many came to him to be instructed; one who had learned, taught another; the art spread rapidly through the nation, and in the course of a very few years, a majority of adult Cherokees had learned to read their own language; and, though elegant penmen are scarce everywhere, yet every one who can read can, by taking pains enough, write so that others can read his writing.

"Christian Cherokees, when they heard passages of Scripture repeated in their own language, would often put them on paper. The interpreters, especially John Arch, had furnished copies of important passages of the New Testament, which had been copied hundreds of times. A translation of the whole was demanded. The committee had long been contemplating such a work. . . . . Mr. Pickering, aided by David Brown, had constructed an alphabet, and proposed to publish a grammar, towards the expense of which the Committee had appropriated

GEORGE GUESS (Sequoyah)

Inventor of the Cherokee Syllabary

$500. But what Guess had done threw all these labors out of consideration at once. The Cherokees would hear of nothing but their own alphabet for their own language. David Brown, their best scholar, must translate the New Testament; and as, owing to his long residence at the north, his knowledge of the Cherokee was imperfect, several of their most skilful orators must assist him. Hicks insisted that he must translate from the Greek, which he had learned at Andover. Whether David, though a very sensible young man, was able to translate much better from the Greek than from the English may be doubted; but the work must go on; and on the 27th of September, 1825, the translation of the New Testament, from the original Greek, into the Cherokee language, by a Cherokee, in an alphabet invented by another Cherokee, was completed. As there were yet no types in existence for printing that language, Brown's version, entire or in parts, was circulated in manuscript."

Such was the state of affairs among the Cherokees when Samuel Worcester arrived. In fact, it was due in part to this state of affairs that he had been sent, for this matter of the Cherokee language needed an expert. There was sure to be bungling in the translation of the Scriptures; there had been, in fact, in the translation of the Gospel of Matthew. John Arch and David Brown were new in the faith and new to those matters of scholarship involved in biblical translation. John Arch, whose Indian name was Asti, had finished his translation of the Gospel of John in the fall of 1824; hundreds of copies of it had been made; it had been widely and wonderingly read by Cherokees who were eager to learn all that the white men knew. In September, 1825, while the Worcesters were on their way to the Cherokee Nation, David Brown had finished his translation of the New Testament, hurried and full of imperfections, and had circulated it among his people at the instigation of Charles R. Hicks, a Moravian convert who was the most influential man in the nation and was later to be elected principal chief. But these men, Brown and Arch and Hicks, represented the most advanced members of the tribe; there was always danger of apostasy because of the strength of the reactionary leaders. Nûñ′nâ-tsune′ga, or White Path, a fullblood of great influence living at Turniptown, in Georgia, cast his dark shadow of opposition over the progressive Christian section, And Yâ′nû-gûñ′ski, one of the chiefs of the eastern Cherokees, had refused to allow the new Gospel of Matthew to be circulated among his people. He was the greatest Cherokee orator of his day; when he stood before his people, very powerful and dark and strangely wise, counseling them to hold to the Indian faith even when they made terms of peace with the white man, he was profoundly convincing. Later, in 1828, when a printed copy of the Gospel of Matthew was brought to him from New Echota, he was only partially won over.[3] He found that it was a very good book, but he did not believe it had been effective. "Strange," he said, "that the white people are not better, after having had it so long." He and White Path and other leaders still advocated the old ceremonies of the green corn dance and of the warpath and the hunt and the ballplay. He believed in the Immortals, and in the Little People; he knew priests and orators who had seen them. There was need of a man like Samuel Worcester to counteract the subtle forces of Satan working through these powerful tribal leaders.

Although the mission at Brainerd had been in existence

3 Bureau of American Ethnology, *Nineteenth Annual Report*, 1897-8, Pt. I, p. 163.

only eight years when the Worcesters joined it, its influences were already far-reaching. John Arch, who now helped as an interpreter and translator, had been one of the early pupils of the mission school. He had written in a beautiful hand—the Cherokee children excelled in singing and handwriting—the copy set before him at school: "Precious in the sight of the Lord is the death of his saints." "Precious to the hearts of many is memory of this amiable and excellent woman." "Assist the needy." But he had gone well beyond his copy book days. He had finished the school at Brainerd with credit, and had been appointed to teach Cherokees in a school opened by the Mission at Creek Path, working very seriously and faithfully. But the white man's ways of living had been disastrous for him; he had fallen into a decline and had made a good Christian end, at the age of twenty-eight, in June of that summer when Samuel Worcester was appointed missionary to the Cherokees.

Elias Boudinot, who was to become Worcester's chief translator and the editor of the Cherokee press, had had more of the white man's educational advantages than had John Arch. He had been educated in the Foreign Mission School at Cornwall, Connecticut, a school which the American Board, in carrying out its dream of uniformity in world evangelization, had founded in 1817 for the education of young men of all the heathen nations. As Galagi'na (the Buck) he had gone there, had learned avidly, and had been given the privilege of taking the name of his patron, the president of the American Bible Society, Dr. Elias Boudinot. He had taken more than that, however. To the consternation of the citizens of the locality, he had taken Harriet Gold, a young woman of excellent birth and rearing, as his wife, and she had gone back with him to his people to live and die and be buried among the Cherokees. That was a development in foreign missions that had scarcely been anticipated. At any rate, Elias Boudinot was one of the leaders of his people for many years, and was Worcester's principal help in the meticulous work of translation.

Perhaps the most brilliant of all the young Cherokees was David Brown. He and his sister Catherine, the children of half-breeds of unusual advancement in white ways of living, had come to the school at Brainerd several years earlier and had been students of great aptitude. David had gone from Brainerd to Cornwall and to Andover Theological Seminary, where he had learned Greek and had worked with Mr. Pickering of Boston on the proposed Cherokee alphabet. While he was at Andover he had received a gift from Switzerland, and had carefully composed an acknowledgment to the donor:

"THEOLOGICAL SEMINARY, ANDOVER, May 1th 1823

To the Hon. the Baron

D. Campaigne

MY DEAR SIR,

"In compliance with the request of my esteemed friend Jeremiah Evarts Esq. with pleasure I now take up my pen to write. Altho' your face I never saw, nor heard your voice, neither do I expect to see you in this world, I feel animated in the hope that I shall ere long meet you in the kingdom of Heaven. There we shall mingle our devotions 'To Him that sitteth upon the throne, & to the Lamb for ever & ever.' Whether we are Swiss, Cherokee, Hottentot, Jew or Pawnee, whether we have sprung from the bases of the Alps or from the wilderness of America, there we shall be one in spirit & 'Christ will be all in all.'

"From my boyhood until lately, I have been taught the religion of my fathers, viz. to reverence the great and supreme Being, love my friends deeply & to take vengeance on my enemies. It is customary with the Indians to spill the last drop of blood in conflict with an inveterate enemy. And on the other hand they will die for a friend; their affection for him being so strong. In their devotion there is nothing like pure religion. Tho' they have faint idea of Deity, yet they are far from loving him with all the heart.

"Christian missionaries of America have already done much, in diffusing light and life among my countrymen. Schools, Churches, & other civil & religious institutions are formed in the Cherokee & Choctaw nations. Missionaries have also gone to various nations of the country & some are erecting the standard of the cross beyond the Mississippi. I flatter myself with the hope, that the period is not far off, when every aboriginal inhabitant of North America shall have the glad tidings of salvation. It makes me glad to reflect that the children of God in Switzerland are praying for us in America. Oh! may their hopes be realized at the day of judgment. I hold out my hand of friendship & Christian love to the benevolent in Europe & thank them for their kind remembrance of us. Oh! could my voice reach the mountains of Switzerland, I would make the Macedonian cry, 'Come over & help us!' I am now studying preparatory to the Gospel ministry. In a year I fondly hope to return to my native land & to unfold to my countrymen the unsearchable riches of Christ. May I 'go in the fulness of the gospel of peace.' Oh! how lovely is the

Christian religion! It fills my soul with delight. Compared with the religion of Christ, how infinite low does every other fall. I anticipate the pleasure of preaching in my own language, as well as in the English. I retain the language of my nation perfectly. I have a strong desire to learn the french dialect, had I books & time; but perhaps I shall not have the pleasure of speaking the language.

"I have lately returned from Washington city, the capitol of the United States. I went on purpose to see some of the Cherokees who had come as delegates from their nation. One of them is my brother. They were all pleased to see me & expressed desire to have me return to their nation as soon as practicable, & preach the Gospel to them. So you see, dear sir, if my life is preserved, I may be the means of good to many who are now roaming in the regions of gloom & death. Please to accept of my thanks for the present you sent me. I shall preserve it many years & cherish a fond remembrance of my venerable friend in Switzerland. I pray that peace & mercy from God the father & the Lord Jesus Christ, may ever attend you.

With high esteem
Hon. & dear Sir
Your Cherokee friend
DAVID BROWN

The Baron de Campagne
[P sessicon]?
   Near Zurich
   Switzerland"

Now David had returned to his people, and was making use there of the language of his nation that he retained perfectly and of his knowledge of English. At Creek Path, Worcester heard him translate the address which an aged chieftain delivered to the children of the mission school there. Even in translation, the oration retained some of the chieftain's dignity and power: "Dear children,—I often speak to you, and encourage you to continue in the pursuit of useful knowledge; such knowledge as will be for your own good, and that of our country. You are engaged in a good thing. I am always pleased to see the progress you are making in learning. I feel that much depends on you. On you depends the future welfare of your country.

"When I was young there were no schools among us. No one to teach us such learning as you are now obtaining. My lot was quite different from yours. You have here many advantages. Improve them. Pursue the paths of virtue and knowledge. Some of your fathers who first agreed for the teachers to come among us are now no more. They are gone.

"It is now some years since a school was established in Creek Path, your native place. I myself aided to build the first school house. At first the children did not learn very fast. But now since the establishment of a school at this place they are doing much better. I have reason to believe you are learning as fast as might be expected. Some of you have been in school five years and some not so long. You have now acquired considerable knowledge. By and by you will have more. This gives me great satisfaction. Remember that the whites are near us. With them we have constant intercourse; and you must be sensible, that unless you can speak their language, read and write as they do, they will be able to cheat you and trample on your rights. Be diligent therefore in your studies, and let

[43]

nothing hinder you from them. Do not quarrel with each other. Aid one another in your useful employ; obey your teachers and walk in the way they tell you."[4]

There was great wisdom in this speech, enough to make amends for what it lacked in tact. Samuel Worcester knew how to value it for its honesty; he was learning how to judge the mission schools by the standard of what they gave the Indian, rather than by any less necessary standard of achievement. Here is his report of the school at Brainerd, following the annual examination in 1827. Though he had not come to teach, he knew the pupils in each class by name and the exact capacity of each boy or girl for the tasks expected of each. "The annual examination of the school at this station is now past, and the task has been urged upon me of giving you some account of their appearance.

"The examination was on June 25th. The assembly convened on the occasion was by no means so great as last year; owing chiefly, I suppose, to the fact, that people had been hindered in their farming by rainy weather until they were very much pressed with business, and to the appointment of a national council on the same day.

"Of the examination I will only say that I think it did not fall below that of last year. But I suppose I can give you a better view of the state of the schools by giving an account of a visit which I made to each a few days previously, when I took memoranda of what was done.

"The girls' school I visited June 19th.

"Nancy Taylor, Nancy Reece, Betsey Taylor, Rachel Murphy, Margaret McDonald, and Eleanor North constituted the *first class*. They read a lesson in Genesis, given out the preceding evening; of thirty-nine questions

4 *Missionary Herald*, XXIII (1827), 381.

on the substance of what they had been reading, all except two were rightly answered.

"Lucy McPherson, Sally Reece, Ann Bush, and Lucy Campbell were the *second class.* They read in Acts XXII, and answered twenty-six questions relating to what they had been reading, with six erroneous answers. These two classes spelt in one. Their lesson consisted of nineteen words from Webster's table of similar words, with their definitions, (Ail, to be troubled,)—errors in spelling or definition, seven.

"Nancy Reese and Nancy Taylor recited from Woodbridge's Geography a lesson which they were preparing for examination. The number of questions was sixty-two, many of which were very comprehensive: for example—the answers to four questions comprise the exact boundaries of the several United States. In answering these sixty-two questions, I noticed no error except in the southern boundary of a single state.

"Eleanor North, Sally Reece, Lucy McPherson, Margaret McDonald, Ann Bush, and Lucy Campbell recited a lesson, which they were preparing for examination, consisting of sixty-four questions from Cummings' *First Lessons in Geography*, in which two mistakes were made. Then eighty-four questions were given, taken promiscuously from different parts of the book, in answering which six mistakes were made.

"The third class were Polly Wilson, Susan Taylor, Elizabeth Shepard, Electa Vail, Christiana McPherson, and Anna McCollister. They read in the New Testament. Of twenty-five questions relating to what they had read, two were answered incorrectly by one girl, and three by another; the rest were correctly answered. They spelt from Webster's *Spelling Book*, Table 12 (difficult monosyl-

[45]

lables,) thirty-six words; of which two were misspelt; recited in punctuation and abbreviations; errors eleven.

"*Fourth class.* Maria [Tsi-na-su,] Catherine Bigbear [Betsey,] and U-ta-yi [Lydia Huntley.] They read (some of them with hesitancy,) in a little book entitled the *Raven and the Dove*, spelt in Webster's Table 21 (achievement, &c,) eleven words; all correct.

"All these classes were in school when you visited it, except Betsey Taylor, who formerly attended at Spring Place. Where names have been altered I have given in brackets those by which they were then known.

"*Fifth class.* Nancy Cherokee, Ku-ta-yi, who entered school Oct. 25, and Jane, Oct. 4, 1826, read and spelt two lessons of twelve words each, in Webster's Table 12, monosyllables. Two misspelt in the first lesson, in the second none.

"Catherine Reece entered Nov. 15, 1826, read and spelt in Table 12, (difficult monosyllables,) ten words, all correct. These with writing and composition, were all the studies to which they were then attending in school. Nancy Taylor has made some progress in arithmetic.

"The next day I visited the boys' school. *First class*, consisting of Thomas Witherspoon, Samuel Worcester, George McPherson, William Brewer, and Lewis C. Strait, read from one of Marshall's *Reading Lessons*, and recited in Cumming's *First Lessons in Geography*. One hundred and sixty-two questions were chosen promiscuously throughout the book, of which three only were incorrectly answered.

"*Second class*, David Spears, William Reece, David Reece, Edward Hopful, John Emerson, and Vinson Gould, read in the book entitled the *Raven and the Dove*; answered questions on the substance of what was read; correctly, seven; not correctly, twenty-one; spelt and defined from Marshall's Table of Definitions (words accented and explained) fifteen words, no error; recited Webster's Table of Abbreviations without error.

"*Third Class*, consisting of Richard Smoker, Wells Gridley, James B. Milson, Josiah Meigs, Moses Hoge, read in a little book entitled the *May Bee*, answered six questions; unable to answer eight; spelt from Marshall's Spelling Book, Table 32, (previous, special, &c.) sixteen words; answered without error a series of questions learned from Webster's *Spelling Book*, relating to the number and names of the months, days of the week, seasons, &c; also tables of money, measures, &c.; and recited Webster's Table of Abbreviations without error.

"*Fourth class*, consisting of John Knox Witherspoon, Adam Empie, Ti-saw-hwi-ski, and U-law-gaw-ti, read in the New Testament, spelt eleven words from Marshall's Table 9, (luminary, &c.) recited from Webster's *Spelling Book* the same questions as the third class, all correctly. In reciting the Table of Abbreviations, six mistakes were made by all but one individual.

"*Fifth class*, Henry Dobson, Reece, Martin, John Langley, and Taw-tsu-waw, the first of whom entered the school in November, 1826, and the other three in October preceding, read pretty well in the New Testament and spelt from Marshall's Table 17, (diaphragm, &c.) twelve words.

"*Sixth class*, consisting of Andrew McPherson, and Charles Gillaspie, both having entered the school in Dec. 1826, read in the New Testament with tolerable fluency, and spelt six words from Table sixth, (Crucifix, &c.)

"*Seventh class*, consisting of Wai-lu-ki-la and Kla-ne-na, both having entered Jan. 1827, read with hesitancy in the New Testament and spelt four words from Table sixth.

[47]

All these were the ordinary lessons of the boys. In spelling, no mistake was made by any scholar. No word was put out (to use the old school expression for pronouncing words for the scholar to spell,) except to the seventh class; but each scholar spelt in rotation from memory.

"Perhaps I ought to state, in regard to the answering of questions on the passages which were read by the second and third class, that they have not been exercised in that way for some time past, and the questions were proposed in this instance at my request.

"The first class have attained a partial acquaintance with the ground rules of Arithmetic, and the first and second have attended to writing, and made some essays at composition. But these things may be stated by the teachers. The object with which I set out, was to show how the schools appeared when I last visited them."[5]

It is obvious, from this thorough account, that Samuel Worcester was in no doubt as to what was required of missionaries. They must preach and teach and translate without relaxation or compromise. There was something like an absolute standard in Samuel's mind, and he found no facile excuse to deviate from it; he expected a mastery of difficult monosyllables, of tables of weights and measures, and of New Testament literature of the children of Cherokees and missionaries alike.

And the Cherokee children responded almost as readily as the white children with whom they went to school. They excelled in singing and penmanship and oratory, and were sometimes a trifle cloudy in their mental grasp of theological points that must have seemed somewhat unnecessary to them. Still, God must have taken a divine pride in the performance of certain Cherokee boys at Creek Path,

5 *Missionary Herald*, XXIII, (1827), 275-7.

CHEROKEE ALPHABET.

CHARACTERS AS ARRANGED BY THE INVENTOR.

Ꭱ Ꭰ Ꮃ Ꮵ Ꮐ Ꮽ Ꮺ Ꮅ Ꮑ Ꮌ Ꭹ Ᏹ Ꮟ Ꮲ Ꭳ Ꮇ Ꮄ Ꭽ Ꮼ

Ꮰ Ꮤ Ᏼ Ꮈ Ꭿ Ꮝ Ᏺ Ꮁ Ꭺ Ꮷ Ꮍ Ꮞ Ꮠ Ꮆ Ꮘ Ꮗ Ꮜ Ꮖ Ꮓ Ꭷ

Ꮸ Ꮢ Ꮒ Ꭶ Ꮩ Ꭸ Ꮦ Ꭼ Ꮻ Ꭲ Ꭴ Ꮥ Ꮂ Ꮫ Ꭻ Ꮶ Ꮙ Ꮔ Ꮎ Ꮳ

Ᏻ Ꮴ Ꮧ Ꮾ Ꮪ Ᏸ Ꮯ Ꭵ Ꮕ Ꮣ Ꮉ Ꮡ Ꮱ Ꭾ Ꮀ Ꮋ Ꮭ Ꮿ Ꮹ Ꮨ

Ꮮ Ꮏ Ꮚ Ꮬ Ꮊ Ꮛ

CHARACTERS SYSTEMATICALLY ARRANGED WITH THE SOUNDS.

Ꭰ a	Ꭱ e	Ꭲ i	Ꭳ o	Ꭴ u	Ꭵ v
Ꭶ ga Ꭷ ka	Ꭸ ge	Ꭹ gi	Ꭺ go	Ꭻ gu	Ꭼ gv
Ꭽ ha	Ꭾ he	Ꭿ hi	Ꮀ ho	Ꮁ hu	Ꮂ hv
Ꮃ la	Ꮄ le	Ꮅ li	Ꮆ lo	Ꮇ lu	Ꮈ lv
Ꮉ ma	Ꮊ me	Ꮋ mi	Ꮌ mo	Ꮍ mu	
Ꮎ na Ꮏ hna Ꮐ nah	Ꮑ ne	Ꮒ ni	Ꮓ no	Ꮔ nu	Ꮕ nv
Ꮖ qua	Ꮗ que	Ꮘ qui	Ꮙ quo	Ꮚ quu	Ꮛ quv
Ꮝ s Ꮜ sa	Ꮞ se	Ꮟ si	Ꮠ so	Ꮡ su	Ꮢ sv
Ꮣ da Ꮤ ta	Ꮥ de Ꮦ te	Ꮧ di Ꮨ tih	Ꮩ do	Ꮪ du	Ꮫ dv
Ꮬ dla Ꮭ tla	Ꮮ tle	Ꮯ tli	Ꮰ tlo	Ꮱ tlu	Ꮲ tlv
Ꮳ tsa	Ꮴ tse	Ꮵ tsi	Ꮶ tso	Ꮷ tsu	Ꮸ tsv
Ꮹ wa	Ꮺ we	Ꮻ wi	Ꮼ wo	Ꮽ wu	Ꮾ wv
Ꮿ ya	Ᏸ ye	Ᏹ yi	Ᏺ yo	Ᏻ yu	Ᏼ yv

SOUNDS REPRESENTED BY VOWELS.

a as *a* in *father*, or short as *a* in *rival*,
e as *a* in *hate*, or short as *e* in *met*,
i as *i* in *pique*, or short as *i* in *pit*,
o as *aw* in *law*, or short as *o* in *not*,
u as *oo* in *fool*, or short as *u* in *pull*,
v as *u* in *but* nasalized.

CONSONANT SOUNDS.

g nearly as in English, but approaching to k. d nearly as in English, but approaching to t. h, k, l, m, n, q, s, t, w, y, as in English.

Syllables beginning with g, except Ꭶ, have sometimes the power of k; Ꭺ, Ꮪ, Ꮫ, are sometimes sounded to, tu, tv; and syllables written with tl, except Ꮭ, sometimes vary to dl.

FROM THE COLOPHON

THE CHEROKEE ALPHABET

when they were given a public examination: "Several single speeches, and a very interesting dialogue, founded on the story of Joseph and his brethren, were spoken uncommonly well. This was indeed novel and unexpected; and though the children had never witnessed any thing of the kind in their lives, yet I am confident I do not exaggerate, when I say that the performance was excellent. The speech of Brutus on the death of Caesar, and that of Mark Anthony on the same occasion, were spoken by two of the boys with great animation. I was much interested in another spoken by a full blooded boy. It was taken from the *Columbian Orator*, attributed to an Indian, and begins with these words—'Fathers, when you crossed the great waters.'—this piece, as you may suppose, appeared quite in keeping with the little Cherokee orator, who delivered it with great propriety."[6]

If there was something slightly inappropriate in these subjects of Cherokee oratory, there was in them, nevertheless, the satisfying element of dignity. That was a thing the Indians could accept at full value, while they gave the Christian God the benefit of the doubt. About God's representative, Samuel Worcester, they need have no doubt; he walked among them, as the Cherokee boy had said during the public examination, of Brutus, like an honorable man. One of them had paid him the compliment, on sending a son to school to the mission teachers, of naming the boy Samuel Worcester. Now, in turn, they must give him a name in their own tongue. What would it be? It must be a name that had a full meaning, that expressed in their language what they saw in the man. "He is very white," an old woman remarked. "Let us name him for the young corn, before it is ripe and

6 *Missionary Herald*, XXIII, (1827), 379.

brown." To this there was objection; they must find a name to tell what the man was, not what he looked like. Charles Reece found the word that suited them all. "He is wise; he has something to say. Let us call him A-tse-nu-sti, the messenger."

Now the Indians change a man's name, if any event justifies a change. But they never gave Samuel Worcester any other name in Cherokee. He continued to be their messenger for the rest of his life. He thought he brought them a complicated message about a God whom the Cherokees must worship instead of their own vague deities; but they simplified his message, and suited it to their own needs. A man's life, they learned from A-tse-nu-sti, may have unity and direction. It needs few words in any tongue to say this, but it needs long years of full living to make the message plain.

Home at Brainerd Mission

THE WOMAN who was Mrs. Worcester had left the girl who was once Ann Orr of Bedford far behind. Under favorable circumstances, Boston was a six weeks' journey from Brainerd Mission; under conditions when the workings of the hand of Providence were undoubted but inscrutable, the distance might lengthen into months of time. A person who traveled out to the wilderness might, though usually at great risk, make his own speed; mail came more slowly and with less certainty; freight sometimes never arrived, though it had a reasonable chance with allowances for low water in the Savannah and accidents in hauling overland from Augusta. Three days before their first Christmas, the Worcesters still had had no letters and no freight from New England. "We suspect," Samuel wrote to the Board, "some failures in the mails. Mrs. Worcester & I have not received one syllable from New England, since we left it, except a letter from my father received at Knoxville, on our way. Nothing has reached this station from the Secretary's department at the Missionary Rooms since our arrival. From the treasurer's office, only Mr. Hill's letter of October 25, containing an invoice of articles, two casks, forwarded by the Brig Helen for this mission. Whether the cask and box which I left at the Rooms have been sent, or whether the two casks which I left at Bedford have been received at the Rooms, and forwarded thence, we are entirely ignorant. We do not yet learn whether anything has arrived at Augusta."

Ann Worcester was learning a degree of patience that Ann Orr had never had to exercise. Still she never doubted that the casks and the box would sometime arrive; Samuel could rope a box and nail a cask as thoroughly as he could work out the logical intricacies of a sermon. Eventually they did arrive, and Ann unpacked and found places for the blankets and feather beds and linens that any good housewife, even the wife of a missionary, considered necessary.

Homesickness would have been natural in that new country that was farther from New England than such a matter as a six weeks' journey would indicate. To have only Indians as neighbors, to see such newspapers as the Boston *Recorder* and the New York *Observer* only rarely and after the news in them was many weeks old, to sit in church with people named Laughing Mush and Big Bear and Long Hair, to be housed among a group of missionaries and teachers instead of in the home of the Honorable John Orr, and in turn to give housing, almost nightly, to any traveler who might ask for it, all this strangeness would have been more than a woman of weaker character could accept. But her husband and her God had both come with Ann to this new land. She had nothing more to ask. For the rest, she made the most of whatever comforts and interests offered themselves, and through the work of her hands and the strength of her heart helped her fellow-workers to build and maintain a New England in the wilderness.

Ann soon learned that commodities which she had

always taken for granted, even in a thrifty New England household, were luxuries here. One drank coffee sparingly, remembering how long it was in reaching the mission station and how unnecessary it might be considered by critical donors to the missionary cause. One of the missionaries to the Cherokees, at Carmel, had thought well to justify his request to the Board for fifty pounds of coffee in an annual list of supplies thus: "You may consider perhaps, the item of coffee large for this station. But we have found by experience that it is quite a saving even in a pecuniary point of view to have coffee at least once a day—for with coffee we always make quite a satisfactory meal although the remainder of what constitutes our meals be coarse & unsavory. We find that a cup of coffee in the morning also greatly revives us and strengthens us for the labors of the day. Another consideration which is not of small moment is that with coffee in the morning all appear satisfied; without it then, to say the least, there would be much unprofitable talk & unholy feelings." But gradually, under these circumstances, the taste for such luxuries wore away. Years later, though Samuel Worcester had long since given up tea and coffee, he was still sending for it, for guests of the mission still expected what the missionaries had gradually learned to do without. In a postscript to a list of necessities for his station in 1841, he added, "Also in my list write 4 lb green tea instead of 2 lb, and strike out the item calomel, and add 1 Mason's Choir.

"We should use but little tea & coffee, but for company. I have not used them for a dozen years or more, my children never. Miss Avery uses none, nor, at present, Miss Thompson. The demands upon our hospitality are exceedingly great, and occasion a very large portion of our

[53]

expenses. We should gladly curtail, but do not see how.....

"An extra session of the Cherokee Council has brought together many who seek a shelter at night; and we, at five miles distance, have had from eight to 15 persons, with their horses, to entertain every night for some time past. One night our number of guests was 19."

Soap, of the kind that came in bars and was bought in stores, was likewise a luxury. "Would you send us five lbs Bar-Soap; it is to be used only for washing dishes & hands," one early order to the Mission Rooms from the Cherokee Mission read. But for such a request an explanation seemed necessary. "We make soap for common washing but the wood that we burn does not afford good ashes and the soap made from them is very poor generally."

Linens were used for the Mission dining tables; propriety demanded them. But they must not be fine and costly. "All came," a letter of 1828 reads, "according to the order nearly except the Table Linen, which was much nicer than we wanted. It was 4/ per yd., I believe; we wanted that which is sold for about 9 d or 1/ per yd. We shall sell it if we can exchange for some other goods."

A woman who came from a good New England home to Brainerd Mission had many practical adjustments to make. First of all, she must be aware, at all times, of the fact that a mission household was not a private one; it was extended to include whatever missionaries, with their wives and children, might be assigned there, the teachers in the schools for boys and girls, the boarding-pupils in these schools, and visitors from every class and station, from a wagoner who needed a night's lodging to the secretary or some other official of the American Board. President Monroe had visited Brainerd in 1819, before he recommended citizenship as the solution of the Indian problem. Indeed, housewives must be ready for any visitor, great or small, ill or well, who might come to the mission threshold. Certainly they must always be in readiness to welcome the parents of their Cherokee pupils who, after the fashion of Indians, were accustomed to paying and receiving long visits. Such visits might be an expense to the Mission, and they were always a drain on the time and energy of those whose days were at best crowded with duties that must not be put off. But Ann must learn, their days were the Lord's, and it was His to plan for them. And the visits frequently were fruitful of good results; they were one of the means by which the principles of Christian living were exemplified for Indian observers. The household of faith must ever serve as a model to those who had not yet learned its ways.

Sundays, being holy days, were never a trial; but they did require a housewife's careful planning. When the sun set on Saturday night, the hurry and effort of the week must cease; until Monday morning there must be no traveling, no unnecessary cooking, no sewing or mending or baking. Everything must contribute to the day of rest and solemnity; if more work came before and more followed after, the Sabbath day must be a day set apart. Departing missionaries had been advised, "In all places, and especially among people superstitiously observant of their own sacred times and seasons, a very exemplary observance of the Sabbath is of the very first importance to Christianity." Saturday meant baking and boiling for two days instead of one, and for probable visitors as well as for the usual family; Monday morning saw an empty larder and a family hungering again for hot foods, but the Sabbath was kept holy.

Supplies were necessarily an uncertain quantity at

Brainerd. Sometimes there was an abundance of food, if an Indian friend brought them venison or if the mission bought a "beef creature" to be butchered. They relished fresh meat, after days without it; but they put aside a thrifty portion to be cured or dried for use at a time when fresh meat was not available. Gluttony was not a habit to foster, when there were always possible lean days ahead. During the summer months, after the orchard had grown large enough to bear fruit and the garden had become productive, there were fruits and vegetables for the table. The surplus must be dried and so made available for winter use; peaches and apples must be sliced, corn husked, and all spread under netting in the sun, with daily turning to insure even drying, and with frequent rescuing from summer showers. New England housewives had their own ways of drying and preserving, in a day when modern methods of canning were unknown. Sometimes, however, they learned a useful idea from their Indian sisters, whose knowledge was simple but not to be scorned. Here are the instructions which Mrs. John Ross gave for "always having corn in a fresh condition, as if newly plucked." "The corn (flint corn in preference) to be plucked when soft & ready for roasting ears. The outer husks to be taken off, and the ears to be boiled thoroughly. The inner husks, after this, are to be drawn back so as to enable it to be tied up in bunches.

"Under a scaffolding raised on poles, it is then to be suspended over a slow fire, till it becomes perfectly dry and rather smoked. It may be some days in undergoing this preparation. When thoroughly dry, it must be removed, and hung in a dry place so as not to mould.

"When wanted for use, the grains must be shelled & boiled over again. At first it will be found shrunken &

as hard as stone; but cooking will bring it out fresh & soft."[1]

Clothing, like food, was the responsibility of the women of the mission. It was never elaborate; yet it must always be respectable. Shoes were of the most serviceable leather— horsehide usually; and when Mrs. Worcester found the wearing of such shoes impossible, her husband made a special explanation on her behalf. "2 pairs women's calf-skin shoes. no. 8—be sure no smaller. *Calfskin*. Those sent last year were horsehide which contracted so that Mrs. W. cannot wear them." And Mr. Worcester explained, when he wrote for "one trimmed Florence bonnet," that a Cherokee young lady would be grateful for it. As for the wives of the missionaries, they contented themselves with a bit of fresh bonnet ribbon, usually black, to rejuvenate the hat of the preceding season, and of several seasons preceding that. Much of the clothing, for school-children, teachers, and missionaries alike, came from eastern donors; and much ingenuity was required to make the articles contained in a gift box suit the exact needs of the group to which they came. The family must never seem ungrateful, or fail to make use of the clothing that came, lest they be misunderstood and cut off from further donations. Such misunderstandings had occurred, as this account indicates. "The customary dress, or rather want of dress, of the Cherokee children, was a hindrance to their attendance at school. Many parents were destitute of the skill requisite to prepare suitable clothing. The female members of the mission were overburdened with other labors, and could not provide clothing for 50 or 60 children. Benevolent ladies at the north, therefore proposed to

1 Manuscripts of John Howard Payne. *Cherokee Notes*, II, p. 51. Newberry Library, Ayer Collection.

furnish clothing for the pupils gratuitously; and finally, public notice was given, that donations of this kind were needed. The notice stated that generally the parents would gladly pay for the garments furnished to the children; so that their value would in fact be given to the Board, for the general objects of the mission. Children's clothes, too, would often purchase articles from the natives, which the mission family needed. The call met with a gratifying response, in all parts of the country. Great quantities of clothing were made and sent to this and other Indian missions. One of the results shows the general character of stories prejudicial to missions. It was reported, that some of these garments had been seen on children who had never belonged to the schools; which, it was supposed, proved that the benevolence of the donors was abused. The truth was, that the garments thus seen had been purchased with corn, or other necessary articles, for the use of the mission, and thus answered the purpose for which they were given."[2]

While they performed their duties as housewives, Ann and her companions must see to it that the Cherokee girls learned these same duties. Some learned rapidly enough, if they were half-breeds or if the white man's utensils and furnishings were not altogether unfamiliar to them. But they moved to a different tempo from that of their white teachers; the Yankee ideal of driving toward the accomplishment of an end was foreign to them. And sometimes, in spite of intelligent effort, they progressed slowly. A little girl might not be able to sew a straight seam of fine stitches, if her heart ached with homesickness for the freer life she had known; she might not watch a boiling pot zealously enough, if her eyes were keen to

2 Tracy, *A History of the American Board of Commissioners for Foreign Missions*, p. 72.

hunt herbs in the meadows. But the mission wives were patient teachers; they combined domestic duties with moral and spiritual training; they gave biblical quotations a literal application to family life that was ingenious and apt. Here is one little girl's letter to Jeremiah Evarts, about her life at Brainerd.

"February 19, 1829.

To Jeremiah Evarts, Esq.:
"I asked Miss Ames if I might write a few lines to you and she said she was afraid you could not read it because I have nor written but a few weeks but she said I might try. I remember you the last time you was at Brainerd. You stood by the fireplace in the classroom and talked to us. I had just come to school and was reading in my *abc*. I have lately heard that I had a little cousin burned to death he was but a child. I then thought death was near us. O how time passes it is now a year since my grandmother died. She was an old woman. She belonged to this Church her soul has gone to God and her body is now mouldering in the grave. I think you would like to hear if we are good children. We are not allowed to do bad things. When we get angry we have to stand in the middle of the floor before all the scholars and say the 29 verse of the 14 chap. in Prov. When we tell lies we say the 22 verse of the 12 chap. of Prov. and Rev. 21 chap. and part of the 8 verse. When our parents bring us sweet potatoes and bean bread if any of the children take it from us without leave they have to repeat the 8 commandment and Cor. 6 chap. and 10 verse. When we break the Sabbath we say the 2 commandment. I wish to be a good girl while I live in this world and when I die to go and be

where God is. I am smaller than the other girls that wrote. I am not nine years old yet. I am sorry that I cannot write better.

from your young friend
CHRISTINA McPHERSON"[3]

Ann Worcester's maternal instinct was strong and her vitality remarkable; she must have found a deep interest in such a child as Christina McPherson, whose mind was alert and whose eyes were bright with observation. Teaching little girls to make their beds properly, to mind their manners and their morals, to live and prepare to die righteously, according to the one strict standard which she knew—this was a duty that Ann accepted as naturally as she accepted the air she breathed. And others labored with her, unquestioningly and untiringly. Women in the mission household taxed their ingenuity and their patience heavily to meet the constantly changing, constantly demanding circumstances. Washing, cleaning, cooking, sewing, candle-making, nursing filled their days; they were indeed servants in the service of their God.

It was part of the training of any New England housewife to be equal to whatever emergency might arise. A house must expand or contract miraculously as visitors came and went; if relatives arrived unexpectedly, they must be entertained; food must be abundant, but never wasted. Here among the Cherokees the same standards must be maintained, as far as possible, under great difficulties. Supplies must be ordered many months in advance, without underestimating and so running short or overestimating and thus alarming the Prudential Committee with an effect of lavish living. Every adult in the

3 Manuscripts of John Howard Payne, *Cherokee Papers*, Vol. VIII, unpaged.

Mission family must help make up the list of supplies, anticipating every possible need and yet tempering the necessity with strict economy. Here is one of the lists Samuel Worcester sent in, in the early years of his life as a missionary:

"Needed at New Echota Mission

15 reams Royal Demi Paper
1 do. Paper suitable for covers, say Retre Cartridge Paper.
1 do. Letter Paper
1 cheap Sand Box
1 doz. Monroe's Pencils
2 Penknives
2 oz. Wafers
1 gill red ink or 1 paper powder
1 Paper Black Ink Powder
½ doz. Reference Testaments, if on hand
A small assortment of simple Sabbath School Books. Among them Hymns for infant minds
½ doz. 24to Watts & Select Hymns
1 Hone
1 Pocket Comb
½ doz. Cakes Windsor Soap
1 lb. Chalk
2 oz. Indigo

2 oz. Gum Arabic
2 phials each 1 oz. E. Tansey
2 bottles Opodeldoc
1 lb. Salt Petre
1 lb. Cream Tartar
1 bottle Tartaric Acid
2 oz. Paregoric
2 lb. Redwood
3 bed cords [Be so kind as to take special pains to have them good; for if we receive such as were sent last year we shall have to send annually.]
1 Oxford Grey Cloth Coat. [My coat last year was too small, yet so that I wear it, but much too fine.]
1 do. Vest
1 pr. do. Cloth or Cassimere Pantaloons
1 pr. Lasting Pantaloons
1 do. Vest

3 pr. men's calfskin shoes, no. 9

1 pr. woman's morocco Walking do., No. 8½ or 9

1 pr. do. calf do. [Mrs. Worcester's feet are such that she cannot comfortably wear horsehide shoes.]

2 prs. calfskin shoes No. 4½

10 yds. brown Tow Cloth

1 piece fine American Gingham

2 yds. English Pink Gingham

2 Handkerchiefs

9 yds. Calico suitable for little girls

2 large Hair Combs

2 Side Combs

3 steel topp'd brass Thimbles

6 fine Darning Needles

6 common mixed do.

2 Tape Needles

1 paper needles No. 5 sharps

1 do. do. No. 4 betweens

1 do. do. No. 6 sharps

1 do. do. No. 7 sharps

1 piece unbleached Cotton Shirting about No. 20

6 yds. red Flannel

2 prs. large woolen Socks

10 lb. Black tea

2 lb. Green Tea

1 oz. Nutmeg

1 oz. Cloves

1 Lantern

1 Sausage Filler

12 sheets Tin Plate

10 cents U. S. copper coin

2 6 qt. Milk pans—tin

½ doz. Cups & Saucers with Teapot and Sugar Bowl

2 small Oval Dishes

2 large Chamber with covers

1 pair Iron Candlesticks, to admit a good-sized candle

1 pair snuffers

1 oz. Beet Seed

½ oz. Early Cabbage Seed

½ oz. Late do. do.

½ oz. Lettuce do.

½ oz. Early Cucumber do.

½ oz. Late do. do.

1 oz. Radish do.

1½ oz. Onion do. [Be so kind as to get from two or three different places, so as to secure seeds that will grow.]

1½ oz. parsnip do.

1½ oz. Carrot do.

1 Roll Paper Hangings

1 bottle Spirits Turpentine

"Mr. Boudinot wishes

50 Reams Super Royal Printing Paper
4 do. Retre Cartridge Paper
2 Canisters Printing Ink
4 lb. Twine
2lb. Full-faced Brevier Capt. Type.
2 lb.   do.   Long Primer   do.
2 lb. Brevier Antique do.
½ lb. small pica letter
½ do.   do.   do.
16 Bevil Column Rules [such as are (apparently) used in printing the N. Y. *Observer.*]
1 ream Letter Paper
1 Sand Box
1 Paper Sand
½ doz. Pencils
2 oz. Wafers
2 Papers Ink Powder
½ doz. cakes Windsor Soap
½ lb. Chalk
2 oz. Ep. Tansey
1 bottle Opodeldoc
1 box Lee's Pills
1 lb. Cream Tartar

1 lb. Peruvian Bark

2 oz. Paregoric
4 good Bed Cords
1 blue cloth Frock Coat
1 pr. do. Pantaloons
1 do. do. best
1 pr. lasting Pantaloons
1 silk Vest. [Mr. Boudinott is 5 ft. 7 in. in height, and 2 ft. 8 in. around the waist. He would like loose pantaloons.]
2 Handkerchiefs
2 prs. woolen Socks
2 prs. cotton   do.
2 prs. dark cotton Stockings
2 pieces dark Am. Gingham
9 yds. Calico for little girls
7 yds. English Buff Gingham, double width
1 pr. good Boots right & left No. 5½
1 pr. Brogs calfskin No. 5½
1 pr. Morrocco pumps No. 5
2 pr. Women's Shoes calf good thick No. 5
½ lb. white cotton thread
½ lb. assortment   do.
½ lb. Sewing Silk
7 yds. British Shirting

15 yds. unbleached Cotton Shirting No. 16
1 large Hair Comb
2 Side Combs
3 fine Darning Needles
3 common   do.
1 paper Needles No. 5 Sharps
1 do.   do.   No. 4
                Betweens
1 do.   do.   No. 6
                Sharps
1 do.   do.   No. 7
                Sharps
6 yds. red Flannel
8 lb. black Tea
2 lb. green Tea
1 oz. Nutmeg
4 sheets Tin Plate
2 long flat Tins
2 10 qt. tin Milk Pans

1 doz. Cups & Saucers
1 block-tin Teapot largest size
1 pr. Iron Candlesticks
1 pr. Steel Snuffers
Garden Seeds [the same as for the Mission]
1 5 pail Brass Kettle-bailed
2 rose Blankets
1 roll Paper Hangings
1 bottle Cayenne Pepper
1 dressing Comb
1 ivory Comb
1 cheap Dressing Glass 8 in. by 10.
1 pair Fire dogs 12 lb. or 15 lb.
1 flute, & directions for playing [cost not to exceed $6]

"Mr. Wheeler will be thankful to have the following purchased for him.

1 4 pail Brass Kettle—bailed
2 rose Blankets
1 piece good Am. Gingham dark
7 yds Calico—good
1 pair iron Candlesticks
1 pair Steel Snuffers
1 Tea Pot

2 lb. black Tea
Garden Seeds—the same as for the Mission
1 pair Cassimer Pantaloons. Same size as for Mr. Boudinott.
15 yds. bleached Am. Shirting
1 piece common Table Linen

I Teakettle [I cannot tell the name of the kind he wants. It is malleable iron cast and tinned within.]"

Four days after he had sent in his original list, Samuel sent a postscript to it. Everyone who had wished items mentioned in the first letter seemed, within four days, to have thought of more; but there seems to have been no impatience with any member of the Mission on that account.

"If it is not too late, a neighbor wishes very much to have me procure for him, through you, the following medicines.

Jewett's improved Vegetable Pills or, German Specific
Dr. Rolfe's Vegetable Pacifick, and Antibilious Pills
    Of each of the above enough for one case of dyspepsia
Vegetable Lithontriptic and Specific Solvent Powders—
    enough for one case of the Gravel.
A little Corn Plaster

"Mr. Weir, a young man who has been at work for me several months, wishes for the following,

I most approved school arithmetic. Not Colburn's
I Goodrich's History of the United States
I Worcester's Epitome of Geography & Atlas—latest
    edition.
I smallest Walker's pronouncing Dictionary
I pair high quartered Calfskin Shoes, no. 9
I best Razor and Razor strap
I silk handkerchief
I waterproof hat. Circumference at the band 23½
    inches

[65]

"Mr. Boudinott wishes added

1 lb. Redwood
1 pair mantuamaker's Shears
1 doz. good common knives & forks
Mr. Wheeler's teakettle, already mentioned, to contain
    6 quarts
"I shall be enabled to oblige some of my neighbors if
    you send me 1 doz. Webster's Spelling Book."

After the list of supplies had been compiled and the postscripts hastily added, there were months to wait before the boxes and barrels containing the goods arrived. Wives had time to wonder whether the gingham would be a pretty shade for the children to wear, and to wish they had asked for blue instead of pink, and then to be glad they had not sent for blue after all; husbands had time to wonder whether this year's overcoat would be more serviceable than the one that had been sent before: teachers had time to wonder how they could do with the small number of books they had asked for. When the shipment finally came, there was great excitement. Samuel Worcester must see that every item had been sent and received in satisfactory condition; Ann must check the list as he unpacked the articles. Then they must put everything away, on shelves and in chests and closets; the cloth must be made into garments; the books must be covered for the schoolroom; the kitchen utensils and the tools must be put to use.

When there is much for the hands to do, and peace in the heart, the days go by in quick succession. Their first Christmas in their new home was at hand before the Worcesters were aware of it. It was a time for solemnity rather than for festivity, and there was a conscious effort to avoid any holiday effect. The festive observances of the papists were to be shunned; fasting, rather than feasting, was to be recommended. There was wonder and beauty enough in the Christmas story itself, without feasting and gift-giving and other unauthorized practices. It was a simple tale that any Indian could learn to understand. Over and over the missionaries and their wives repeated the story to the listening Indians.

The Indians were pleased with the account. They were glad the mother of the baby Jesus had a stable for her housing and straw for her bed. Most of them now had comfortable cabins, but they could remember when shelter had been less certain than it now was. Indian babies had been born without warmth or shelter, they knew. They took a just pride in knowing that this Jesus who was their Savior was well born.

On November 7, 1826, before their second Christmas among the Cherokees, the Worcesters' first child was born. Births were not uncommon among the missionaries, and no wife in those days went back to New England for the sake of medical care and safety. Sometimes, by the hand of Providence or for want of a doctor and the proper medicines, a woman died in childbirth. Every mission churchyard had its stone markers naming these sad happenings. But Ann had no fear of her ordeal, though it proved to be a hard one and she made a slow recovery.

"It is a bow or a meal-sifter, the Messenger's child?" the Indians asked when they heard of the event.

"A meal-sifter," they were told, for the baby was a girl.

They baptized the baby Ann Eliza, in the little church at Brainerd Mission. The Indian women, who were wise in such things, said she was a remarkably fine baby; her eyes were bright and her body was strong. Some of them had advice to offer to Ann: to feed the pretty infant on cockle-bur brew so that things might stick in her mind and her memory be strong, to give her the heart of the huhu (which is the mockingbird) so that she would learn quickly, like her father the Messenger. And though Ann did not follow their advice, the baby grew fast and developed rapidly, just as if her mother had used all of the Indians' lore in rearing her.

When the second Christmas in the wilderness came for the Worcesters, Ann Eliza could smile at her parents from her cradle. She was a radiant child, from the first, and she never lost her quality of radiance. The wilderness as birthplace held no sense of harm for her; in her parents and in the mission home she had complete security. Like the little Lord Jesus, she was well born.

The Cherokee Phœnix

THE CHEROKEES were an ancient race, with a history that reached back beyond definitely calculated time into the vague boundaries of a long ago when tradition fathered history. If this history had had only oral transmission from one generation to the next by those men whose powers of memory and of narration won them the place of "traditioners" among their people, it was nevertheless definite and heroic. Migrations and floods and famines, battles and hunts and ball-plays, councils and treaties and assemblies, these were the events that comprised this history. They had had a culture of their own of a high order, and a moral code that by its simplicity and its assumption of the strict honor of every man, rather put to shame the white man's complicated system of enforcing order and justice. None of these elements of the Cherokee culture, however, found regard in the opinion of the white man. He wrote his history in books, instead of relying on the book of his own mind; he had a written code of many laws for his government, with many penalties for many crimes; he maintained order in his land by a series of punishments for violations of the rules of order. And he had a God that was new to the Cherokees, the true God, whose seat was in heaven and whose words were all written in a holy book called the Bible. He and his brethren

[69]

spread over the land that had been the red man's, and no authority stayed him in his claim for more and more territory. Obviously this way of life that was the white man's was the right way; those who followed it increased and prospered.

Once the Cherokees had hoped to remain in isolation from the whites; now, having lost thousands of square miles of their lands and suffered constant encroachments from traders and trappers and road-builders, they began to see that the part of security lay in being like the white invaders. With a rapidity equalled by no other tribe of Indians, the Cherokees took up the ways and the teachings of the white men, although not without bitter and prolonged opposition by the more conservative, or the less readily persuaded, members of the tribe. In the beginning of the nineteenth century, America was too sure of its own cultural values to set high store by those of any other people; the mythology, the art, and the religion of its primitive inhabitants must be exchanged as soon as possible for approved American brands. Protestant Christianity was not ready to make allowances for any culture other than the one in which it flourished. The missionaries, in their sincerity bringing Christianity, brought its whole American environment; the Indians, embracing Christianity, embraced the mode of dress, the manners and customs, the form of government that accompanied it. Quick changes, then, were in store for the eager Cherokees.

Before the beginning of the nineteenth century, some of the Cherokees who resented the encroachments of white settlers had moved west of the Mississippi where hunting was more plentiful and the influence of white civilization less powerful. Year after year other members of their tribe followed them. By 1817 they had become numerous enough to be recognized by the United States as the Western or Arkansas Cherokees, and to acquire a grant of land there through a treaty arrangement with the Osages. The larger body of Cherokees remaining in the East opposed any official recognition of their brothers in Arkansas Territory, suspecting the United States of encouraging the western band as a means of persuading them all, eventually, to move west of the Mississippi. By 1819, when Thomas Nuttall, the naturalist, made his journey through the territory of Arkansas, he found Cherokees there to the number of several thousands, and a degree of civilization that indicated the inevitability of progress even among the most conservative and farthest removed. Both banks of the Arkansas, he wrote, "were lined with the houses and farms of the Cherokee, and though their dress was a mixture of indigenous and European taste, yet in their houses, which are decently furnished, and in their farms, which were well fenced and stocked with cattle, we perceive a happy approach toward civilization. Their numerous families, also, well fed and clothed, argue a propitious progress in their population. Their superior industry either as hunters or farmers proves the value of property among them, and they are no longer strangers to avarice and the distinctions created by wealth. Some of them are possessed of property to the amount of many thousands of dollars, have houses handsomely and conveniently furnished, and their tables spread with our dainties and luxuries."[1] No missionaries were required to teach them avarice and class distinctions; Christian business men and traders and statesmen had already taught them the elements of these traits.

But shortly after Nuttall wrote this, the first Christian

1 Bureau of American Ethnology, *Nineteenth Annual Report*, 1897-8, Pt. 1, p. 137.

missionaries to the Western Cherokees had arrived. Through their principal chief, Tollunteeskee, they had asked the American Board for a mission and a school, and now, in 1829, Dwight Mission had been moved west near the point where the Illinois joins the Arkansas River. They found themselves, in their bewilderment, asking for the very influences of religion and education that they had come west to avoid. Theirs had been a simple standard of right; how could they avoid mental confusion when the government which in one treaty guaranteed them "the remainder of their country forever" began almost immediately after that treaty was signed to ask for more land, and when what were subtly called "silent considerations" —rewards of land and money for the chiefs who brought about the agreement to a treaty—were imposed upon the bewildered leaders? "Forever," strangely enough, was a brief time; men who called themselves followers of Christ grasped all they could lay hold of; statesmen spoke with two tongues; the Great White Father sometimes turned a deaf ear to his red children. Civilization was indeed a complicated matter. Language, even when it was written, seemed to undergo quick changes of meaning.

As early as 1808, the Cherokees had made a beginning at a reorganization of their government on a plan similar to that of the United States. Gideon Blackburn, a Moravian missionary who had lived among them several years, wrote in a letter dated September 16, 1808: "The period has at last arrived, on which I have long fixed my eager eye. The Cherokee nation has at length determined to become men and citizens. A few days ago, in full council, they adopted a constitution, which embraces a simple principle of government. The legislative and judicial powers are vested in a general council, and lesser ones subordinate. All criminal accusations must be established by testimony; and no more executions must be made by the avenger of blood."[2] In 1810, they had made another advance in their tribal government by abolishing, in council, the whole custom of revenge by clans.

"In Council, Oostinaleh, April 8, 1810.

"1. Be it known this day, That the various clans or tribes which compose the Cherokee Nation have unanimously passed an act of oblivion for all lives for which they may have been indebted one to the other, and have mutually agreed that after this evening the aforesaid act shall become binding upon every clan or tribe thereof.

"2. The aforesaid clans or tribes have also agreed that if, in future, any life should be lost without malice intended, the innocent aggressor shall not be accounted guilty; and, should it so happen that a brother, forgetting his natural affections, should raise his hands in anger and kill his brother, he shall be accounted guilty of murder and suffer accordingly.

"3. If a man have a horse stolen, and overtake the thief, and should his anger be so great as to cause him to shed his blood, let it remain on his own conscience, but no satisfaction shall be required for his life, from his relative or clan he may have belonged to.

"By order of the seven clans."[3]

Black Fox, principal chief, and the seven chiefs of the separate clans, made their marks in token of their agreement to these new laws which their orators had framed and which they had written on the white man's "talking leaves." They must have found themselves astonished at their own advancement.

2 Tracy, *A History of the American Board of Commissioners for Foreign Missions*, p. 66.
3 Bureau of American Ethnology, *Nineteenth Annual Report*, 1897-8. Pt. 1, pp. 86-7.

Next, thanks to George Guess, the Cherokees came into possession of a form of writing of their own, and were becoming a literate people. True, this had not come about without struggle—the personal struggle of Guess to devise his system and the struggle of the national council to convince everyone of its value. Later, when they had a national newspaper, the *Phœnix*, it printed an account of the achievement of the man whom their government agent called the American Cadmus. "Mr. Guess is, in appearance and habits, a full Cherokee, though his grandfather on his father's side was a white man. He has no knowledge of any language but the Cherokee, consequently, in his invention of the alphabet, he had to depend entirely on his own native sources. He was led to think on the subject of writing the Cherokee by a conversation which took place one evening at Santa. Some young men were making remarks on the superior talents of the white people. One said, that white men only put a talk on paper, and sent it to any distance, and it would be understood by those who received it. They all agreed, that this was very strange, and they could not see how it could be done. Mr. Guess, after listening to their conversation for a while, raised himself, and putting on an air of importance, said, 'You are all fools; why, the thing is very easy; I can do it myself;' and picking up a flat stone, he commenced scratching on it with a pin, and after a few minutes read to them a sentence, which he had written by making a mark for each word. This produced a laugh, and the conversation on the subject was ended. But the inventive powers of Guess' mind were now roused to action; and nothing short of being able to write the Cherokee language would satisfy him. He went home, purchased materials, and sat down to paint the Cherokee language on paper. . . . .

"Nor could he succeed [in convincing his people that he had found a way to represent the Cherokee language on paper], until he went to the Arkansas and taught a few persons there, one of whom wrote a letter to some friends in this nation, and sent it by Mr. Guess, who read it to the people. This letter excited much curiosity. Here was a talk in the Cherokee language, which had come all the way from the Arkansas sealed up in a paper, yet it was very plain. This convinced many that Mr. Guess' mode of writing would be of some use. Several persons immediately determined to try to learn. They succeeded in a few days, and from this it quickly spread all over the nation, and the Cherokees (who as a people had always been illiterate,) were in the course of a few months, without school or expense of time or money, able to read and write in their own language."[4]

Now the Cherokees were realizing the first practical results of the education in eastern schools of some of their young men. David Brown, Elias Boudinot, Leonard Hicks, David Carter, John Ridge, and John Vann had all come back to the Cherokee Nation from eastern schools, where they had stayed for varying periods of time. Leonard Hicks, son of the chief Charles B. Hicks, had been too homesick to remain long, and David Carter had been dismissed for some obscure reason from the Foreign Mission School at Cornwall, which the American Board had founded for the education of heathen youth. There had probably been some puzzlement in the minds of the people of Cornwall over the appearance of some of these redskinned youths. In a public examination, it was said that "the Indian pupils appeared so genteel and graceful on the stage that the white pupils appeared uncouth beside

4 *Missionary Herald*, XXIV (1828), 330-1.

them."[5] Major Ridge, commander of the Cherokees in the Seminole War, had come to visit his son John at Cornwall in 1819, "a large, tall man in white top boots," who wore a coat trimmed in gold lace and had "waiters in great style." He "came in the most splendid carriage that had ever entered the town." When he returned to the Cherokee Nation, John had brought back with him more than the education he had acquired at Cornwall; he had brought back a bride from the town. "In January, 1824, he was married to Sarah Bird Northrup much to the disturbance of the people of Cornwall. After the marriage of John and Sarah they lived in Georgia in great splendor. John frequently transacted business for his nation in Washington while Sarah dressed in silk every day, remained at home looking after her three children and thirty servants."[6]

David Brown had gone to Andover, as well as to Cornwall, and he had returned to his people with a knowledge of Hebrew and of theology. Since his return he had served the Cherokees as translator and interpreter; he had acted as secretary of their council; and he had made a tour of observation among his people, for the sake of giving accurate information about them in a report to the Secretary of War. According to this report, "numberless herds of cattle grazed upon their extensive plains; horses were numerous; many and extensive flocks of sheep, goats and swine covered the hills and valleys; the climate was delicious and healthy and the winters were mild; the soil of the valleys and plains was rich, and was utilized in the production of corn, tobacco, cotton, wheat, oats, indigo, and potatoes; considerable trade was carried on with the neighboring states, much cotton being exported in boats

5 *Chronicles of Oklahoma*, Vol. VII, No. 3 (September, 1929), p. 246.
6 *Ibid.*, p. 247.

of their own to New Orleans; apple and peach orchards were quite common; much attention was paid to the cultivation of gardens; butter and cheese of their own manufacture were seen upon many of their tables; public roads were numerous in the nation and supplied at convenient distances with houses of entertainment kept by the natives; many and flourishing villages dotted the country; cotton and woolen cloths were manufactured by the women and homemade blankets were very common; almost every family grew sufficient cotton for its own consumption; industry and commercial enterprise were extending themselves throughout the nation; nearly all the merchants were native Cherokees; the population was rapidly increasing, a census just taken showing 13,563 native citizens, 147 white men and 73 white women who had intermarried with the Cherokees, and 1,277 slaves; schools were increasing every year, and indolence was strongly discountenanced; the nation had no debt, and the revenue was in a flourishing condition; a printing press was soon to be established, and a national library and museum were in contemplation."[7] Elias Boudinot, back among his people after his years of study at Cornwall and Andover, had made a compilation of statistics for the year 1826. "At this time there are 22,000 cattle; 7,600 horses; 46,000 swine; 2,500 sheep; 762 looms; 2,488 spinning wheels; 172 waggons; 2,943 ploughs; 10 sawmills; 31 grist-mills; 62 blacksmith-shops; 8 cotton machines; 18 schools; 18 ferries, and a number of public roads. In one district there were, last winter, upwards of 1,000 volumes of good books; and 11 different periodical papers both religious and political were taken and read."[8]

7 Bureau of American Ethnology, *Fifth Annual Report*, 1883-4, p. 240.
8 *Missionary Herald*, XXIII (1827), 116.

With these conditions prevailing among a people who were by nature both proud and intelligent, the establishment of a national press was a move to be expected. To them, and rightly, the founding of the Cherokee Press marked a peak of achievement in their climb toward the white man's culture and ways of living. The speeches of Boudinot indicate that the national council voted to establish the press in 1826 and appropriated money for it, but more than a year passed before any printing could be done. They were dependent upon Samuel Worcester for the execution of the whole project. Through him, they arranged to have their types cast in Boston and their press purchased there, the arrangements all being made by detailed correspondence with the American Board. It was no easy matter, since no one in Boston knew Cherokee and Guess' characters were very much like a Chinese puzzle to those who cast the types.

Press, types, and furniture must be shipped by steamboat from Boston to Augusta and then hauled overland to the Cherokee national capital at New Echota, Georgia. Although they were sent about the middle of November, in 1827, they did not arrive in the Cherokee nation until the first day of February, 1828. And when they did arrive, it was found that no printing paper had been shipped. Printing must therefore be delayed until a temporary supply could be brought by wagon from Knoxville. Still, the news that the equipment was on its way was encouraging to the anxious leaders among the Indians, and Jeremiah Evarts' letter sent out to them from the Missionary Rooms on November 8, 1827, was like the confirmation of a hope that seemed almost impossible of fulfillment. "The types & press, & furniture for the office are to be ready for shipping by the close of this week. The types

& furniture have been ready for several weeks; but we have delayed purchasing a press, because we supposed that the printer who would be employed, would wish to have some voice respecting the kind. We have this morning engaged one called the 'union press'—it is an iron press; but seems simple in its structure—easily set up—& not likely to get out of repair.

"Drawings of the press, with directions for putting it up and working it, will be forwarded to you. It weighs about lbs. 1000, the types & furniture—say—1200. All will be well packed & sent as soon as possible, to Augusta.

"The whole will be addressed to John Ross, Esq., Newtown, Cher. Na.—to the care of Brewster & Prescott, Augusta. Mr. Ross will give directions to some waggoner. I hope the council have made some provision for the support & employment of Mr. Boudinot. In regard to his connexion with the mission, I think that question must be left till our expected visit, in the course of the ensuing winter."

Meanwhile, plans for the work of the press had gone forward to the very point of printing. Samuel Worcester, still the Messenger to the Cherokees, was to supervise all the work of the press, with the permission of the American Board. He had learned their language with amazing rapidity; he used the system of writing invented by Guess; he was eager to see the Cherokees have books and periodicals in their own language. And he was a tireless, constant worker for the enlightenment of the Cherokees.

It had been voted to establish a weekly journal to be called the *Cherokee Phœnix*, with Elias Boudinot as its editor. This was to be printed partly in Cherokee in the characters of Guess' invention, and partly in English. Its object, according to the prospectus which Samuel

Worcester prepared and distributed, was "the benefit of the Cherokees," and for the accomplishment of this object the following subjects were to fill its columns:

"1. The laws and public documents of the nation.

"2. Accounts of the manners and customs of the Cherokees, and their progress in education, religion, and the arts of civilized life, with such notices of other Indian tribes as our limited means of information will allow.

"3. The principal interesting news of the day.

"4. Miscellaneous articles, calculated to promote literature, civilization, and religion among the Cherokees."9

The enlightenment of the whole tribe being the aim of the *Phœnix*, a special system of charging for subscriptions was devised. Those who could read Cherokee only received the journal free of charge. "To subscribers who could read English, the cost was $2.50 annually, if paid in advance; $3 if payment is delayed 6 months; and $3.50 if not paid till the end of the year."

Meanwhile, everything that could be done in anticipation of the arrival of the press was under way. John F. Wheeler, the printer who had been hired, has left an account of these preparations and of the early activities after the arrival of the press. "We arrived at New Echota about the 23rd of December, 1827. We found the press, type, etc., had not arrived, they having to be transferred from Augustine, Ga., in wagons, a distance of over 200 miles. We found the Rev. Samuel A. Worcester, a missionary under the American Board, with his family, and Elias Boudinot, the editor of the paper, with his family, at New Echota, both of whom had just removed there,

9 *Ibid.*, XXIV (1828), 133.

and both intending to engage in the translation of the Scriptures into the Cherokee language, to be printed with the newly invented characters. Mr. Worcester had systematically arranged the characters, which can be better understood as something like the English *ba, be, bi, bo,* etc., using the Cherokee vowels at the head of each line. Mr. Worcester furnished Mr. Harris and myself with a written copy, (for there was no printing in the Cherokee language) to learn the alphabet. We had nothing to do for three or four weeks but to learn the alphabet, and it was more and more incomprehensible to us than Greek. For myself, I could not distinguish a single word in the talk of the Indians with each other, for it seemed to be a continuance of sounds. While we were waiting for the type and press it was ascertained that no printing paper had been ordered from Boston with the material. A two-horse-wagon was procured and Harris started for Knoxville, where was a paper mill, for paper. He was gone about two weeks, when he returned with a sufficient supply for the present wants. At that time, 1828, paper was moulded, each sheet separate. This was the kind of paper on which the first number of the *Phœnix* was printed.

"The press and type did not arrive until the latter part of January, 1828. While waiting we had devoted a portion of our time to learning the alphabet.

"The house built for the printing-office was of hewed logs, about 30 feet long and 20 wide. The builders had cut out a log on each side 15 or 16 feet long and about two and a half feet above the floor, in which they had made a sash to fit. This we had raised, because the light was below the cases. Stands had to be made, a bank, and cases for the Cherokee type. The latter was something entirely new, as no pattern for a case or cases [to accomodate] an alphabet containing 86 characters could be found. After considering the matter over for a few days, I worked upon making cases with boxes corresponding to the systematized alphabet as arranged by Mr. Worcester. Accordingly we had the cases so made, one case being about three feet by three and one-half feet. This brought all the vowels, six in number, in the lower or nearest boxes, but the letters in the latter part of the alphabet were in the upper boxes, and hard to reach. It took over 100 boxes for figures, points, etc., to each case. There were no capitals.

"The Cherokee font was cast on a small pica body, and, as several of the Cherokee characters were taken from the English caps, the small caps of small pica were used. The press, type, etc., arrived about the middle of January. The press, a small royal size, was like none I ever saw before or since. It was of cast-iron, with spiral springs to hold up the platen, at that time a new invention.

"Mr. Green, the Secretary of the Mission Board, came out at the same time the material arrived. It was a part of his business to put up the new press. It was a very simply constructed hand press, and any country printer could have put it together. At that day we had to use balls made of deerskin and stuffed with wool, as it was before the invention of composition rollers.

"The first number of the *Cherokee Phœnix* (Tsa-la-ge Tsi-le-hi-sa-ni-hi) was issued about the middle of February, 1828. There were three hands in the office—Harris, myself, and John Candy, a native half-blood who came as an apprentice. He could speak the Cherokee language and was of great help to me in giving words where they were not plainly written. . . . .

"We had no impression [*sic*] stone, and had to make up each page of the paper on a sled [?] galley, put it on the

[82]

press, and take proofs on slips of paper, and then correct it on the press, a very fatiguing way of correcting foul proof, which was the case with my first efforts at setting Cherokee type. It was a very foul proof, and a very troublesome and fatiguing job to correct it, as I did not know or understand a word of the language. But after a few weeks I became expert in setting up Cherokee matter, and as every letter or type had a thick body it amounted up pretty fast. Translation from English into Cherokee was a very slow business; therefore we seldom had more than three columns each week in Cherokee."[10]

In spite of some inaccuracies in this account, and in spite of his own disparagement with regard to the Cherokee language and its representation in Guess' alphabet, Wheeler became indispensable in the operation of the press. He went west at the time of the Removal, and was as zealous there at printing and binding as he had been in the old nation. The goodness and the zeal of the Worcesters seems to have had an increasing influence on the printer, as it had on most of the people with whom they came in contact. He not only remained a faithful laborer, but became a contributor to the Mission. Out of a salary that probably never exceeded four hundred dollars annually, he made contributions as large as five dollars. To his mind, the proof of the cause was in the lives of the men who represented it.

Always Samuel Worcester had a double problem in his life: to attend to every detail of his work as missionary, minister of the Gospel, supervisor of the secular affairs of his mission station, translator, and head of the press; and to walk without deviation from the path of right-

10 James C. Pilling, *Bibliography of the Iroquoian Languages* (Washington: Government Printing Office, 1888), pp. 41-2.

eousness after the manner of the saints. There was no separation of the two aims; every letter that he wrote shows them interwoven inextricably. In the following letter, details of the press and a temperance dilemma are of equal concern:

"NEW ECHOTA, June 10, 1828

"DEAR SIR:

"The printing paper, except two boxes which exceeded a wagon load, has arrived in good order. The two boxes remain at Augusta. The box of articles for this station has also arrived in perfect order. We will endeavor to write briefly to the donors. We were quite disappointed in the printing paper on account of its size. I know not what is the ground of the mistake, and am unacquainted with the sizes of paper; but this, though charged super-royal in the invoice, is what the printers here call imperial. It is between that of the N. Y. *Observer* & that of the Boston *Recorder* of the present year, both of which I have supposed to be called imperial. Paper of a better quality and of the proper size might probably have been procured for the same price. If the *Phœnix* is printed on this it must look badly on account of the quantity of blank space, and would though the form were made as large as the chase would possibly admit. I am sorry for the mistake, but do not know that there can be any remedy.

"I think I stated in my last that the invoice of printing paper had not been received. It afterwards came to hand.

"In answer to your inquiry I state that I have received from the Treasurer of the Cherokee Nation

Balance due for press, types, &c.		$487.31
Brewster & Prescott's bill of freight	$142.39	
Deduct freight of articles for mis-		
sion	8.05	134.34
Postage of letters relating to the press		.75
		613.40

"The payment for paper I have not yet obtained.

"I might have mentioned before this that there is a deficiency in the Cherokee fount of type, some *accents* which are charged in the bill not being to be found. Some other trifling deficiencies I believe the printers have mentioned. An additional supply of type for headings &c. is needed. I shall write particularly respecting this soon.

"I expect to need presently a few reams of paper for printing hymn books; and a few more soon after, I hope, for the Gospel of Matthew in Cherokee. The paper on which the *Herald* is printed is such as I would like. Folded in 24to it would be of very suitable size for hymn books. I shall include printing paper in my list of articles needed by the station. Would the Committee object to my employing a printer from abroad to print hymn books, if it should seem necessary?

"I have read Dr. Beecher's sermons on intemperance with great pleasure, and should have been glad if this had been one of the stations to which they were sent. I have also rejoiced much in noticing the progress and influence of the Temperance Society. I should like to have your opinion, I mean that of the officers of the Board, in the following case. I need vinegar, and must purchase something to make it of. I can make it either of whiskey or sugar. Made of whiskey it will be less costly, and perhaps somewhat better. Shall I buy or shall I not buy?

"I know not that I have any special intelligence to communicate, but remain, with much affection to you all,

"Your servant in the Gospel,
S. A. WORCESTER

H. HILL, Esqr.
Treas. A.B.C.F.M."

Practical affairs and religious and moral issues both claimed attention in letters which the Board sent out. Jeremiah Evarts, Worcester's former teacher, was the one to answer his letter of inquiry about the employment of a printer and the making of vinegar. "The business part of your letter has doubtless all been attended to," Mr. Evarts wrote. "In regard to your question of conscience respecting the obtaining of vinegar, I advise

"1. To get it, if you can, by requesting some of your Cherokee friends, who live on the borders of Tennessee, to import it in the form of vinegar.

"2. To use no more of it than is conducive to health, which, if your constitution is like mine, will be a very small quantity.

"3. To make it from sugar rather than whiskey, though it cost more & be not quite so good. There are two objections to your having whiskey in your possession—the first, that it furnishes a pretext for others obtaining it, who would not use it so harmlessly—the second, that the Cherokee laws forbid the introduction of it, if not in all cases, at least generally.

[86]

"I do not know as I understand your question about employing a printer from abroad for your hymn books. Is it whether you may send the book to be printed at another press than that of the Cherokees? Or did you think of bringing in a printer to work off that particular work on the Cherokee press? I see no objection to either course, if the interests of the mission require you to adopt either. But, if the national press & national printer can do your work, I would recommend that you employ them.

"The exertions for the promotion of temperance are favored beyond all expectation. Wonders are performed, of which you would hardly conceive. In some places the consumption of ardent spirits is diminished three-fourths —in many others fully one-half—in short drinking is rapidly going out of fashion."

One of the details involved in beginning the work of the press was the removal of the Worcesters to New Echota. Samuel and Ann had lived at Brainerd Mission a little more than two years; they had found the life there a pleasant, if strenuous one, with congenial fellow-workers and the plain but secure comforts that the excellent management of the Mission had afforded them. Now they must leave this place that had been their first home together, with its farm, its orchard, its schools for boys and for girls, its meetinghouse, for a new home where they must establish such things for themselves and their neighbors among the Indians. But they had no lack of courage for the undertaking that was before them. Knowing themselves to be the servants of God, they had no dread of any place or any work to which He might call them. Ann repacked the linens and the blankets and the books and the furniture that belonged to them, and on the twenty-ninth of November, 1827, they moved from

[87]

Brainerd Mission to New Echota. They had only a borrowed house for the winter, but it would shelter them, and when spring came they were to build one for themselves. There were three of them now to be sheltered and clothed and fed—Samuel, Ann, and Baby Ann Eliza.

Two days after their arrival at the Cherokee capital, Elias Boudinot and his family arrived. He, like his cousin John Ridge, had married one of the young ladies of Cornwall, and though at the announcement of their engagement the church bells were tolled for hours and the betrothed white girl and her Indian lover were burned in effigy, the marriage was a happy one. Harriet Gold Boudinot had not come all the way from Connecticut to Georgia to pine for the security she had left behind; she busied herself rearing children and setting up a domestic establishment like those of the New England she had left. Ann Worcester and Harriet Boudinot had the instincts of home-making; this could be achieved among Indians as well as among white neighbors. When Harriet's parents made a forty-seven-day journey to visit their daughter in her New Echota home, in 1829, they seem to have found her environment beyond their criticism. "She has a large and convenient framed house," her father wrote, "two story, 60 by 40 ft. on the ground, well done off and well furnished with comforts of life. They get their supplies of clothes and groceries—they have their year's store of teas, clothes, paper, ink, etc.,—from Boston, and their sugars, molasses, etc., from Augusta; they have two or three barrels of flour on hand at once.

"This neighborhood is truly an interesting and pleasant place; the ground is smooth and level as a floor—the center of the Nation—a new place laid out in city form,—one hundred lots, one acre each—a spring called the public spring, about twice as large as our saw-mill brook, near the centre, with other springs on the plat; six framed houses in sight, besides a Council House, Court House, printing office, and four stores all in sight of Boudinot's house."[11]

New Echota, then, had become the center of the Cherokee national life. Those who were to direct that life had come there to live; the council house was there; the press was there in its new log housing. On February 21, 1828, the first issue of the *Cherokee Phœnix* was printed. A new chapter in Cherokee history had begun.

11 *Chronicles of Oklahoma*, Vol. XI, No. 3 (September, 1933), p. 929.

Gold

THE CONSTANT concern of Samuel Worcester was to keep the spiritual aims that prompted all his efforts foremost in the minds of those he served. To him the advancing civilization of the Cherokees was a matter for rejoicing because it implied the advance of Christianity, also, among them; their increasing literacy, to his mind, meant the probability of their learning more about the Bible and about the one true way of belief represented in Calvinistic theology. He was of necessity involved every day—except the Sabbath—in secular affairs; but he had a way of combining them with spiritual matters, of turning them to purposes of religion, that only a Yankee with a shrewd mind and a true heart could have achieved. He wished above all things to eschew worldliness; he must on the other hand depend in part on success in worldly affairs for the accomplishment of salvation among the Indians.

Already the mission to the Cherokees had been charged with the fault of worldliness. Brainerd, beginning humbly with a farm only partly cleared for cultivation, had grown and prospered, and by its very prosperity had drawn criticism upon itself. It had been said to function as a farm, as a blacksmith's and mechanic's shop, as a boarding school, and as an hostelry, without functioning in the saving of Cherokee souls. It had been referred to as a "great establishment, which had the appearance of wealth and profit, and excited envy, and gave rise to injurious reports of the worldliness of the mission."[1] Consequently, the size of the mission was cut down in 1824; the missionaries were distributed to new and smaller stations set up in various parts of the Cherokee nation, and schools were established in outlying places where there was an interest in education. In 1827 the annual report of the American Board indicated seven missionary stations comprising the Cherokee mission: Brainerd, Willstown, Creek Path, Hightower, Haweis, Carmel, and Candy's Creek, each one "as small as can be consistent with the care of a large family." There were, in all, thirty-four missionaries and assistants. The charge of worldliness seems to have been soon thoroughly eradicated, for 1827 was reported as "a year of moderate progress, with no remarkable changes."[2] But Samuel Worcester's heart could take deep joy in another statement in the report, that "there was some special seriousness and some were added to the churches, at several of the stations."

However pressing his duties were in connection with the press, the farm that he must supervise, and the schools that he must follow in minute detail, he found time for an incredible amount of work as a missionary of the Gospel. In those days when there were fewer mechanical aids than the present time offers and fewer distractions from whatever work might be under way, there was time for the accomplishment of everything. How many sermons Samuel Worcester prepared carefully and preached ardently, how many religious gatherings of Indians he attended,

1 Tracy, *A History of the American Board of Commissioners for Foreign Missions*, p. 132.
2 *Ibid.*, p. 170.

will never be known; but if there be a Golden Book where a tireless man's most sincere efforts are recorded, his name may lead all the rest. One of his daughters, late in her life, remembered of him, even more than his immense vitality and his unfailingly sympathetic understanding, "his living faithfully up to the declaration, 'I am determined to know nothing among you, save Jesus Christ, and him crucified.' He made this mean that he would never preach a sermon, on whatever subject, in which he would not before its close, so plainly bring in Redemption by Christ as that all might embrace it if they would. His skill in making this come in naturally, with whatever subject or text he might be handling, seemed to me remarkable."[3]

Like nearly all the missionaries among the Indians who were themselves not of Indian extraction, he never learned to preach in their language. He always wished to, and always hoped until the latter years of his life that in time he might free himself from other duties long enough to perfect his speech to the point of preaching in Cherokee and so dispensing with an interpreter. Ordinary speech he learned to manage readily, but preaching was another matter. Only the expert could make sure he was not misleading his hearers into false ideas of doctrine, because of the nature of the Cherokee tongue; and false doctrine, either in preaching or in translating, must be avoided at any cost. "There is," Worcester wrote, "a peculiar definiteness about the Cherokee language, which compels us to settle many questions, which the English and Greek leave ambiguous. *Definite* we must be, whether definitely *right* or definitely *wrong*; and as we *wish* to be right, we are obliged to spend much time in settling ques-

3 Couch, *Pages from Cherokee Indian History*, p. 24.

tions which other translators leave for the commentator." He was humble about his failure with respect to preaching in Cherokee, as a letter written to the Board as late as 1851 proves: "The fact that none of us preach in Cherokee, or are likely to, is indeed a difficulty, and the want of an adequate number of suitable interpreters is a greater one. And I think it now highly probable that no white missionary will hereafter acquire it. Yet if the state of things were as when I came, I would say, send a young man with even as great a faculty for acquiring languages as I possessed when I was young, which was not great, and let him make that his first aim, and he will acquire the language so as to preach in it. You will ask, why did not *you* do it? My answer is, that the Providence of God seemed plainly to point out the work of translation as the leading object of my attention, and that precluded the other."

Almost as soon as he arrived at Brainerd, Samuel Worcester set about his work as an evangelist. No time was to be lost; to men of his type of theology salvation was likely to be a slow and gradual process; the sooner it was begun, the greater men's chances were of escaping damnation. Within a few months after his arrival, he was at Haweis where, through a misunderstanding, preparations had not been made for the organization of a church, but where an interesting meeting was held nevertheless. "Probably," he wrote, "150 adult Cherokees were present on the Sabbath. Besides a sermon from Mr. Butrick, interpreted by David Steiner, and one from Mr. Chamberlain, interpreted by Steiner, and one from me, interpreted by John Ridge, on the Sabbath, there was a meeting on Saturday afternoon, in which all the services were performed by Cherokees, in their own language, a prayer meeting early on Sabbath morning, a meeting for addresses by native Cherokees in the afternoon, and another in the evening: and the Monthly Concert on Monday morning, attended by 50 adult Cherokees. Exhortations in Cherokee were made by John Huss, Samuel J. Mills, Archibald Downing, and a young man, a member of the church at Willstown. Another young man, also, who was baptized here, but has not conducted worthily, made a speech, confessing his faults. Huss spoke several times, and, I believe, in a very interesting manner. Mills also spoke at different meetings; and an address from him at the Monthly Concert I judged to be an hour in length, in a very animated strain. I do not know that there was an instance of hesitancy, or the repetition of a single word, throughout the whole. I think I never heard a specimen of fluency to be compared with it in any language."[4] It is evident, from this account, that the Cherokees loved eloquence and were disciplined to receive it in large quantities; they had been trained to this for generations before they heard the eloquence of Christian ministers and laymen.

Even the public examinations held at the schools were made occasions for sermons and meetings of a deeply religious nature. Mr. Worcester wrote of the examination held at Brainerd in August after his arrival. "Our first meeting was a lecture preparatory to the Lord's Supper, on Saturday afternoon. Mr. Reece interpreted the sermon, after which Mr. Huss and Mr. Downing addressed the people in their own language. In the evening, there was another meeting, at which time, except that spent in prayer and singing, chiefly in Cherokee, was occupied by addresses from Mr. Mills and Mr. Reece, in the same

4 *Missionary Herald*, XXII (1826), 353.

A Missionary, preaching to Indians.

"Go . . . teach all nations." Matt. 28: 19.

"GO . . . . TEACH ALL NATIONS"

language. On the Sabbath morning there was a meeting for prayer. After that, a sermon and the communion service were interpreted by Mr. Reece. By this time, so great a number of people had collected, that the schoolhouse, with all the seats for which room could be found, was crowded to the utmost, and the number excluded by want of room was considerable. At another meeting in the afternoon, addresses were made by a man called the Whirlwind, a member of the Methodist church, and by Mr. Huss, in their native tongue. In the evening, Mr. Huss and others went into a room in the house and began singing. Immediately the room was crowded with Cherokees, and Mr. Huss and Mr. Reece successively addressed them. At all these meetings, a part, and in the two last all, of the singing and prayers were in the Cherokee language. We regarded it, all together, as an animating scene.

"A man by the name of Atisitihi, and his wife, were received on Saturday, as candidates for baptism, with a view to recommend them, as such, to the notice of the church to be formed at Haweis."[5]

There was, indeed, a depth and earnestness about the Cherokees at this time such as is seldom found in any people. At Haweis (named for the English donor of fifty pounds to the American Board for the cause of Indian Missions) there was matter for wonder at the transformation that had taken place. The man whom they called Samuel J. Mills had come, troubled and distraught, to Brainerd in the summer of 1821 to made inquiry about the religion they taught there; a few weeks later he had been baptized and had taken the name of the young student of Williams College through whom the present

5 *Ibid.*

missionary movement had begun; now, at Haweis, he worked tirelessly for the salvation and the improvement of his people. At Brainerd they still talked of the beauty and the brilliant work of Catherine Brown, sister of David Brown, who had on account of her elegant person and manners, "probably received more attention than any other girl in the nation, and was haughty, vain, and loaded with trinkets." She had been baptized, had worked diligently in the school at Brainerd and later become a teacher in the school organized at Creek Path. She had become the idol of the mission and its patrons; but she had succumbed to tuberculosis at what seemed the beginning of her career. She had come a long road, at the time of her death in her early twenties; the missionaries wrote of her that "her end was peace." John Arch, too, had been made new by the influences of the Cherokee mission. "According to his own account, he had attended school for a short time in his childhood, and had learned to spell a little. After he left school, he had a desire to learn to read, and studied his spelling-book at times till it was worn out; after which he had nearly forgotten the little that he once knew. . . . . He heard. . . . that a school has been established for the instruction of the Cherokees. He determined to come; and after travelling 150 miles on foot in seven days, arrived at Brainerd on the 26th of January. He did not know his own age, but supposed it to be about 25. He could converse in English, and his countenance indicated a mind capable of improvement; but he had the dress and dirty appearance of the most uncultivated part of his tribe; and his age and wild and savage aspect seemed to mark him as one unfit for admission to the school. But it was difficult to refuse him. He readily agreed to the terms of admission and continuance. He

[96]

cheerfully sold his gun, his only property, and the dearest treasure of an Indian, to procure suitable clothing. He was admitted on trial. He applied himself diligently to his studies, and made good proficiency. He soon showed a thoughtful concern for his soul, and appeared desirous to know the way of life and to walk in it. In October, his father came to take him away; but at the earnest request of John and his instructors, after staying a few days and becoming acquainted with the mission, willingly permitted him to remain. In November, he was examined as a candidate for admission to the church, and employed as an interpreter to Mr. Buttrick. At this time he said that he often felt inclined to tell the Indians about God and the Savior, but he knew so little that he thought it would not please God; and he desired to obtain an education, that he might be able to do it."[6] He continued his work as interpreter as long as he lived, traveling tirelessly from meeting to meeting in all seasons and under all conditions. When the Worcesters arrived among the Cherokees, John Arch had recently died, "as became a Christian." The Indians were learning, Samuel saw, how to live and die in the Lord.

The outlook for the Cherokees was indeed hopeful. Two years of residence at New Echota, at the very heart of the affairs of the tribe, convinced Samuel Worcester that the civilization of the whole people, as well as their evangelization, was not an impossible dream. There were, he well knew, contrary influences, but the trend was in the right direction. Even the letter he wrote to William S. Coody, secretary of the Cherokee delegation at Washington, tempered as it was by the strict honesty that must characterize statements made for the public, showed his

6 Tracy, *A History of the American Board of Commissioners for Foreign Missions*, p. 78.

optimism. "I cheerfully comply with your request, that I would forward to you a statement respecting the progress of improvement among your people, the Cherokees. Whatever might be said of the propriety or impropriety of missionaries discussing the question of the removal of the Indians, it can hardly be doubted that it is proper for one to give a statement of what passes under his observation, in regard to the present condition of the tribes interested in that question. I shall not say anything in this communication, which I shall be unwilling to have come before the public, accompanied with my proper signature, if occasion require.

"Whatever deficiencies there may be in my statement, I shall use my utmost endeavor, that nothing colored, nothing which will not bear the strictest scrutiny, may find a place.

"It may not be amiss to state, briefly, what opportunities I have enjoyed of forming a judgment respecting the state of the Cherokee people. It was four years last October, since I came to the nation; during which time I have made it my home, having resided two years at Brainerd, and the remainder of the time at this place. Though I have not spent very much of my time in traveling, yet I have visited almost every part of the nation, except a section on the northeast. Two annual sessions of the General Council have passed while I have been residing at the seat of government, at which times a great number of the people of all classes and from all parts are to be seen.

"The statistical information which has been published respecting this nation, I hope you have on hand, or will receive from some other source; it goes far toward giving a correct view of the state of the people. I have only to say, that, judging from what I see around me, I believe that a similar enumeration made the present year would show, by the comparison, a rapid improvement since the census was taken.

"The printed constitution and laws of your nation, also, you doubtless have. They shew your progress in civil polity. As far as my knowledge extends they are executed with a good degree of efficiency, and their execution meets with not the least hindrance from anything like a spirit of insubordination among the people. Oaths are constantly administered in the courts of justice, and I believe I have never heard of an instance of perjury.

"It has been well observed by others, that the progress of a people in civilization is to be determined by comparing the present with the past. I can only compare what I see with what I am told has been.

"The present principal chief is about forty years of age. When he was a boy, his father procured him a good suit of clothes, in the fashion of the sons of civilized people; but he was so ridiculed by his mates as a *white* boy that he took off his new suit, and refused to wear it. The editor of the *Phœnix* is twenty-seven years old. He well remembers that he felt awkward and ashamed of his singularity, when he began to wear the dress of a white boy. Now every boy is proud of a civilized suit, and those feel awkward and ashamed of their singularity who are destitute of it. At the last session of the General Council, I scarcely recollect having seen any members who were not clothed in the same manner as the white inhabitants of the neighboring states; and those very few (I am informed the precise number was four) who were partially clothed in Indian style were, nevertheless, very decently attired. I have seen, I believe, only one Cherokee woman, and she an aged woman, away from her home, who was not clothed in, at least, a decent long gown. At home only one, a very aged woman, who appeared willing to be seen in the original native dress; three or four, only, who had at their own houses dressed themselves in Indian style, but hid themselves with shame at the approach of a stranger. I am thus particular, because particularity gives more accurate ideas than general statements. Among the elderly men there is yet a considerable portion, I dare not say whether a majority or a minority, who retain the Indian dress in part. The younger men almost all dress like the whites around them, except that the greater number wear a turban instead of a hat, and in cold weather a blanket frequently serves for a cloak. Cloaks, however, are becoming common. There yet remains room for improvement in dress, but that improvement is making with surprising rapidity.

"The arts of spinning and weaving, the Cherokee women, generally, put into practice. Most of their garments are of their own spinning and weaving, from cotton, the produce of their own fields; though considerable northern domestic, and much calico, is worn, nor is silk uncommon. Numbers of them wear imported cloths, broadcloths, &c., and many wear mixed cotton and wool, the manufacture of their wives; but the greater part are clothed principally in cotton.

"Except the arts of spinning and weaving, but little progress has been made in manufactures. A few Cherokees, however, are mechanics.

"Agriculture is the principal employment and support of the people. It is the dependence of almost every family. *As to the wandering part of the people, who live by the chase, if they are to be found in the nation, I certainly have not found them, nor ever heard of them, except from the floor of Congress, and other distant sources of information. I do not know of a single family who depend, in any considerable degree, on game for a support.* It is true that deer and turkies are frequently killed, but not in sufficient numbers to form any dependence as the means of subsistence. The land is cultivated with very different degrees of industry; but I believe that few fail of an adequate supply of food. The ground is uniformly cultivated by means of the plough, and not, as formerly, by the hoe only.

"The houses of the Cherokees are of all sorts, from an elegant painted or brick mansion, down to a very mean cabin. If we speak, however, of the mass of the people, they live in comfortable log houses, generally one story high, but frequently two; sometimes of hewn logs, and sometimes unhewn; commonly with a wooden chimney, and a floor of puncheons, or what a New England man would call slabs. Their houses are not *generally* well furnished; many have scarcely any furniture, though a few are furnished even elegantly, and many decently. Improvement in the furniture of their houses appears to follow after improvement in dress, but at present is making rapid progress.

"As to education, the number who can read and write English is considerable, though it bears but a moderate proportion to the whole population. Among such, the degree of improvement and intelligence is various. The Cherokee language, as far as I can judge, is read and written by a large majority of these between childhood and middle age. Only a few who are beyond middle age have learned.

"In regard to the progress of religion, I cannot, I suppose, do better than to state, as nearly as I am able, the number of members in the churches of the several denominations. The whole number of native members of the Presbyterian churches is not far from 180. In the churches of the United Brethren, are about 50. In the Baptist churches, I do not know; probably as many as 50. The Methodists, I believe, reckon in their society, more than 800; of whom I suppose the greater part are natives. Many of the heathenish customs of the people have gone entirely, or almost entirely, into disuse, and others are fast following their steps. I believe the greater part of the people acknowledge the Christian religion to be the true religion, although many who make this acknowledgment know very little of that religion, and many others do not feel its power. Through the blessing of God, however, religion is steadily gaining ground.

"But, it will be asked, is the improvement which has been described, general among the people, and are the full-blooded Indians civilized, or only the half-breeds? I answer that, in the description which I have given, I have spoken of the mass of the people, without distinction. If it be asked, however, what class are most advanced, I answer, as a general thing—those of mixed blood. They have taken the lead, although some of full blood are as refined as any. But, though those of mixed blood are generally in the van, as might naturally be expected, yet the whole mass of the people is on the march.

"There is one other subject, on which I think it due to justice to give my testimony, whatever it may be worth. Whether the Cherokees are wise in desiring to remain here, or not, I express no opinion. But it is certainly just, that it should be known whether or not they do, as a body, wish to remain. It is not possible for a person to dwell among them without hearing much on the subject.

I have heard much. *It is said, abroad, that the common people would gladly remove, but are deterred by the chiefs, and a few other influential men. It is not so.* I say, with the utmost assurance, it is not so. Nothing is plainer, than that it is the earnest wish of the whole body of the people to remain where they are. They are not overawed by the chiefs. Individuals may be overawed by *popular opinion*, but *not by the chiefs*. On the other hand, if there were a chief in favor of removal, *he* would be overawed *by the people*. He would know that he could not open his mouth in favor of such a proposition, but on pain, not only of the failure of his reëlection, but of popular odium and scorn. The whole tide of national feeling sets, in one strong and unbroken current, against removal to the west."

In the last paragraph of this letter, Worcester approached a matter that, for all the advancement achieved by the Cherokees in the direction of the white man's civilization, threatened them alarmingly. This was the question of their removal westward. During the administration of Thomas Jefferson, removal of the Indians to lands west of the Mississippi had first been given consideration as a solution to the whole Indian problem. It was a solution for the white man, not for the Indian. Jefferson himself had favored the plan, and it had been as a result of his proposal that part of the Cherokee tribe, principally those of the Lower Towns who preferred to live largely by hunting and fishing rather than by farming and raising stock and learning trades, had sent a delegation to the west to look for new lands and had finally, to the number of more than three thousand, removed there. Those who chose to live a settled life, mostly those who lived in the northern part of the Cherokee nation and were called the Cherokees of the Upper Towns were, he proposed, to "be placed under the same government of the United States, become citizens thereof, and be ruled by our laws; in fine, to be our brothers instead of our children." Congress, he assured them, wished nothing more sincerely than to render their condition secure and happy. He spoke, apparently, in good faith, without a knowledge of how complicated the Indian question was soon to become. "Tell your people," he concluded his communication, "that I take them all by the hand, that I leave them free to do as they choose, and that whatever choice they make, I will be their friend and father." But the next year after he wrote these words he went out of office; Madison, his successor, was too busy with events connected with the War of 1812 to attend to the troubles of the Indians, and Monroe was involved in matters of commerce and foreign policy. Monroe favored Indian citizenship and individual allotment of lands, but he did not attempt to bring them about.

Meanwhile, the states to the north were outstripping those of the south in population and in manufacturing and industry; the State of Georgia grew increasingly anxious to rid itself of the handicap imposed upon it by the existence of an Indian nation, sovereign and independent, within its own borders. Of the Creeks, who were less powerful than the Cherokees and lacked their organization, the Georgians had managed to rid themselves in 1827. But the Cherokees spoke of a prior right, and would not be ousted. In fact, they recalled the terms of the treaty of Holston, signed in 1791, by which, "If any person, not an Indian, shall settle on any of the Cherokees' lands, he shall forfeit the protection of the United States, and the Cherokees may punish him." But white men pressed against the Cherokees on all sides; they looked upon the

Cherokees as inferior and without authority; the Cherokees looked upon them as intruders. The situation had, by the beginning of Jackson's administration in 1829, become more complicated than Jefferson had ever anticipated. As the *Cyclopædia of Political Science* explains, "The state of Georgia was thus threatened with the permanent establishment of an *imperium in imperio* over which state laws did not operate, a district of refuge within which any criminal, if agreeable to the Indians, might set state officers and writs at defiance. . . . . With this grievance as a vehicle, it was natural that the greed for the rich Creek and Cherokee lands should urge not only private speculators, but the state government also, to active efforts to oust the rightful owners, despite the supreme law of the land, and the solemn guarantee given by the United States."[7]

To Georgia, removal was the only solution; but to the Cherokees who were settled and established within the boundaries of Georgia, living lives of decency and order under their own constitution, the idea of removal was untenable. They had decided against removal, years before, and had been told that they might follow their own decision. They were not a people who changed their minds. The *Phœnix*, which in the beginning had room for translations from the Gospels and for articles of general cultural interest, came soon to be filled with denunciations of the removal schemes. Even Samuel Worcester, knowing that Christianity could not advance among a people who were grieved and wronged, could not begrudge the space their controversial articles required; he must pray for power to bridle his own temper and stop his own pen lest he become too ardent a partisan in the

7 *Cyclopædia of Political Science*, I, 391.

Cherokee cause. He understood, as Congress and the State of Georgia did not understand, how fundamentally opposed to change the Cherokee temperament was; he read with a great swell of pity in his heart a contribution sent for publication in the *Phœnix* by the citizens of Aquohee District.

"To our beloved Brother Elias Boudinot: We understand that rumors are in circulation, which are calculated to induce our friends to believe, that we are willing to leave our country. In order to counteract the injurious tendency of such reports, we wish to communicate to the public our own testimony on the subject.

"The emigrating scheme has been proposed to us, and we have considered it deliberately, and the result is, that not a single citizen of this District has agreed to the plan. The bones of our fathers lie here in security, and we cannot consent to abandon them to be crushed beneath the feet of strangers.

"Most of our old men have lived here from infancy to old age, and our young men inherit the same disposition. The lands we possess are the gift of our Creator. They are moreover recognized by the United States, and *guaranteed to us forever*. Our limits on all sides are permanently fixed and well known. Within these limits we consider ourselves at home, and have no doubt to the goodness of our title. And the pure air of our country, the wholesome springs and fertile soil are well suited to supply our wants and to promote our happiness. In the enjoyment of these blessings, our rising families are making rapid advance in knowledge and industry and good order.

"Our Creator has not given us the land beyond the Mississippi, but has given it to other people; and why should we wish to enter upon their possessions?

"We have not been in the habit of moving from place to place as the white people have, and we think those of our white brethren who are so anxious to take possession of our lands might with a little trouble, keep on to the west and settle the lands which they recommend to us. We feel injured and aggrieved in being continuously harrassed with solicitations to part with our last refuge on earth. When a person owns certain property and a brother wishes to purchase it, if the owner refuses to sell we think the other ought to cease his importunity and should never think of having recourse to unfair and forcible means to obtain it.

"Our peaceful homes, our cultivated fields, and our friendly neighbors are daily acquiring stronger hold on our affections. Our laws encourage virtue and industry, and punish vice. Our chiefs use their influence to diffuse light among the people and their efforts are crowned with success. Veneration for the laws is felt to the remotest corner of the land, and a peaceable and orderly disposition pervades the whole population. Being placed in these favorable circumstances by the goodness of our Creator, we have no inclination to relinquish our inheritance for the uncultivated wilds in the vicinity of lawless and hostile savages. In fact it would be ruinous to us to do so. We entertain friendly dispositions towards the citizens of the United States, and our enemies themselves cannot charge us with the violation of good order in our intercourse with them. Though we are sorry to say that some of our white brethren, forgetting the superiority which they claim over us, frequently cross the line to steal horses and other property and strange as it may appear are screened from punishment by the laws of a Christian people who call us savages. We have borne these injuries in silence, relying on the justice of the United States Government to make good her solemn engagements for our protection."[8]

How much the Indians had yet to learn about the ways of Christian people; how much about the good faith and guarantee of a government where a chance for unjustifiable profit was concerned! How acutely a gentle savage might suffer, at the hands of a Christian gentleman! And how blind were the eyes of the Creator of all men! Had not the Book of Matthew, circulated among them bit by bit and published chapter by chapter in the *Phœnix*, taught them how the Father saw all and bade them have no fear: *Are not two sparrows sold for a farthing? and one of them shall not fall on the ground without your Father. But the very hairs of your head are all numbered. Fear ye not therefore, ye are of more value than many sparrows.*

In 1828 occurred the event that determined the expulsion of the Cherokees from Georgia. Gold was discovered near Dahlonega. This was in the center of the Upper Towns, scarcely more than fifty miles from New Echota. A negro slave found a nugget, grew excited over his discovery, and made it known. The news spread like a kindled fire, and from then on the rightfulness of the policy of removal, that had been a debatable question in the minds of many people before, was established beyond question. When gold existed in paying quantities, the rule of might was the only rule that was recognized. Samuel Worcester feared, from that time, that his hope for the permanence of the Cherokees in Georgia was a lost hope; the only chance, he believed, lay in struggling with all his powers of body and mind, and in prayer. With God,

8 *Cherokee Phœnix*, Vol. II, No. 27, October 14, 1829.

he knew, all things were possible; but the ways of God were intricate and beyond man's comprehension.

The existence of gold in Georgia had been known before 1828. Spanish explorers had been the first white men to find it there, and although the policy of the Spanish government had kept it secret, old mining shafts and fortifications had disclosed the Spaniards' mining operations to Oglethorpe's settlers. About 1815 a little boy, playing on the bank of the Chestatee River, had found a shining pebble and brought it to his mother. She washed it, found it to be a nugget of gold, and sold it to a white man in the settlement nearby. Though she seems to have concealed the exact place from which the nugget came, the general location of its origin was known. Men talked of how the dreams of De Soto were to come true in the Cherokee country. By 1819, the whole territory east of the Chestatee had been lost to the Cherokees by compulsory cessions. Now, with the discovery of gold on Ward's Creek, a western branch of the Chestatee, the remainder of the Cherokee lands was imperiled.

The election of Andrew Jackson to the presidency, in the fall of 1828, precipitated the Cherokees' misfortune. No one doubted what his attitude would be; he had been an Indian fighter and was an Indian hater. The constitutionality of laws passed against the Cherokees need not be considered, with him in the presidential chair. Within a month after Jackson's election, the first of these new laws discriminating against the Cherokees was passed. This law, which was to be effective June 1, 1830, annexed to Georgia all the lands of the Cherokees within the state, made null and void the laws and customs established by the Cherokees, and forbade any person of Indian blood to act as a witness in a suit in which a white man was the defendant. Justice was impossible, under such legislation; it would have been unlikely anyhow, with the desire of the white settlers strongly against it. John Howard Payne, who spent some time among the Cherokees preceding their removal and became ardent in their cause, has left this description of the dignity of the courts: "At one of those log-hut courts, where the business was begun before the hut was finished, the trunks of the felled trees were left standing inside for seats, and on the amplest sat the judge, paring the nails of his nether fingers. 'Why don't that tarnation jury come, Sheriff?'

" 'Please your honor,' said the Sheriff, 'they can't be long now; I've got nine of 'em tied with hickory wyths, & five men and two dogs out a'ter the other three.' "[9]

Force began, indeed, to be the greatest element of the law. White men seized land wherever they could oust an Indian family, or bought it for a pittance, often with the aid of whiskey. The Indians struggled to maintain the rights which they still held the Creator had given them. Jackson represented their claims to the land as faulty, since they claimed tracts they had never lived upon; they argued, logically, that their claim was more just than that of a people who got their charter from a British king who was never less than three thousand miles from the land. But it was no time for logic; while the Cherokees reasoned, individuals were dispossessed. The parents of David and Catherine Brown appeared at Brainerd, pushed out of the house they had built and deprived of the abundance they had had for many years. Ta-che-che, according to a story related by John Howard Payne, lost part of his farm "in a way not uncommon in other cases. The Georgia

9 Manuscripts of John Howard Payne, *Cherokee Notes*, II, p. 25. Newberry Library, Ayer Collection.

law forbade the Cherokees to clear more land or make further improvements. But sometimes a white family would come, plead destitution, & ask to remain a few days. The family would clear some ground, put up a shack, and so outwit the law for the Cherokee. Thus he would be robbed of his field for his kindness. Mr. George Hicks gave a white man a home with him, & did not send him away at once under the new law. Then the man appeared & ordered him to take away his wife and family, as he wanted the house. Hicks finally offered $2 a day for the house till he could get another for his family, but it was refused. He took his family to the shelter of an old sugar-camp in the woods. The house was of hewn logs, with shingle roof & good floors, & had good furniture which was mostly lost to him."[10]

Efforts were made to strengthen the Cherokees' resistance. An old law was revived, inflicting the death penalty on any member of the tribe who sold land without the consent of the tribe. Instances of sale were comparatively few, and were usually forced, but the Cherokees clutched at straws now for aid. Womankiller, of Hickory Log District, spoke eloquently in the Council in favor of the bill. "My Children: Permit me to call you so, as I am an old man and have lived a long time, watching the well being of this Nation. I love your lives, and wish our people to increase on the land of our fathers. The bill before you is to punish wicked men, who may arise to cede away our country contrary to the consent of the Council. It is a good law—it will not kill the innocent but the guilty. I feel the importance of the subject, and am glad the law has been suggested. My companions, men of renown, in

10 Manuscripts of John Howard Payne, Vol. VIII, unpaged. Newberry Library, Ayer Collection.

Council, who now sleep in the dust, spoke the same language, and I now stand on the verge of the grave to bear witness to their love of country. My sun of existence is now fast approaching to its sitting, and my aged bones will soon be laid underground, and I wish them laid in the bosom of this earth we have received from our fathers who had it from the Great Being above. When I shall sleep in forgetfulness, I hope my bones will not be deserted by you. I do not speak this in fear of any of you, as the evidence of your attachment to the country is proved in the bill now before your consideration. I am told, that the Government of the United States will spoil their treaties with us and sink our National Council under their feet. It may be so, but it shall not be with our consent, or by the misconduct of our people. We hold them by the golden chain of friendship, made when our friendship was worth a price, and if they act the tyrant and kill us for our lands, we shall, in a state of unoffending innocence, sleep with thousands of our departed people. My feeble limbs will not allow me to stand longer. I can say no more, but before I sit, allow me to tell you that I am in favor of the bill."[11]

In general, the policy of the missionaries had been to advise and encourage the Indians to exercise their full rights. Unexercised, these rights would soon enough be lost; exercised, there was at least a chance of maintaining them. The missionaries made no effort to share in the gold that had been found; that was not their function, but they did encourage the Indians to mine gold within their own territory. And Jeremiah Evarts, in Boston, wrote a series of articles under the pseudonymn of William Penn, in which he reviewed the Indian treaties and set

11 *Cherokee Phœnix*, Vol. II, No. 29, October 28, 1829.

forth the solemn obligation of both the United States and the state of Georgia to defend the rights guaranteed to the Indians. These were copied in many periodicals throughout the country, among them the Cherokee *Phoenix*, and did much to create public sympathy for the Indian cause. But sympathy was ineffective now.

In June, 1830, the Governor of Georgia issued a proclamation prohibiting the Indians from taking any more gold from their lands. "A proclamation by his Excellency, Geo. R. Gilmer, Governor and Commander-in-Chief of the Army and Navy of this State and of the Militia thereof.

"WHEREAS it has been discovered that the lands in the territory now occupied by the Cherokee Indians within the limits of this state, abound with valuable minerals, and especially gold—AND WHEREAS the State of Georgia has the fee title to said lands, and the entire and exclusive property in the gold and silver therein; AND WHEREAS numerous persons, citizens of this and other states, together with the Indian occupants of said territory. . . . . engaged in digging for gold in said land, and taking therefrom great amounts in value, thereby appropriating riches to themselves which of right equally belonged to every other citizen of the state. . . . I have thought best to issue this my proclamation notifying all persons whom it may concern that the jurisdiction of this state is now extended over all the territory in the occupancy of the Cherokees, included within the limits of this State, and which was by an act passed by the last legislature of this State made a part of the counties of Carroll, DeKalb, Gwinnett, Hall or Habersham. . . . and to warn all persons whether citizens of this or other states or Indian occupants, from all further trespass upon the property

[113]

of this State, and especially from taking any gold or silver from the lands included within the territory occupied by the Cherokee Indians. . . and to direct all persons to quit possession of said lands and depart from said territory without delay. . . and to require all officers of the State within the counties aforesaid to be vigilant in enforcing the laws for the protection of the public property, and especially to prevent any further trespass upon the lands of the State or the taking of any gold or silver therefrom."[12]

Samuel Worcester read the proclamation with a sinking heart, when it was sent for publication in the *Phoenix*. The Cherokees followed it with assurances to their people that violence would not be resorted to, and that prudence and forbearance would be the practice of the tribe. They thought, apparently, that as converts to Christianity they could practice Christian principles in a land where gold had just been found! And John Huss and Archibald Downing, Indian converts who were ardent in their efforts to cooperate with the missionaries, were spending much time at the gold fields, holding divine services among the Indians.

Word came to New Echota that an old Cherokee, despondent over the white man's greed for gold and sure of the destruction of his people at the white man's hands, had hanged himself from a tree in his own field. Truly the ways of God were strange, and past all finding out!

12 *Ibid.*, Vol. III, No. 10, June 26, 1830.

Prisoner of the Lord

THE WORCESTERS found no time for idleness at New Echota. Ann Worcester had served her apprenticeship as housewife for the large and changing make-up of a mission family at Brainerd. She knew that there were few times when her household at New Echota would number only her immediate family, any more than it had done so at Brainerd; the teachers appointed for the schools in the neighborhood of New Echota probably would live with them; missionaries who had business with the press or with the Cherokee officials would often be with them for several days at a time; Indian friends, who liked the giving and receiving of hospitality, would come to pay them visits; white travelers would expect a welcome at the door of the principal white resident of the town; visitors from the American Board, inspecting the mission stations, would come from time to time. There would never be a period when Ann, as a housewife, could relax and allow things to take their own course. Every member of the household helped with its duties, it is true, but the responsibility was always Ann's.

Sometimes, it must be noted, the housewife's duties were far from delicate, as the request in an early list of supplies for "1 ridding comb" would indicate. Another letter asked, however, for a "small assortment of simple

Sabbath School Books. Among them Hymns for Infant Minds," and (for Mr. Boudinot) for "1 flute, & directions for playing. Cost not to exceed six dollars." Pain and pleasure blended at New Echota.

If a day promised less work than usual, Ann had learned to seize upon it as a time for duties that must be wedged in between the more regular tasks—for soap-making and candle-dipping and for the sewing and knitting and mending that were always lying ready for her hands. Always, no matter how many candles she dipped, there seemed to be need of more. Samuel burned his candle far into the night, writing letters, going over accounts, working at his translations, composing his sermons. Many religious gatherings were called for "early candle-light" or for "candle-light"; this meant, literally, that the candles Ann had made would be used to illuminate the meetinghouse. Cooking and cleaning and washing and ironing were part of the daily routine, and caring for her baby was a more or less constant task; these duties must be managed so well that they allowed time for extra undertakings—drying peaches and apples and corn, curing or frying down meat, polishing the pewter, making butter and cheese, sewing new garments for the next baby. Yet all was done without a sense of haste and confusion; and there was always time for morning prayers with the family, and for a hymn and a benediction at night.

Somehow, Ann found less and less opportunity to write letters to her old home; she must content herself, while her hands were busy in her kitchen, with letting her mind take her back to her New England girlhood at Bedford and to her school days at Ashfield. She was glad, always, of the presence of another white woman of her own ways of living at New Echota; she and Harriet Boudinot, living within sight of each other's doorways, could support each other in the daily trials of housewifery; they could sit together occasionally for an hour's sewing or knitting, talking serenely while their needles flew, of some item they had read in the Boston *Recorder*, or of some neighborhood happening, or of New England memories held in common. However much she might rejoice that Mrs. Laughing Mush showed marked evidence of piety or that Mr. and Mrs. Drowning Bear manifested a promising interest in the church, there were times when she, like any other woman, craved the companionship of one of her own kind by birth and training. But she had no time, even if she had had inclination, for gossip; it was never to be said of her, as of some of the other wives of missionaries, that she busied herself with matters outside her own province as assistant missionary or that she was a bearer of tales and a monger of scandals. Her shining floors, her neat chests, her full larder, bore evidence of her steady industry.

If there was a precariousness about life in this new land, the baby Ann Eliza was none the worse for it. She grew steadily in body and in mind, glad of each day's unfolding of new sights and sounds. She had no fear of racing horses or fluttering wild birds or dark Indians because she had always known all these things; she had no awe of the big iron press and the cases of type; she was learning to understand all these things by that excellent method of observation and participation. Affection tempered the discipline with which she was reared; her mother was patient when she tore a stocking or lost a mitten; her father was painstaking when he answered her eager questions. Ann Eliza learned to sing almost as soon as she learned to talk; she knew hymns in both Cherokee and

English. She was the perpetual joy of her parents' hearts as long as they both lived.

Before they had lived in New Echota a year, another child was added to the Worcester family. Ann Eliza, almost two years old, was full of joy at the presence of this baby sister, whose name was Sarah and who was fairer and whiter than the dark-eyed babies of the Indians. And Sarah lay in a cradle, instead of being carried on her mother's back in a blanket.

Even missionaries and teachers in mission schools, devoted to the cause of the world's evangelization, had their shortcomings in disposition and ability to coöperate with others in the same cause. However holy their purpose, they remained human and fallible. This the Worcesters were soon to discover; they confessed it in themselves; they witnessed it in others. Again and again it was to fall to them, as missionaries who knew how to live serenely under trying circumstances, to help others less disciplined to bear disappointment and make adjustments. A disgruntled teacher in their household became tractable; an angry employe, transferred to their jurisdiction, found his wrath turned to industry. The Worcesters never thought of these transformations as the results of any psychological effect; they saw in them the workings of the grace of God in erring hearts. One of the first of these cases was that of Sophia Sawyer, who had come as a teacher to Brainerd and had proved to be fiery and untractable. She had gone out well recommended, and even after derogatory letters about her went back to the Mission Rooms, the Prudential Committee were reluctant to recall her; they wrote that they hoped she might yet prove quiet and useful. They sent her from Brainerd to New Echota, knowing that if she learned to adapt herself to mission life, with its hardships and its emergencies, it would be under the influence of the family life of the Worcesters. "I do not know," David Greene wrote to them from Boston, "how far she may be permanently useful in your family; yet I do not think of any place where she can probably be more contented & turn her labors to better account. Perhaps she may do something at teaching a few scholars in the place. Of this you must judge." Within a few months, Samuel and Ann Worcester had led her into a way of peace and usefulness, and David Greene had written his joy in the fact that she was "in a way to do some good, after the manner of her choice."

Sophia Sawyer became one of the really successful teachers of the Cherokee Mission; indeed, no other teacher showed more zeal in the education of Cherokee girls or had more evident success. Samuel and Ann Worcester had turned her fiery energy into its proper channel. After a year or two we find her ordering, "for her school one of Holbrook's globes, which we see advertised by Allen & Ticknor." And a later letter to Mr. Hill of the American Board, accompanied by a letter and a donation from some of the children of her school, shows to what extent she had devoted herself to her work as a teacher. "Please to accept & dispose of this small offering for the Grecian youth," the children's letter began. "It is the avails of industry. We have earned the small sums annexed to our names by remaining every Wednesday after school hours to sew. We have done this at the suggestion of our teacher that we might have the pleasure of giving something to liberated Greece. We know something about the former greatness of that nation. Parley tells us stories about them & we read Mr. Brewer's letters in the *Youth's Companion*.

Please to give the money we send to Mr. Brewer the American Missionary to help support the little Grecian Paper.

"On our maps we have crossed the Atlantic—entered the Mediterranean, & visited the shores of Greece—seen by description the beautiful green islands with which the sea is spotted. Parley tells us of the mildness of the climate—that while we are glad to sit by the fire the Grecians are sporting beneath the trees in the open air. We have seen some of the animals in Parley's *History* & have learned from him also that the oppression from the Turks, on this once great nation, has made the people artful, & to some extent faithless. We know that they are making efforts to rise as a nation, & from the sufferings of our own people we would learn to pity & help other oppressed nations.

"Mary Fields, Secretary	30 cts.
Mary Vann	30
Nancy Martin	30
Rachel Martin	30
Elvina McCoy	30
Nancy Vann	30
Delilah Hicks	30
Jane L. Hicks	30
Mary Ann McCoy	30
Ann Eliza Worcester	30
Eleanor Susan Boudinot	30
Lucretia Tiger	30"

"The letter," Miss Sawyer explains, "and the last six names were written by Mary Fields. The ages of the writers are from nine to thirteen years. You will see, Sir, the object was not to add much to the Treasury but to form habiths of industry, self denial, & benevolence." There, witness to New England scrupulousness, is a postscript: "When I say the letter was *written* by Mary Fields, I refer only to the penmanship. The composition is my own. I have put nothing into the mouths of the children which they cannot say with truth. . . . . If you think best, Sir, please to send for my own use E. H. Burnet's *Geography of the Heavens* accompanied by a *Celestial Atlas* with a view of the Solar System illustrated by Engraving."

Samuel Worcester's brief note, accompanying what Miss Sawyer and her pupils had written, explains these avails of industry. "Please to acknowledge the receipt of a bedquilt from the girls of Miss Sawyer's school, valued at $5.10, from which deduct $1.50 paid for quilting, leaving a balance of $3.60, the amount of the several sums specified in her letter above. . . . . Also acknowledge the receipt of $10 from Mr. Joseph Vann of Springplace, Cherokee Nation, for Miss Sawyer's school."

Sophia Sawyer had, indeed, found her vocation. Her whole heart turned now, not to dissension with circumstances that governed mission life, but to efforts for the children she taught. No trouble was too great, if it contributed to the success of her school. Here is a fervent addition, in her handwriting, to one of Mr. Worcester's letters to the Board: "If any of the supplies are yet in Boston for any of the stations, will you please have the goodness to forward the books &c mentioned in a letter from me to Mr. Greene? Especially do we need Hull's *Geography for Young Children*. We have some little ones that I do not know how to keep understandingly busy without these geographies. The prospect is of a large & difficult school. I hope we have your prayers, especially the prayers of mothers who feel the need of Divine aid in training children." Reading such expressions of Miss Sawyer's fervor as a teacher, Samuel and Ann Worcester considered, thankfully, that the Lord had found His way with her. Through them, He had.

It was with this same purpose of serving the Board in every way that Samuel undertook the duties of postmaster at New Echota. Letters came and went slowly enough at best, but with a postmaster who might be indifferent to the interests of the mission and of the press they would often have been even more belated. He was quick to think and alert to act, and he expedited the delivery of many letters for which someone in the neighborhood of New Echota was anxiously waiting. By serving as postmaster he was able, too, to save some expense to the Board, for he never charged the customary postmaster's fees on letters connected with the mission. Even the smallest saving must be practiced, he knew, wherever there was opportunity. And all, to the quarter-cent, must be accounted for in his quarterly reports of finance to the Prudential Committee.

Accounts were always one of Samuel Worcester's greatest trials, though he never gave up his cheerful efforts to keep them for his station. Small wonder it is that he found them complicated, with personal items for the teachers, the school children, the printers and mechanics who might be temporarily employed, the editor of the *Phœnix*, and the neighbors who wanted purchases made for them in the East through the mission, all to carry on books that sometimes he was unable to bring up to date for many days at a time. When his first quarterly account would not balance, he was painfully surprised. Years afterward, he was still being surprised at the same happening, for always a different set of circumstances—such a variety of circumstances, surely, no institution other than an Indian mission could invent—had occasioned the error. Sometimes it was delay in the arrival of expected supplies, necessitating temporary purchases: "You may perhaps notice that we have consumed a considerable amount of flour. It was occasioned by the failure of a contract for corn, and the impossibility of procuring it for some time, so that we were under the necessity of using flour almost exclusively. Some additional expense has been occasioned by the failure of the agents at Augusta to send us new supplies when requested. . . . . Our supplies have not yet arrived, nor have we heard from them. The Savannah river has been very low." Or again it was an advance payment that complicated his accounts: "I do not yet succeed in making my accounts square off exactly. I will try again. . . . . You may notice $12 paid in advance for corn. In consideration of that advance I have the use of a milch cow, which, with her calf, is worth nearly that sum, to be redeemed with the corn in the fall."

The second year's accounts at Brainerd were, to Samuel's disappointment, no easier to keep than the first had been. "I seem," he wrote to Henry Hill, treasurer of the Board at the end of the first quarter of 1829, "to be unable to make my accounts balance exactly at a quarter's end, with however much pains I attempt it. At the end of last quarter I credited $3.03½ for error in account. I find on looking at my private memorandum a deficiency of a little more than $4.00, which seems to throw the balance on the other side. Let it however stand. . . . . Mr. Boudinot is quite in arrears, and I choose to indulge him awhile, unless you order otherwise." In October he was again balancing figures uncertainly, and entering an item that he named "error" to right his balance. "On the third page of this sheet," he explained, "you have my account for four months. I should have made it out at the end of three months, but for an impression which I had that my last account included the month of June.

"I can account for the error of $1.07½ only on the supposition that I must have paid out some small items when my books were not at hand and forgotten to minute them.

"I shall probably have to pay out all I have on hand in a short time for the printing of books, a supply of corn and fodder for another year, &c. Your last order of $12 to be paid to the editor of the *Phœnix* I have not yet paid. I will be much obliged to you to forward to me another check of $100 or less immediately on the receipt of this, or to inform me if you cannot."

Balancing books never ceased to be a kind of mental acrobatics which God and the Board required of Samuel Worcester. He had fresh wonder and amazement for the outcome of every quarterly account, most of all when it happened to balance exactly to the quarter-cent. Fortunately, he was too busy with other efforts, which succeeded better than his keeping of accounts did, to brood over his failures in bookkeeping. His work of translation lay nearest his heart, and that went forward steadily. It progressed slowly, it is true, for Cherokee was still fairly new to him, and the lack of any written literature in the language, from which to find examples and make comparisons, was a constant handicap. Sometimes he got what seemed to be contradictory information when he asked one person after another about the meaning of a word; in such a case he must sift all his gleanings for the sake of accuracy. From the beginning he had worked at the translation of hymns, for the Cherokees sang with great enthusiasm and they were first drawn to the services of the church, often-times, by the music. By the fall of 1829 he had thirty-three hymns so carefully translated that he felt they were ready to print, and he issued them in a book of fifty-two pages, printed in Guess' characters. "I paid, you will see," he wrote in regard to his accounts, "$30 on account of the printing of hymn books. I had 800 copies printed. I apprehend the edition is too small, but the type for 28 pages is kept standing. I have disposed of near 370 copies, most of them to the mission stations, where I have re-quested them to be credited to this station at $8 per hun-dred. This sum, I suppose, will a little more than cover the expense. At the stations they retail them at 12½ cents, but whether they will give away enough to reduce the sum received below the average of eight cents each I know not. Pray can you tell me what would be in Boston the ordinary cost of folding, stitching, covering & trimming a hundred such books as the Cherokee Hymnbook?"

To have a hymn book in their own tongue was grati-fying to all the Cherokees who leaned toward civilization according to the white man's standards, but to Samuel Worcester this was a secondary achievement. He was concerned that they have the very bread of their new spiritual life, the Gospels. In time they must have the whole Bible; they would begin, however, with that essen-tial portion which David Brown had already put into crude translation, the book of Matthew. Samuel dared not, with his limited knowledge of Cherokee, proceed alone with a translation, but he could expedite his labor by shaping his plans to suit Elias Boudinot's. Boudinot, as editor of the *Phœnix*, must constantly turn to Wor-cester for help and advice; Worcester, on the other hand, claimed his services as translator whenever he found time to turn to translation. As they finished a chapter or a unit of a chapter, they published it in the *Phoenix*. Thus, among the Cherokees, the Gospel of Matthew was circulated serially before it was issued as a whole. On July 29, 1829, Worcester wrote to the Board of what seemed to him the achievement of deepest spiritual importance in the history of the mission. "We completed the translation of Matthew yesterday. The proof of the fifth form has been struck off today, leaving the last chapter and a few verses of the 27th to make a little additional form." Books were not easily come by, even in English, in those days, and printed matter like copies of the *Phœnix* was passed about and handled as something of great price. Now, before the end of 1829, the Cherokees had two books in their own characters and language.

Except for Samuel Worcester's constant help, the *Phœnix* could not have been published. It was a national undertaking, with which he had no official connection, but he functioned in every capacity. Now his boyhood experiences in his father's print shop at Peacham stood him in good stead; he wished only that he had learned more before he left New England. But he sought from the Board advice regarding what he did not understand; and when there was no time to wait on letters, he solved the problem in hand by his own ingenuity. We find him writing in almost every order to the Missions Rooms for something needed for the press, as in this extract from a letter of July 2, 1828. "Mr. Boudinott wishes the following articles for the Printing Office—

2¾ lb. line long primer Type [which was charged in Baker & Greele's Bill but not sent]

2 oz. Cherokee mark [/\/] to meet the corner of a letter
   thus Ḙ

4 oz. Cherokee mark [:] [These two are not found in the
   office, but they may have been overlooked. The matrices are charged.]
2 lb. 2 line Pearl Capitals like those already sent
2 lb. 2 line nonpareil meridian shaded capitals
2 lb. long primer antique capitals
3 lb. space rule
5 reams wrapping paper suitable for doing up Newspapers
P. S. I wrote in a former letter that I should be glad of
   such paper as the *Herald* is printed on. Good paper is
   more important for Cherokee than English."

Obtaining printing paper was a constant problem, since
what they could purchase in Tennessee was too costly,
while what they ordered from the east did not correspond
in size and quality to that sold by the same designations
in the south. "It will probably be too late now to correct
a mistake," he wrote once, "as I requested an immediate
purchase; but if not too late, I suppose that I should have
said medium paper, instead of royal. I wished the same
size with that which was sent last, which Mr. Wheeler,
(my printer) called royal, and one bundle of which was
marked royal on a label—but on looking since at the invoice, I find it is charged 'medium paper.' The names
and corresponding sizes of paper at the South do not agree
with those at the North, which, with my ignorance of the
subject, is the occasion of mistakes. If you have already
purchased, and the paper is too large, the only difference
will be a little waste by having too large a margin."
   The choice of printers, too, was a recurring problem.

Sooner or later the morals, as well as the skill, of a printer came under consideration, if he stayed long enough to do more than help with one or two issues of the *Phœnix*. John Wheeler stayed on year after year, his heart prompting the work of his hands, but the assistants under him came and went. Of the first of these, Isaac Harris, the report was not good, and Mr. Boudinot was soon inquiring, through Samuel Worcester, for someone to take his place. "In regard to the printer, Mr. Boudinott wishes me to say that it is altogether probable he will be wanted, but nothing can be decided till the meeting of the Council, who alone have the power. Mr. B. wishes that you will have the kindness to ascertain whether the man will come, and if so to have testimonials respecting his character and qualifications forwarded in season to be communicated to the National Committee in October next. The time for which Mr. Harris is engaged will expire in December. Mr. B. wishes to have these testimonials forwarded only on the supposition that you judge the man to be one who will come for the sake of doing good, and not for the sake of the payment merely, and in other respects suitable for the undertaking. We wish to see a man whose influence shall be in favor of good things.

"The price of board is from $1.50 to $2.00 per week. Other necessary expenses, except clothing, for a single man would be, as far as I can perceive, almost nothing." Perhaps, in this last sentence, lay the explanation of the difficulty regarding printers, tramp printers having, besides their wanderlust, a heightened sense of *joie de vivre* which life at New Echota might not long satisfy.

It became plain to the enemies of progress among the Cherokees that Samuel Worcester was largely responsible for this progress. His energy, his intelligence, his skill in everything connected with the press, his standing among the leaders of the tribe—all were convincing evidence of the influence he exerted among them. He became a noxious presence to the white enemies of the Cherokees. These white men were ingenious in their schemes to undermine Worcester's standing, going about it through some of the weaker, more easily influenced members of the tribe and through those who were staunch conservatives in the matter of Cherokee religion and culture. As a matter of fact none of the white people among the Cherokees—with the exception of a few individuals such as John Howard Payne who came to the Cherokee country from New Orleans in 1835—put any value on Cherokee culture for its own sake, because of its mythology, its ceremony and ritual, its simple and dignified conception of life: the missionaries condemned it as pagan; the enemies of the missionaries were equally ready to condemn it as a unifying and strengthening influence among the tribe.

Samuel Worcester was not aware of the forces working against him; but his first written evidence of opposition came to him through the American Board, which had received a complaint from Colonel Thomas McKenney, chief of the Bureau of Indian Affairs. "We received," Jeremiah Evarts wrote to New Echota, "yesterday, from Col. Mc-Kenney, a letter containing a charge against you, forwarded to his office from the nation. The charge was, interfering with the press, & writing scurrilous articles respecting officers of government & other public men. The letter was answered & the charge declared by us to be unfounded. The number of the *Phœnix* containing your disclaimer, was forwarded to him. Col. McKenney gave no opinion as to the credit attached to the article in the War Department.

"Do what is right, & you need not fear."

Doing what was right, however, was less simple than it sounded. It needed the wisdom of a serpent and the harmlessness of a dove. Samuel Worcester—being of Yankee shrewdness and of the saintliness that has no geographical associations—possessed that rare combinanation; but trouble was in store for him. Georgia enacted her law—to be effective March first, 1831,—requiring all white persons except women, children, and minors residing within the Cherokee Nation to take an oath of allegiance to the state; it was aimed particularly against the missionaries stationed at Carmel, Hightower, Haweis, and New Echota. The oath, if taken, would have jeopardized their position with the Cherokees and canceled their citizenship in the states from which they had come. In March, Mr. Proctor, Mr. Thompson, and Mr. Worcester, and in May Mr. Butler, missionaries of these four stations, were made prisoners without civil authority by the "Georgia Guard," but were soon released by Judge Clayton on the evasive ground that the law, which the Judge refused to consider unconstitutional and void, did not apply to them because they had been agents of the government in administering the Indian Civilization Fund. Governor Gilmer foresaw difficulty in enforcing the law in so far as the missionaries were concerned, particularly in Worcester's case because he held the office of postmaster. But constitutionality—in theory as firm as rock—is in practice as flexible as economic conditions are variable. By May 16, 1831, the Governor had bent the firm rock of constitutionality enough to write a personal letter to Worcester. "Sir," he began with something less than customary southern courtesy, "It is a part of my official duty to cause all white persons residing within the territory of the state, occupied by the Cherokees to be removed therefrom, who refuse to take the oath to support the constitution and laws of the state. Information has been received of your continued residence within that territory, without complying with the requisites of the law, and of your claim to be exempted from its operation, on account of your holding the office of postmaster of New Echota. You have no doubt been informed of your dismissal from that office. That you may be under no mistake as to this matter, you are also informed that the government of the United States does nor recognize as its agents the missionaries acting under the direction of the American Board of Foreign Missions. Whatever may have been your conduct in opposing the humane policy of the general government, or exciting the Indians to oppose the jurisdiction of the state, I am still desirous of giving you and all others similarly situated, an opportunity of avoiding the punishment which will certainly follow your further residence within the state contrary to its laws. You are, therefore, advised to remove from the territory of Georgia, occupied by the Cherokees. Col. Sanford, the commander of the Guard, will be requested to have this letter delivered to you, and to delay your arrest until you shall have had an opportunity of leaving the state."[1]

Colonel Sanford, however, had a regard for human suffering if not for constitutionality. There was a new baby in the Worcester home, for Jerusha, the third child, had been born on February 27. A difficult confinement, followed by an attack of one of the fevers common in the region, had kept Ann Worcester to her bed for many weeks. The little baby did not thrive, and Ann became so ill that removal anywhere was impossible. Scarcely any household help was available, when a nurse and a doctor

1 *Missionary Herald*, XXVII (1831), 248-9.

were both needed as well as a housekeeper. Samuel wrote Colonel Sanford that he must be with his wife if it were at all possible, and Colonel Sanford under these pitiful circumstances could not bring himself to make the arrest. Samuel hoped, meanwhile, that a letter to Governor Gilmer, such as one gentleman might write to another in case of a misunderstanding, would clear the whole situation.

"NEW ECHOTA, CHER. NA., June 10, 1831.

"*To His Excellency George R. Gilmer, Governor of the state of Georgia.*

"SIR—Your communication of the 15th ult. was put into my hand on the 31st, by an express from Col. Sanford, accompanied with a notice from him, that I should become liable to arrest, if after ten days, I should still be found residing within the unsettled limits of the state.

"I am under obligation to your excellency for the information, which I believe I am justified in deriving by inference from your letter, that it is through your influence, that I am about to be removed from the office of postmaster at this place; inasmuch that it gives me the satisfaction of knowing that I am not removed on the ground of any real or supposed unfaithfulness in the performance of the duties of that office.

"Your excellency is pleased to intimate that I have been guilty of a criminal opposition to the humane policy of the general government. I cannot suppose your excellency refers to those efforts for the advancement of the Indians in knowledge, and in the arts of civilized life, which the general government has pursued ever since the days of Washington, because I am sure that no person can have so entirely misrepresented the course which I have pursued during my residence with the Cherokee people. If by the humane policy of the government, are intended those measures which have been recently pursued for the removal of this and other tribes, and if the opposition is no more than that I have the misfortune to differ in judgment with the executive of the United States, in regard to the tendency of those measures, and that I have freely expressed my opinion, I cheerfully acknowledge the fact, and can only add that this expression of opinion has been unattended with the consciousness of guilt. If any other opposition is intended, as that I have endeavored to bias the judgment, or influence the conduct of the Indians themselves, I am constrained to deny the charge, and beg that your excellency will not give credit to it, until it shall be sustained by evidence.

"Your excellency is pleased further to intimate, that I have excited the Indians to oppose the jurisdiction of the state. In relation to this subject, also, permit me to say, your excellency has been misinformed. Neither in this particular am I conscious of having influenced, or attempted to influence the Indians among whom I reside. At the same time, I am far from wishing to conceal the fact, that, in my apprehension, the circumstances in which providence has placed me, have rendered it my duty to inquire whose is the rightful jurisdiction over the territory in which I reside; and that this inquiry has led me to a conclusion adverse to the claims of the state of Georgia. This opinion, also, has been expressed—to white men with the greatest freedom; and to Indians, when circumstances elicited my sentiments.

[133]

"I need not, however, enlarge upon these topics. I thought it proper to notice them in a few words, because I understood your excellency to intimate that, in these respects, I had been guilty of a criminal course of conduct. If for these things I were arraigned before a court of justice, I believe I might safely challenge my accusers to adduce proof of any thing beyond that freedom in the expression of opinions, against which, under the constitution of our country, there is no law. But as it is, the most convincing evidence of perfect innocence on these points would not screen me from the penalty of the law, which construes a mere residence here, without having taken a prescribed oath, into a high misdemeanor. On this point, therefore, I hope to be indulged a few words in explanation of my motives.

"After the expression of my sentiments, which I have already made, your excellency cannot fail to perceive, that I could not conscientiously take the oath which the law requires. That oath implies an acknowledgment of myself as a citizen of Georgia, which might be innocent enough for one who believes himself such to be, but must be perjury for one who is of the opposite opinion. I may add, that such a course, even if it were innocent of itself, would in the present state of feeling among the Indians, greatly impair, or entirely destroy my usefulness as a minister of the gospel among them. It were better, in my judgment, entirely to abandon my work, than so to arm the prejudices of the whole people against me.

"Shall I then abandon the work in which I have engaged? Your excellency is already acquainted, in general, with the nature of my object, and my employment, which consist in preaching the gospel, and making

[134]

known the word of God among the Cherokee people. As to the means used for this end, aside from the regular preaching of the word, I have had the honor to commence the work of publishing portions of the holy scriptures, and other religious books, in the language of this people. I have the pleasure of sending to your excellency a copy of the gospel of Matthew, of a hymn-book, and of a small tract consisting chiefly of extracts from scripture, which, with the aid of an interpreter, I have been enabled to prepare and publish; and also of another tract, which, with my assistant, I have translated for the United Brethren's Mission. The tract of scripture extracts has been published since my trial and acquital by the superior court. This work it would be impossible for me to prosecute at any other place than this, not only on account of the location of the Cherokee press, but because Mr. Boudinott, whose editorial labors require his residence at this place, is the only translator whom I could procure, and who is competent to the task. My own view of duty is, that I ought to remain, and quietly pursue my labors for the spiritual welfare of the Cherokee people, until I am forcibly removed. If I am correct in the apprehension that the state of Georgia has no rightful jurisdiction over the territory where I reside, then it follows that I am under no moral obligation to remove, in compliance with her enactments: and if I suffer in consequence of continuing to preach the gospel and diffuse the written word of God among this people, I trust that I shall be sustained by a conscience void of offence, and by the anticipation of a righteous decision at that tribunal from which there is no appeal.

"Your excellency will accept the assurance of my
sincere respect.

S. A. WORCESTER."[2]

The letter did not pacify Worcester's opponents, or
make the missionaries' position in the Cherokee nation
more secure. Early in the summer, Mr. Proctor, Mr.
Thompson, and Mr. Butrick (a missionary who had thus
far escaped arrest) removed their familes to Cherokee
territory outside the boundaries of Georgia, but Worces-
cester and his family remained at New Echota. Ann was
still ill, though improving slowly, and her husband divided
his time between caring for her and working with Boudinot
on his translations. He could not see that he had any
choice in the matter.

But the Georgia Guard was still active. When the missionaries returned to preach or to look after the schools
at their old stations, they were arrested; and on the seventh
of July Samuel Worcester was arrested and taken to Camp
Gilmer where the other white prisoners were in custody.
He learned that their trial was not to take place until
September, and that meantime discharge or release on
bail was to be disregarded. Since his family could not yet
be removed and the danger of arrest was constant, even
after a release on a writ of habeas corpus and the giving
of bonds to appear for trial, Worcester retired to Brainerd.
Catherine Fuller and Sophia Sawyer, free from the duties
of teaching school for a time, could be trusted to look
after Ann and the children with intelligence and affection.
But even loving care could not stay disease, and though
Ann's fever slowly yielded to their efforts, the baby
Jerusha loosed her slight hold on the troubled life to which

2 *Ibid.*, pp. 250-1.

[136]

she had been born. On the fourteenth of August, 1831, she died.

There was grief and a heavy sense of trouble in the Worcester household. The little girls, Ann Eliza and Sarah, went about bewildered by their weight of sadness and sickness and loneliness, puzzled by the strange presence of death and alarmed at their mother's helpless grief. They had a feeling that their father might have stayed the onset of trouble, but he was away in Tennessee. The messenger that was sent for him could not bring him back in time for Jerusha's funeral. Elias Boudinot conducted the funeral service, and the little girls' sense of the heaviness of sorrow was lifted, in that strange scene at the baby's new grave, by his comforting, tender words. For as long as Ann Eliza lived, until 1905, it was her most vivid early memory.

Then, after the funeral, the little girls' father came home, and they felt a security and peace that nothing but his presence could bring them. But the second night after his return, he was arrested on his own doorstep, to be released later when Colonel Nelson of the Georgia Guard learned the circumstances of his brief visit home. To the children, nothing seemed lasting or certain, save trouble and uncertainty.

A month later, on the sixteenth of September, the trial was held. Eleven white men, including Samuel Worcester, his colleague Dr. Butler of Haweis, and his printer, J. F. Wheeler, were tried for violation of the Georgia law. The jury brought in a quick verdict of guilty against the entire number, but the sentence was not pronounced until the next day. The judge condemned them to four years of hard labor in the penitentiary.

"I Was In Prison,
And Ye Visited Me"

THOSE of the eleven who had been imprisoned before knew what to expect now in the way of discomfort and humiliation. Under previous arrests they had been compelled at the whim of the guards to walk in a straight line through the center of the road, in mire and water, a day's journey of thirty-five miles; Dr. Butler had been chained to the neck of a horse until the horse stumbled and the soldier mounted on it fell, breaking two ribs and relenting somewhat in his discipline; Worcester and his fellow-prisoners had been chained, two by two or to their bedsteads at night; and they were compelled to listen to the obscenity and profanity of one Sergeant Brooks, a member of the Georgia Guard, who was a master of cursing and reviling. Worst of all to them, they were obliged to go on with their journey to Camp Gilmer on the Sabbath, in spite of their scruples against journeying on the Lord's day, and to march into the prison camp, after twenty-two miles of tramping, under sound of fife and drum on that day of rest. "Remonstrance would only have irritated," Samuel explained in a letter. "We were under command of armed men, and must travel on." When they entered the jail, Brooks, who must have had a genius for melodramatic villainy, remarked, "There is where all the

enemies of Georgia have to land—there and in hell."
But the prisoners had cleaned the filthy floor and enlarged
some holes already made in the daubing of the log walls
for light and air, and had "under the care of a merciful
Providence," enjoyed good health and dwelt in peace until they were released. And always their difficulties were
mitigated by kindnesses that were unofficial but comforting. Their situation had aroused much sympathy
among all classes and kinds of people; opposition to them
and their cause was by no means general. Sometimes, on
the march, a soldier had mounted one of them on his own
horse for a while; once some of the soldiers had asked
that a religious meeting be held for them by their prisoners; and at their trial General Harden of Athens,
Georgia, had defended them at his own request and without fee. Colonel Nelson had refused the soldiers' request
for religious services rudely, it is true, writing on the outside of their petition, to the missionaries who had been
asked to hold them, "We view within request as an imper-
tinent one. If your conduct be evidence of your character
and the doctrines you wish to promulgate, we are sufficiently enlightened as to both. Our object is to restrain,
not to facilitate their promulgation. If your object be
true piety you can enjoy it where you are. Were we
hearers we would not be benefitted, devoid as we are of
confidence in your honesty."[1]

There was no want of support from the American Board
as to the stand its missionaries had taken. Indeed, letters
from the Board reveal something like a spirit of rejoicing
in the fact that events reached the point of imprisonment.
The time was ripe for a martyr to appear. Some of that
attitude by which martyrdom consists in not being mar-

[1] *Missionary Herald*, XXVII (1831), 301.

tyred—or at least in not having a martyr sacrificed to the cause—prevailed. The situation, put into modern terms, was good publicity for missions. Jeremiah Evarts, writing for the Prudential Committee, had made this plain, point by point, in an earlier letter to Worcester.

"1. You are clearly in the path of duty & engaged about your Master's work.

"2. There is no pretence, from any quarter, that you are violating any law of God by being where you are.

"3. You are where you are by the authority and under the protection of the United States & the Cherokees—under the protection of the highest & most sacred laws of the U. S.—plainly expressed. And there is no human authority, except of the U. S. & of the Cherokees, which has any right to interfere with you. This is a perfectly clear case. If it were doubtful you would be justified in staying still till it should be decided; but it is not doubtful.

"4. By standing firm in this case, & being willing to suffer for righteousness' sake, you will do much to encourage the Cherokees. Courage is the thing they want, i.e., long continued courage or fortitude; it is the very point, in my judgment, where they will lose their country, & their earthly all, if Georgia shall finally prevail against them. I have always feared for them on this point. I have often said, 'White men, in a high state of civilization, are alone competent, & expect deliverance by the slow progress of law. Such men have been the Hampdens, the Sydneys, & Baxters & Bunyans of every age.' These things I have said many months ago. Now God is likely to bring this trial upon white men of a select character, who went out for a holy purpose; that is, to give their labor & their lives, if need be, to the Cherokees.

"5. If you leave, I fear the Cherokees will make no stand whatever, & that they cannot wait till deliverance comes. It is true that the same law cannot operate upon them as upon you; but they can be easily vexed & frightened by other laws, which can be executed more oppressively than their letter would warrant. If Georgia sees that they can be easily frightened, she will certainly frighten them.

"Indeed, it strikes me that your leaving in these circumstances, would greatly endanger, if it did not utterly ruin, the cause of the Cherokees.

"6. If Georgia should carry some of you to prison, the fact would rouse this whole country, in a manner unlike anything which has yet been experienced. It would call forth the prayers of all God's people for you & the Indians. It would call forth petitions to the President and to the next Congress, & very possibly to the governor of Georgia. I cannot believe you would be detained in prison long. But what if you were?. . . . I think I never knew, or read of, a case in which so much good would be done, by submitting (only a few persons) to a groundless & most odious persecution. You would not only benefit the Cherokees, but your case would be known through the civilized world. You would do good to the poor and oppressed everywhere.

"7. But if you leave the ground, and other of the Cherokees are frightened away, the people of the U. S. would say the case is hopeless, & will fold their hands in apathy or despair. The most intelligent members of Congress, are of opinion that the Supreme Court will sustain the Indians, & that the people of the U. S. will yield & a settlement will be made. That this would be done is the only earthly hope of the Cherokees, & it is of immense importance to this country, & to the civilized world—it is of more value than millions, uncounted millions of money —& many thousands of lives—as it will save money & lives to an incalculable extent."

Mr. Evarts had concluded his letter, "You will commend the whole matter to God. May He direct you." And to Catherine Fuller, who remained at Hightower to look after the property of the station there and to teach the school, David Greene wrote from the offices of the Board: "For you to be insulted, driven from the house, & have the property of the station seized before your eyes may be the saving of the Cherokees and of the country."

It had been expected that the prisoners would set out for the penitentiary at Milledgeville on Saturday, the seventeenth of September, but the sheriff was detained in getting certain necessary papers. On Sunday morning, everything was in readiness for the march to Milledgeville, except the hearts of those prisoners who held it wrong to travel on the Lord's day. They were mindful of their instructions to uphold the Sabbath before the heathen and unbelievers, and they wrote a petition to the sheriff requesting delay. His reply was gratifying.

"REV. S. A. WORCESTER, and other applicants.

"Yours of this morning is received and in reply I have to state that your request is readily complied with. In taking this step you must be sensible that I incur considerable responsibility; for the expense of the guard (to prevent the necessity of confining you in jail,) is considerable; but, believing that it is not the wish of the public authorities of the state, and knowing that it is not my desire, to offer the least disrespect to religion through harsh treatment of any of its professors, on account of conscientious scruples, much less to aggravate the sufferings of a condition already sufficiently painful, I take much pleasure, with a hope that it will be approved by my fellow-citisens, in affording you this evidence how much your feelings and misfortunes can be respected by a public officer.

"Yours very respectfully,

"THOMAS WORTHY, Sheriff."[2]

Thanks to Thomas Worthy, they rested on that Sabbath.

Of eleven possible martyrs, only two entered the prison doors. When they reached Milledgeville, Governor Gilmer offered to pardon and release them all on condition that they take oath to sustain Georgia in her measures against the Cherokees or abandon their missionary labors and withdraw from the state. The Inspector of the Penitentiary left a record of the conversation with each convict, and of the conditions by which nine of the convicts, all of the eleven but the two missionaries of the Board, were freed. Official records are free from personal reactions; otherwise this Inspector might have noted an amusing inconsistency in the proceedings by which the nine prisoners were released. The testimony of Samuel Worcester and Elizur Butler as to the general good character of each of their fellow-convicts was required before they were pardoned and released! But still the state had not gained its point. It hoped to establish a principle; so did the two missionaries. For hours the two men were urged to accept the terms accepted, for the sake of expediency or necessity, by the others; and at intervals the gate of the prison was opened and closed again, grating on its iron hinges

2 *Missionary Herald*, XXVII (1831), 364.

with a sound intended to produce terror in the hearts of the listeners. Apparently the sound strengthened their resolution, for in the end they were taken inside, clad in prison garb, and assigned to prison labor. That, of course, was not the end Governor Gilmer had had in mind. But there was now nothing for it but to proceed in the direction events had taken; four years of imprisonment at hard labor must satisfy him, in lieu of compliance.

Meanwhile, Ann Worcester stayed on at New Echota. Slowly her fever ran its course and she regained her health. She must regain it, to carry on as well as a woman might the duties that her husband had left by the abrupt interruption of arrest. She must write his letters, attend to his business at New Echota, see Indians who came to consult her in his place. But in spite of the strength of faith and the pressure of duty, there were hours when she knew her own weakness. Sometimes she wished she might give herself up to grief for the baby she had lost, and to loneliness for Samuel. Death and insecurity were realities to her now. Word had come to her, by the usual slow course of ill and good news alike, of the death of their dear friend Jeremiah Evarts. His letters to them had been their support; his work as a member of the American Board had been their inspiration; his writings and his influence at Washington had been a source of help in their trials among the Cherokees. Now that human source of strength and wisdom was removed from them. And Dempsey Fields, A Christian Cherokee whose help had been valuable to the mission, had died three days after the date of Mr. Evarts' death. "No doubt," the *Missionary Herald* had observed in mentioning both deaths, "they had a very unexpected and happy meeting in their Father's house." Ann had no doubt of this; she believed in the resurrection of the dead and in the heavenly mansions.

Worcester was in the penitentiary before word of consolation came to them for their loss in the death of Jerusha. David Greene wrote as soon as he heard of their loss. "I see by the *Phœnix* rec'd this morning that the Lord has visited you with another form of affliction, & cut off your little daughter. I trust that you & Mrs. Worcester, in this day of trial, are enabled to look at these events not as visitations of anger, but as the affectionate chastisements of a gracious Father & Redeemer, in whom you have piously trusted, to whom you have near access in this time of need, and who is even now, from amid all these clouds, revealing himself to you in love, filling you with joy & peace & awaking in you immortal hopes. May the Lord bring light out of darkness, & joy out of all this sorrow. I hope you are able to visit Mrs. Worcester in this time of affliction & comfort her." A woman like Ann Worcester could find comfort in these words. She could believe that in their Father's mansion the baby Jerusha was not comfortless; the Christian Indian Dempsey Fields would not seem strange to the baby Jerusha, and Samuel's old teacher, Jeremiah Evarts, would be kind to the infant daughter of his former pupil. Heaven was a place of very happy connections; but a mother's arms ached with emptiness unless she kept herself constantly reminded of them.

Ann could not help feeling a constant anxiety about her husband. Were his surroundings decently clean? Were there blankets enough for his bed, now that winter was coming on? Was the prison labor assigned to him more than his strength could bear? She knew he would not write her of these matters, however uncomfortable he might find himself; he might not, alas, in his interest in the prisoners and his absorption in affairs outside himself, even be aware of them. If she could only see his prison room and assure herself that his needs were satisfied, she could have peace of mind; if she could talk with him about problems of the mission that had arisen since his departure, she could act for him more intelligently. Elias Boudinot had an Indian's quiet understanding; he sensed Ann's desire to see her husband in his prison surroundings and he set about to make this possible. Soon he brought her twenty-three dollars, which several Cherokees had contributed to send Ann to Milledgeville; later, from a journey to Chatooga where he had gone for a meeting of the Council, he sent her fifteen more. John Ross, the chief, had contributed, and Cherokee men like Joseph Vann and John Ridge; Captain McNair, a white man with a Cherokee family, had given five dollars, and George Lavendar, a white man who did overland hauling for the mission, had given two. "Perhaps," Mr. Boudinot wrote Ann, "you will now have enough to bear your expenses to Milledgeville and back, and to purchase for Mr. Worcester a couple of blankets. I could collect as much more if it were needed before you start. I wish you a pleasant journey and a pleasant interview with your beloved husband. Give my *best, kindest* regards to him & tell him that the Cherokees sympathize with him. He lives, and will live, in their affection & remembrance."

On November 4, 1831, Catherine Fuller wrote the news of the station at New Echota to the Board. "I am happy to inform you that Mrs. Worcester's health is so far restored that she has ventured to leave us today on her proposed journey to Milledgeville. We are not without hope it will be beneficial. Mr. and Mrs. Chamberlin &

Mrs. Butler are in company with Mrs. Worcester. The family here is comfortably situated."

On the afternoon of the twelfth of November, Mrs. Worcester and Mrs. Butler visited their imprisoned husbands for the first time. They found them cheerful, busy, and obviously loved and respected by the criminals with whom they were imprisoned. They were allowed to spend all of that Saturday afternoon in the penitentiary, since they were not to be admitted at all on the following day. Mr. Worcester asked questions about the church and its Indian members, about the press and the sale of Matthew and the hymn book, and about the two little girls whom he had not seen for many weeks. On Monday and Tuesday the two women were allowed to visit their husbands again, and to bring in blankets, books, and some provisions. They were permitted to visit the workshops in the penitentiary, and to see the occupations and activities of the place. On Wednesday, they began their journey home, far less depressed and terrified at the situation of the two men than they had been before they had seen it with their own eyes. Ann knew, now, that no external conditions could disturb her husband's equanimity, and that felons and thieves had no power of felony or thieving in his presence. They found themselves drawn to him, and they felt no embarrassment or offence in his genuine piety. He, on the other hand, had much to learn from them and from the work shops in the penitentiary. A missionary, he held, had need of every kind of mechanical skill and knowledge; here was a chance to learn much that he had not known before. It would stand him in good stead when he was again a free citizen.

Ann was, as her friends had hoped, stronger after her return from Milledgeville. She could think of Samuel as she had seen him among the other prisoners, respected and deferred to by them all. She could remember the kindness of citizens of Milledgeville, whose loyalty to Georgia did not prevent their seeing the injustice that had been done the missionaries. She could look forward with faith to what might be accomplished at the next Monthly Concert for Prayer for Foreign Missions. On this, the first Monday night in December, churches throughout the land had been asked to pray for the deliverance of the missionaries and for the victory of the cause for which they stood.

Shortly before Ann's visit, Samuel had written a letter to the Missionary Rooms, giving them some account of his state of mind and of affairs.

"Although without being informed of it we should have the consolation of *believing* that we may enjoy the sympathies and prayers of Christians extensively, yet it affords us much happiness to be *assured* of it, as we have been by your letter and others. Great indeed is the comfort arising from the assurance that our lot is in this respect what that of Peter was, when 'prayer was made without ceasing of the church unto God for him.' We also enjoy peace of mind, which we hope proceeds from the favor which God manifests to his own children, and we hope that among your prayers for us you will not forget to ask that we may not be left either to do anything, nor indulge any feelings, which shall render necessary the withdrawal, even temporary, of the light of our Father's countenance. For myself, although I cannot say that I do not feel the pain of the deprivation of liberty, and of other trials necessarily connected with our situation, yet, on the whole, I have enjoyed quite as large a share of happiness as has commonly fallen to my lot, during an equal space of time. My cheerfulness has been uninterrupted, without even an hour's depression of spirits. When I say as large a share of happiness as has commonly fallen to my lot, you will remember that it is the expression of one to whom God, in his great kindness, has given a cheerful heart.

"In regard to our situation in prison, it is perhaps sufficient to say that we get along with a good degree of comfort.

"We have opportunity to make some attempts at doing good among our fellow prisoners. Since the burning of the penitentiary, of which you may have heard, (it occurred in May last,) there are but four lodging rooms for the prisoners; most of them lodge in three rooms, and between two of these is a free communication. Dr. Butler and I have separated our lodgings at the request of some of the prisoners, for the sake of having evening worship every night in two rooms. On the Sabbath we are in the same rooms as at night. By permission of the keepers I preach in the morning in my own room, and in the afternoon in the other, so that most of the prisoners who are disposed have opportunity to hear. The number usually present in both rooms taken together is between sixty and seventy. Dr. Butler also holds a meeting in the forenoon in the room where he lodges. Pray that these efforts may be followed with the divine blessing.

"We are expecting before long, perhaps next week, a visit from Mrs. Worcester and Mrs. Butler, accompanied by Mr. Chamberlin. Mrs. W. says, under date of October 28, 'Mr. Boudinot, who is now absent at

Chattooga to attend the sitting of Council, put into my hands the sum of 23 dollars for the purpose of defraying the expense of my journey to Milledgeville, contributed by five individuals at his solicitation. The plan, I believe was entirely his own. The persons who contributed did it very cheerfully, and promised, if that sum should not be sufficient, to give more.'

"From what we gather respecting public sentiment in this state, we are led to believe that a good deal of sympathy is excited in our behalf among the pious, who, while they do not approve the course we have taken, give us credit, nevertheless, for the uprightness of our motives. This is what I feared we should not obtain, not knowing but that the falsehoods with which it has been attempted to blacken our characters, might gain credit even among the good, whose esteem we cannot but highly prize. It is a great happiness to be esteemed a deluded good man, rather than an ill-designing hypocrite. Let my name be sounded abroad as a weak, misguided enthusiast, yet a sincere lover of Jesus, *anything* consistent with sincere devotion to the cause of the Redeemer, rather than told with the highest commendation man can bestow, and yet withhold the reputation of being a servant of Christ. Yet after all, it is a light thing to be judged of man's judgment. We stand or fall at a higher tribunal.

"With much love to yourself and your associates in the labors of the Missionary Rooms and your families and connections, and to all who inquire for the prosperity of the missionary cause.

"I remain yours in the bonds of the gospel,
"S. A.. WORCESTER

"P.S.—Dr. B. joins in love. We are both well. You

will understand that we are steadfastly of the same mind."

Ann, back at New Echota after her visit to the penitentiary, had a new zeal and a new strength for her duties. She wrote David Greene, at the Missionary Rooms, an account of their visit to Milledgeville, and gave an account of the work of the press. "The first form of the second edition of the Gospel of Matthew is printed. The number of copies is three thousand. We are now folding the second edition of the Hymn Book. With the assistance in the family which I have had the year past, I think we shall be able to do all that is required except trimming the books. Mr. Boudinot says we shall not have to return any paper to the *Cherokee Phœnix*, so that sent by Mr. Hill to which Mr. Worcester alludes, will be of the right kind for printing Matthew."

The War Department had called for a report from each of the Indian schools maintained by the missions; it was Ann Worcester's task to prepare this in her husband's absence. It was concise, specific, and excellently written; it must have given the Honorable Lewis Cass a moment of surprise at its faultlessness. No degree of piety gave excuse for slovenliness at New Echota, he discovered.

"SIR,
   In the absence of my husband (who, as you know, is in confinement in the Penitentiary of the State of Georgia, for reputed illegal residence at this place) it devolves upon me to answer a series of questions proposed by the War Department through the American Board of Commissioners for Foreign Missions respecting the school at this station.

"It is necessary to state that the establishment of a school was never the object of this mission station. Indeed at the commencement, a school was hardly contemplated at all. The object was the preaching of the Gospel, & the preparation & publication of books, especially religious books in the Cherokee language. The latter object has been so far accomplished as to publish in that language three successive editions of a Hymnn Book, one of the Gospel of Matthew, one of the United Brethren Litany, for the use of their missions, & one tract consisting chiefly of portions of the Sacred Scriptures. A second edition of the Gospel of Matthew is now in progress.

"To the questions of the War Department, I presume it is sufficient to refer by numbers, as you doubtless have copies at hand.

"1. The mission was commenced in Nov. 1827; but no school was opened till April, 1830.

"2. No aid has been received from Government, & no particular appropriation made for the school distinct from the other objects of the station.

"3. There is no school house;—the school has been taught in public buildings belonging to the Cherokee Nation.

"4. Buildings, fences, &c may be valued at thirteen hundred dollars, which, however, would be precisely the same independently of the school.

"5. The sum expended for the school by the station has been about ten dollars per annum, independently of the board & clothing of the teacher. This has been for books, other expenses of the scholars, including fuel for the school, being defrayed by the parents.

"6. No debts or incumbrances.

"7. One teacher, Miss Sophia Sawyer, is engaged in the instruction of the school, who receives no compensation beyond her food & clothing. I am, in the absence of my husband, the only other person connected with the station in the capacity of missionary or assistant missionary, & receive the subsistence of myself & children for the time being.

"8. The whole number who have attended the school more or less is fifty. Average number twenty-two. Whole number of males, fourteen, of females, thirty-six. Names of the present pupils*———

"The greater part of the present pupils are under twelve years of age, & are taught reading, spelling, Mental arithmetic, Natural History, Rudiments of Geography, &c.

"Of those who formerly attended school, one was instructed in Grammar, History, Ancient Geography; four, in Penmanship & Composition. The scholars have generally been punctual in attendance, & have made good proficiency in their studies.

"I do not know that any report has ever before been made to the War Department.

"Yours respectfully,

ANN O. WORCESTER."

* These I omit in this copy, as they have been forwarded to the Missionary Rooms.

Meanwhile, efforts were being made to liberate the missionaries through higher powers than those of the state of Georgia. The proceedings were complicated, since issues far beyond the liberation of two imprisoned missionaries were involved. President Jackson was openly on the side of the state of Georgia and anxious to avoid the appearance of the test case, for as such it was regarded by constitutional authorities, before the Supreme Court. Governor Lumpkin, who had succeeded Governor Gilmer, was skillful in avoiding any finality. With these complications, the legal proceedings are difficult to follow, but Joseph Tracy has summarized them briefly and simply— and apparently without any warping of facts—in his *History of the American Board*. "Their case was brought, by a writ of error, before the Supreme Court of the United States, and argued by William Wirt and John Sargeant on the 20th, 21st and 22nd of February. No one appeared before the Court in behalf of Georgia. On the 3rd of March, Chief Justice Marshall pronounced the decision of the court in favor of the missionaries, declaring the laws of Georgia, extending her jurisdiction over the Cherokee country, to be repugnant to the constitution, treaties and laws of the United States, and, therefore, null and void. The mandate of the Court was immediately issued, reversing and annulling the judgment of the Superior Court of Georgia, and ordering that all proceedings on the indictment against the missionaries 'do forever surcease,' and that they 'be, and hereby are, dismissed therefrom.' On the 17th of March, Mr. Chester, supported by Mr. Underwood and Gen. Harden, moved, in the Superior Court of Georgia, that this mandate be received and recorded, and the prisoners discharged. The Court refused to obey the mandate. According to the regular course of law, a record of this refusal should be carried up to the Supreme Court of the United States, which should then proceed to enforce its own decision. To prevent this, the Court refused to allow its own decision, or any matter relating to it, to be recorded. To supply this deficiency, for which the statutes had made no provision, Mr. Chester made his affadavit of these facts, which, Judge Clayton certified, was sworn before him. Mr. Chester then applied by letter to the Governor, Lumpkin, to discharge the prisoners, but he refused to answer in writing; saying, 'You got round Clayton, but you shall not get round me.' "[3]

At the end of 1832, then, affairs were at a deadlock. President Jackson made no pretense of intention to see that the decision of the Supreme Court was carried out. His unofficial remark was, 'John Marshall has made his decision; now let him enforce it.' The supremacy of the Supreme Court, it appeared, was not a matter for the President's concern.

Meanwhile, with the missonaries and with the Board, dignity and a decent sense of honor must be maintained. The attorneys who had given their time and energy without stint in the cause of the imprisoned missionaries must be given some financial reward. Worcester, in charge of affairs for the mission, must see that they were paid, even though the expenditure had been in his behalf. The Board wrote him to reward General Harden and Judge Underwood according to his own discretion, out of the mission treasury. "We do not wish," they wrote, "to squander money on the cause, & still we do wish to do what is proper & honorable." From the penitentiary Samuel wrote the Board of his proper and honorable settlement of the indebtedness. "Mr. Chester was here last week. After consulting with him respecting the amount of compensation which ought to be made for the services of Judge Underwood and Gen. Harden, I have this day written drafts on you, which I shall immediately forward to them, to the amount of two hundred and fifty dollars payable to the

3 Tracy, *A History of the American Board of Commissioners for Foreign Missions*, p. 226.

order of Wm. H. Underwood, and one hundred dollars, payable to the order of Edward Harden."

Whatever might be their constitutional rights to freedom, Worcester and Butler were still not free. They waited developments patiently, performing whatever labors were asked of them and making no tactless distinctions between themselves and other prisoners. Samuel had asked that they might receive newspapers and some journal of medicine that would enable them to learn more, during their enforced absence from active missionary duties, about the practice of medicine. Medical knowledge was vital, for their own families, and for the Indians who came to the mission for help. David Greene wrote that he had sent the Boston *Recorder* as soon as he found that the prisoners might receive papers. But, he explained, "I do not think we have any medical journal that is worth sending, at least the physicians here say that we have not. The *Youth's Companion* is sent to Haweis. Is it worth while to send it to you & Dr. B. in prison?" Worcester went on, too, with his carpentry and cabinet-making. If he was ever free again, he would know all he needed to know about the building of a mission. Several years after his release, David Greene made a comment on Samuel's carpentry while in prison, a sample of which had been taken back to the Missionary Rooms in Boston. "Since I wrote your name above, I have had a very pleasant call from your father & your brother Isaac. The former thinks himself to be in unusually good health, & Isaac says that he is better than he was two months ago, while still the disease on the lungs is not removed & he fears that no permanent check is given to it. They are making a tour among their friends & are soon to return to Littleton. Among other things, they saw and heartily laughed over the box you made while you were in the Georgia penitentiary."

While Worcester was making his box, reading his copies of the *Recorder*, directing the Cherokee Press *in absentia*, and preaching to and teaching any of his fellow-prisoners who desired preaching and teaching, legal matters were taking a strange and complicated course. Tracy's account of the procedure continues: "The course of events had fixed the attention of politicians, as well as of the churches, intensely upon the imprisoned missionaries. The doctrine of 'nullification,' that is, of the right of a State to declare a law of the United States unconstitutional, and to prevent its execution within her limits, had become predominant in South Carolina. A convention, called by the legislature of that State, had published an ordinance, 'nullifying' the existing revenue law of the United States, forbidding the courts of the United States, their officers, and all other persons, to attempt to enforce that law in South Carolina, and declaring that if the general government should attempt to enforce it, South Carolina would withdraw from the Union; and the State had drafted men and provided military stores to sustain its ordinance by force. If the missionaries should persevere in their suit, and the Supreme Court of the United States should attempt to enforce its decision in their favor, it was feared that Georgia would join the 'nullifiers,' and that Alabama and Mississippi, where similar unconstitutional laws had been enacted, would follow the example. . . . . Georgia wished to support the President against the 'nullifiers,' but dared not, while it was so probable that she should soon find it expedient to join them.

"These embarrassments had been foreseen, ever since it was ascertained that the missionaries could not be frightened, and would not accept a pardon; and the Governor had sent them word that he intended to release them from confinement at some future time, When, in November, they gave notice of their intention to move the Supreme Court for further process, the Governor saw the necessity of a speedy extrication from his difficulties. But there was only one way to escape. The missionaries must be persuaded to withdraw their suit. He and his friends grew active. Gen. Coffee, Judge Schley, Mr. Cuthbert, and other leading politicians, visited them in the prison, and told them that they had conversed with the Governor, and had his unqualified assurance, that if they would withdraw their suit, they should be unconditionally discharged immediately after the adjournment of the Supreme Court. The Hon. John Forsyth called on Mr. Wirt, to persuade him to advise the missionaries to withdraw their suit, and assured him that, immediately on being informed that no motion would be made in the Supreme Court, they would be released. He gave this assurance 'unofficially'; yet he was authorized by the Governor to give it.

"The decision of the Supreme Court had established the right of the missionaries to a discharge from confinement, and the right of the Cherokees to protection from the President from the aggressions of Georgia. . . . . The law under which the missionaries had been imprisoned, had been repealed; and if released, they could now return to their stations and resume their labors. In this state of things, they believed that by withdrawing their suit, they should gain all that they could expect to gain by prosecuting it, and in a shorter time; and should save the country from whatever danger there might be of a civil war with the 'nullifiers.' They immediately wrote to the

Prudential Committee, stating their views and asking advice. . . . . The question was very fully discussed at a meeting of the Committee on the 25th of December, 1832. The prevailing opinion was, that it was expedient for the missionaries to withdraw their suit, and a letter was immediately written by Dr. Wisner, communicating that opinion. This letter was received on the seventh of January, 1833. The next day they wrote to their counsel, instructing them to make no motion in their behalf before the Supreme Court, and to the Governor and Attorney General of Georgia, informing them what instructions they had given their counsel. . . . . At length, on the fourteenth, Col. Mills told them he had received orders to discharge them from confinement, and took them from prison to his own parlor. The Governor sent them no written discharge, but issued his proclamation, stating that they had appealed to the magnanimity of the State, and had been set at liberty. With a horse and wagon furnished by Col. Mills at his own request, they returned to their homes and their labors."[4]

The long legal struggle was over, but the victory was scarcely a complete one for any of the parties concerned. Economic interests, rather than the constitution, had come off with the advantage; but the moral victory lay with the missionaries. They had won the friendship of their fellow-prisoners, and the complete confidence of more Cherokees than they might have hoped to reach by many years of quiet labors among them.

To Mrs. Worcester and the two little girls, the principal matter was that Samuel Worcester had come home to them. To Ann Eliza and Sarah, their father who sat again in their house and led their family prayers, did not look

4 Tracy, *op. cit.*, pp. 238-9.

like a bad man who had been behind prison bars. Nor did he look like St. Paul, whose picture they had seen in their story books, although St. Paul, too, had been in prison. He looked like their own dear father, kind of face and voice, eager of eye, shining of spirit.

A House Divided Against Itself

THE PROBLEMS of life in the penitentiary had been simple as compared with those Samuel Worcester found awaiting him when he reached home again early in 1833. There was no longer a routine so rigidly imposed that it left only a limited amount of time at his own disposal; there was, instead, the necessity to accomplish every day more than was humanly possible and so to offset the state of confusion and demoralization among the Cherokees due to pressure for their removal. The need was imperative for a leader who could see the outcome of the whole controversy and direct the bewildered Cherokees. But such a leader was not to be had, for no one could foresee what the end was to be. The nation had no definitely stated and stabilized Indian policy; it asserted, if it did not follow, a desire for the welfare of the Indians and a respect for their rights. Hope lived among the Cherokees on these assertions; if they saw that their own good lay in continuing where they were, might the Government not learn to see eye to eye with them and leave them unmolested? President Jackson's attitude toward the Indians, it is true, was known to be unfriendly, and his promises to them had proved precarious; the Indians said he spoke with two tongues. Years earlier, he had acknowledged that he owed his victory over the Creeks at the Battle of the Horseshoe in 1814 to the valor of the Cherokees, but he had forgotten his indebtedness. The Great White Father obviously had not drunk the brew of cockleburs which Cherokees knew had power to make a man's memory long; or, if his memory was long enough, his sense of obligation was short. But Tsunu lahun ski, one of the chieftains of the East Cherokees in North Carolina, had not forgotten. "If I had known that Jackson would drive us from our homes, I would have killed him that day at the Horseshoe," he said bitterly.

As late as 1832, while Worcester was still imprisoned, the Indians had high hopes of the election of a new Great White Father who would replace Jackson and whom they could trust to be mindful of their own rights. Henry Clay, if elected to the presidency, would not forget the red children. But Henry Clay was not chosen; Jackson was reëelected and felt he had free rein to continue with the policies he had begun. Those Cherokees who understood the significance of national affairs were more deeply discouraged than they had been before; removal westward seemed to a small but increasing number to be their only hope of survival as a people.

The principal chief, John Ross, held stubbornly to the rights of the Cherokees east of the Mississippi. At the time of Worcester's release, Ross was in Washington, heading a delegation composed of Richard Taylor, John F. Baldridge, and Joseph Vann, that had gone to defend the rights of their people at the capital. Word had come back that Ross had refused the Great White Father's offer of three million dollars for all of the Cherokee lands east of the Mississippi other than those in North Carolina, declaring that the gold mines alone were worth more than that. On his return, Ross' nephew William Shorey

Coody, John Ridge, and Elias Boudinot opposed his stand; they could see no peace ahead in this land where white men seized their farms and houses, plied them with whiskey and bribes, and deprived them of all right to give testimony in court.

It was difficult for Samuel Worcester to remain an on-looker, when he saw individual cases of injustice among his own Indian friends, and when he yearned with his whole heart to devote himself to the welfare of the people he had come to save. How could he save their immortal souls, when he could not even save their bodies and their property? At times, he knew with remorse, he had over-stepped the bounds of neutrality. Once David Greene had written him disapprovingly: "I was sorry to see one of your letters in the Northampton papers, presenting things before the public in just that shape & at just that time." Since that reproof, he had prayed fervently that he might practice discretion and do his Indian friends no harm in his desire to help them. But he must not, on the other hand, be too meek in his work among the Indians and their white oppressors; if he were he would soon find himself and his cause effaced. His colleague, John Thompson, had dis-covered this danger and had denied with spirit a false charge against the missionaries. Governor Gilmer, Thomp-son wrote, had informed the late Secretary of War that the missionaries had "found their stations *too lucrative* to yield them up willingly. . . . . I will not say that Governor Gilmer has originated this allegation; for it is as old as the hostility to missions. . . . . All I ask, and all I obtain for my labor among this people is a bare support."[1] The essential frugality of life as the Worces-ters and all their fellow-workers lived it, the hard tasks

1 *Missionary Herald*, XXVIII (1832), 22.

that Ann and Samuel both performed without ceasing, the knowledge that they had of the faithfulness and self-sacrifice among the Indian missionaries made the charge of mercenary interests seem, for a moment, cruelly unjust. But the moment passed; there was so much for them to do that they had not time to dwell on injustice and breed embitterment. There were gratifying incidents frequently enough to make the hard tasks appointed them seem well rewarded. One of the most surprising and gratifying of these concerned the expenses of the press, which the Mission had heretofore paid with scrupulous exactness for all the printing done for the Mission rather than for the nation. He wrote the Board. "Heretofore we have always paid the Cherokee nation for the use of press & type; and I had already paid Mr. Hicks $23 for printing Matthew, Poor Sarah, and the Acts of the Apostles, when the late council, at the suggestion of Mr. Boudinott, passed a resolution allowing us the use of the press & types gratuitously from the date of the resolution."

In spite of threats from the Georgia Guard, the Cherokee press went on with its work. Boudinot still edited the *Phœnix*; there was a general agreement that it must go on. But Boudinot had committeed himself to the policy of emigration for his people, for whom he saw no hope in their present surroundings, and he met with much opposition among the leaders of the Cherokees. Like most of his fellow-tribesmen, he was not subtle; he had none of that craftiness that is almost generally native to Americans. David Greene, reading the *Phœnix* in Boston, had discovered this lack of subtlety, and had written Samuel Worcester about it. "It seems to me now not impossible that the whole matter would have passed off so, had not Mr. Boudinott noticed the arrest & trial in so irritating a manner; and in addition let the Georgians into the secret that the U. S. Government had withheld its appropriations, and thus ceased to renew its recognition of you as agent. . . . .

"While noticing this in the *Phœnix*, I will also mention the manner in which Mr. B. remarks on the probable arrangement of the P. O. route by Spring Place and New Echota, in which he tells how the operations of his press might be the most embarrassed. The Georgians will find that out soon enough. It is hardly worth while to tell an enemy how he may vex & injure you most effectually."

With or without American subtlety, the *Phœnix* continued to do all in its power to promote intelligent loyalty among the Cherokee people. On that necessity all factions could agree. They must know what greatness of leaders and events lay back of them; in their new interest in the white man's culture these things were being forgotten. Such accounts as this one recalling the succession of chiefs who had ruled the people were frequent; they called up stirring memories among the old and awoke a new sense of loyalty among the younger members of the tribe.

"Cherokee Nation,
Nov. 24, 1831.

Editor of the Cherokee Phœnix,

"For publication if you think proper, I send you a list of the names of the principal chiefs of the Cherokee Nation, given by and from the memory of Noonday, an aged man. You will discover the dates of the times when each flourished are not given and which is impossible to obtain from any man 'on the mortal side of existence.'

"All the chiefs mentioned in this list were seen by

Noonday except the first, who flourished before his recollection, but was still well known to fame when he arrived at the age of discretion. His name was *Etuk-kungsta*.

"*Occunstota* succeeded this chief, and had for his vice-chief *Sahwahooka* who administered the government as principal, when the first chief became very old; notwithstanding the old chief was exceedingly beloved, honored and well obeyed to the day of his death.

"Under the administration of these two chiefs flourished the great war and civil chief called *Attacul-culla*, or *Wood-leaning-up*, who is noticed by some of the British writers.

"*Eknngyeahdahhee*, or the *Firstkiller*, succeeded *Sah-wanooka*,—to him succeeded the famous chief,—

"*Kungnitta*, or the *Little Turkey*, whose benignant influence at last achieved the establishment of durable treaties of peace with the United States. To this chief was addressed a friendly letter, written on vellum, and to which was attached a golden chain as an emblem of the purity of the faith of the United States, by Dearborn, Secretary of War, acting under the special instruction of the President. After his death,

"*Enolee*, or the *Badger*, became the chief. In his time the people of the Nation became divided into parties, the civil and the vagrant, or as they are now well known by the designation of the 'lovers of the land' and the 'Arkansas Emigration' parties. Little was this chief qualified to tranquilize the discordant elements then rising into flame, or to oppose the 'malign influence' of the U. S. officers who blew the coal of contention, to enable themselves as friendly mediators to effect treaties, ceded large tracts of land by compromise, and

[166]

which enured to the advantage of the U. S. The patriotic party, claiming themselves to be the representatives of forty and some odd towns, deposed the chief under the charge of bias to the Arkansas party &c. but in a subsequent Council of the nation he was reinstated to the dignity of the office, but from the wound inflicted upon his reputation he never recovered to the day of his death. Then commenced the administration of

"*Nungnoheeahdahee*, or the *Pathkiller*, supported by *Charles R. Hicks*, who became the assistant principal chief, and other powerful chiefs, distinguished for their firmness, resolution, eloquence and wisdom, who effectually counteracted the tide of emigration opened by Gen. Jackson, in the treaty of 1811, and closed the breach, by the last treaty of 1819, concluded with J. C. Calhoun then Secretary of War. The spirit of civilization infused itself in all the acts of the Nation, which now established a written code of laws in conformity with the advice and written instructions of President Jefferson to the Cherokee Nation. The Great Council was then divided into distinct bodies, with power to negative each other's acts, and whose concurrence became necessary to the passage of any law. A constitution was also received by these chiefs, which was made by convention, the members of which were elected by the people. Previous to the operation of the Constitution and one year before the change was effected, it pleased the Great Chief to call these good men from the state of human existance. To fill this vacancy, thus occurring, for one year, devolved upon the members of the Council who held their seats under the ancient and immemorial usage: who appointed by ballot *William Hicks*, Senior, brother of the late *Charles R. Hicks*, to be the Principal

Chief, and John Ross, President of the Council at that period, to be the assistant principal chief. At the expiration of the term for which these chiefs were appointed, the members of the General Council elected under the new Constitution, chose by ballot John Ross and George Lowrey Senior principal and assistant principal chiefs, for four years, whose term of service will terminate in October, 1832.

FLYING CLOUD."[2]

But all attempts to unify the Cherokees were hopeless now. Confused by the misrepresentations of white men among them in Georgia and at Washington, baffled by a succession of treaties the terms of which were abandoned as soon as new terms seemed more advantageous to the white treaty-makers, they were completely demoralized. Some of them, sure that they would soon be forced to emigrate, planted no crops and followed no industry. What was the use, they asked, if they must leave their crops to grow for the white man's harvesting and surrender their homes and property for the white invaders to possess. Officials of the state of Georgia and of the United States used bribery without scruple; and those Indians who accepted bribes sold their national cause without realizing what they were doing. In their inexperience they did not know the insidious nature of a bribe. It was a new method to them then. John Rogers was offered "a liberal reward which would place myself and family in easy circumstances for the ballance of my life"; Jack Walker, who had been active in promoting the cause of removal and whose influence was strengthened by the fact that his wife was a niece of the Indian agent,

2 *Cherokee Phœnix*, Vol. IV, No. 21, December 3, 1831.

Return J. Meigs, was suspected of selling his influence and was assassinated; Sam Houston, friend of Chief Jolly of the Western Cherokees, was charged with the expectation of large profit from the exercise of his influence among the western division. Distrust and dissension ruled. There were rumors of attempts to bribe John Ross, though he remained staunch in his opposition to emigration. To the minds of the Cherokees, no men in high places were now to be trusted. How could they be, when the Secretary of War, a few years earlier, had made a record of his official attempt to bribe each of the Cherokee chieftains to the extent of two thousand dollars?

In the winter of 1835 two rival factions represented the Cherokee Nation in Washington. Ross, still heading his party, stood staunch against removal; Ridge favored yielding to the demands of Georgia and the United States. The Reverend Mr. J. F. Schermerhorn, of a somewhat shadowy political reputation, was appointed by President Jackson to treat with the Ridge faction, since—although Ross' place as principal chief was unquestioned—it was the Ridge party with whom Jackson preferred to make a treaty. Schermerhorn's co-worker was to be General William Carroll of Tennessee, but Carroll's ill health and perhaps his distaste for so difficult and unfair an undertaking prevented his acting as Commissioner for the United States. Schermerhorn seems to have had no fear to act alone, with the knowledge that he was backed by the President. The agreement which Schermerhorn and the Ridge party reached in Washington must be presented to the whole body of the Cherokees in council in October. After spending the entire summer and the early fall in efforts to reconcile the tribe to the Ridge agreement, Schermerhorn met the full council at Red Clay. To his

great disappointment the Ridge treaty was overwhelming-
ly rejected and he was obliged, after the council disbanded,
to report unfavorably to Washington. "I have pressed
Ross so hard by the course I have adopted that although
he got the general council to pass a resolution declaring
that they would not treat on the basis of the $5,000,000
yet he has been forced to bring the nation to agree to a
treaty, here or at Washington. They have used every
effort to get by me and get to Washington again this
winter. They dare not do it. You will perceive Ridge and
his friends have taken apparently a strange course. I
believe he began to be discouraged in contending with the
power of Ross; and perhaps also considerations of personal
safety have had their influence; but the Lord is able to
overrule all things for good."[3]

With or without the overruling of the Lord, Schermerhorn's defeat was only temporary. He gave notice that
the Cherokees were to meet the Commissioners at New
Echota in December, and warned them that those not
present would be counted as favoring the treaty that
would be drawn up. In spite of this warning, however,
there were present only from three to five hundred men,
women, and children out of a population of more than
seventeen thousand. Yet a treaty was drawn up and
signed on December 29, 1835. By the terms of this treaty,
the Cherokee Nation ceded to the United States its whole
remaining territory east of the Mississippi for the sum of
five million dollars and a joint interest in the lands of the
Western Cherokees. Improvements were to be paid for,
and the Indians were to be removed at the expense of the
United States, with subsistence for a year following their

3 Bureau of American Ethnology, *Fifth Annual Report*, 1883-4, p. 280.

removal. Emigration was to be completed within two years after the signing of the treaty.

William Carroll was again absent when this treaty was drawn up, and neither John Ross nor any other official of the Cherokee Nation was present. It was ratified by Congress, however, on May 23, 1836. In protest, Ross and the national delegates presented a memorial with signatures representing nearly sixteen thousand of the Cherokee people, and councils were held in various parts of the Cherokee Nation denouncing the methods used to secure the treaty and declaring it null and void. General Wool, in charge of federal troops in the Indian country, forwarded their protests to Washington, explaining: "It is, however, vain to talk to a people almost universally opposed to the treaty and who maintain that they never made such a treaty. So determined are they in their opposition that not one of all those who were present and voted at the council held but a day or two since, however poor or destitute, would either receive rations or clothing from the United States lest they might compromise themselves in regard to the treaty. These same people as well as those in the mountains of North Carolina, during the summer past, preferred living upon the roots and sap of trees rather than receive provisions from the United States, and thousands, as I have been informed, had no other food for weeks. Many have said they will die before they will leave the country."[4] The President rebuked General Wool for forwarding the protests, declaring them disrespectful to the Executive, the Senate, and the American people. But Major W. M. Davis, appointed to enroll the Cherokees for removal and to appraise their property, supported General Wool's attitude. "I conceive," he wrote to the

4 *Ibid.*, 1897-8, Pt. I, p. 127.

Secretary of War, "that my duty to the President, to yourself, and to my country reluctantly compels me to make a statement of facts in relation to a meeting of a small number of Cherokees at New Echota last December, who were met by Mr. Schermerhorn and articles of a general treaty entered into between them for the whole Cherokee nation. . . . . Sir, that paper. . . . called a treaty, is no treaty at all, because not sanctioned by the great body of the Cherokee and made without their participation or assent. I solemnly declare to you that upon its reference to the Cherokee people it would be instantly rejected by nine-tenths of them, and I believe by nineteen-twentieths of them. There were not present at the conclusion of the treaty more than one hundred Cherokee voters, although the weather was everything that could be desired. The Indians had long been notified of the meeting, and blankets were promised to all who would come and vote for the treaty. No enumeration of them was made by Schermerhorn. The business of making the treaty was transacted with a committee appointed by the Indians present, so as not to expose their numbers. The power of attorney under which the committee acted was signed only by the president and secretary of the meeting, so as not to disclose their weakness. . . . . Mr. Schermerhorn's apparent design was to conceal the real number present and to impose on the public and the government upon this point. The delegation taken to Washington by Mr. Schermerhorn had no more authority to make a treaty than any other dozen Cherokee picked up for the purpose. I now warn you and the President that if this paper of Schermerhorn's called a treaty is sent to the Senate and ratified you will bring trouble upon the government and eventually destroy this the Cherokee

Nation. The Cherokee are a peaceable, harmless people, but you may drive them to desperation, and this treaty cannot be carried into effect except by the strong arm of force."[5]

And now John Ridge, who had been the leader of the treaty party, saw taking place the depredations that General Wool feared. Trusting to the President's sense of fairness, he addressed a letter to him. "We now come to address you on the subject of our griefs and afflictions from the acts of the white people. They have got our lands and now they are preparing to fleece us of the money accruing from the treaty. We found our plantations taken in whole or in part by the Georgians—suits instituted against us for back rents for our own farms. These suits are commenced in the inferior courts, with the evident design that, when we are ready to remove, to arrest our people, and on these vile claims to induce us to compromise for our own release, to travel with our families. Thus our funds will be filched from our people, and we shall be compelled to leave our country as beggars and in want.

"Even the Georgia laws, which deny our oaths, are thrown aside, and notwithstanding the cries of our people, and protestation of our innocence and peace, the lowest classes of the white people are flogging the Cherokees with cowhides, hickories, and clubs. We are not safe in our houses—our people are assailed by day and night by the rabble. Even justices of the peace and constables are concerned in this business. This barbarous treatment is not confined to men, but the women are stripped also and whipped without law or mercy. . . . . Send regular troops to protect us from these lawless assaults, and to

5 *Ibid.*, 1897-8, Pt. I, pp. 126-7.

protect our people as they depart for the West. If it is not done, we shall carry off nothing but the scars of the lash on our backs, and our oppressors will get all the money. We talk plainly, as chiefs having property and life in danger, and we appeal to you for protection."[6]

Property and possessions were no longer safe in the Cherokee Nation. License to seize what belonged to the Cherokees began with the excitement over gold, and extended everywhere. Joseph Vann, one of the wealthiest of his tribe, had been compelled to abandon his plantation with its expensive home, and with his family to wade through the snow to Tennessee where he had found shelter in an open log cabin with a dirt floor. And during one of his early absences in Washington, John Ross' beautiful home on the Coosa River had been seized. He now lived in a one-room cabin beyond the Georgia boundary in Tennessee, near the temporary Council Grounds that had been set up when New Echota no longer seemed safe for tribal gatherings. Shortly after the council in the fall of 1835, Ross was captured, at his new home in Tennessee, by twenty-five members of the Georgia Guard, and with all his private papers and the records of the Council he was taken to Spring Place, held twelve days, and then released without apology or explanation. John Howard Payne was also captured, held a prisoner for thirteen days, and then ordered out of the country. A few days before the seizure of Ross and Payne, the Georgia Guard had appeared at New Echota, accompanied by Elias Boudinot's brother Stand Watie, suppressed the *Phœnix*, and taken possession of the printing plant. Nothing was to be left by which tribal unity and morale might be maintained.

Long before the treaty was ratified, the missionaries

6 *Ibid.*, pp. 127-8.

[174]

had accepted the fact that they could accomplish nothing in Georgia. They knew, as the Cherokees themselves knew, what to expect if removal became necessary: it would take place under the most difficult circumstances. The Choctaws had agreed to go with more readiness than the Cherokees felt, but they had undergone terrible hardships. Once during the Choctaw removal, a body of several hundred on the march westward had stopped near the mission station at Martyn. More than nine-tenths of the women and children were barefooted; they were cold and hungry and in need of blankets; they needed, more than all else, some sense of hope to make their sufferings endurable. One party of Choctaws had come to Martyn to beg an ear of corn for each member, to appease their hunger. So, all knew, it would be with the Cherokees.

Things were going none too smoothly for the missionaries themselves. By force and fraud, Dr. Butler was driven from the station at Haweis, and in February, 1834, he removed his family to Brainerd in order to be beyond the jurisdiction of Georgia. Soon afterward, the mission premises at New Echota were seized by a claimant under the Georgia lottery, and the Worcesters were threatened with homelessness. It was particularly hard to be uprooted now, for there was a new baby in the household, and Ann was in frail health from hard work and the birth of the child, "Another meal-sifter," the Indians had said when they learned the new baby was a girl. "Her name is Hannah," Samuel and Ann had announced, "for she is the child of grace." And now, with the tiny baby, they must go back to Brainerd to live until their future as missionaries to the Cherokees could be decided. Whatever the Lord had in store for them, east or west of the Mississippi, they were ready to accept.

[175]

By the spring of 1835, it had been decided that the Worcesters would go west. The press had been threatened, and was sure to be seized sooner or later; and there was small hope that affairs among the Cherokees in Georgia could ever again be so settled that work in translating and publishing could go on without interruption. Now that the house was divided against itself, through no fault of its own, no advancement could be expected. Whatever missionaries could accomplish for the Cherokees, other than to teach and preach wherever the Indians could give any thought to teaching and preaching, must be done in the West.

On the eighth of April, 1835, the Worcesters bade farewell to Brainerd. On the twenty-ninth of May, they arrived at Dwight Mission, in the Cherokee Nation West. How many weeks and how many hundreds of miles of travel they had added to the distance between themselves and their former New England homes, they did not consider. They had made the journey with speed and comfort, in fifty-one days, in "a two-seated ambulance," while their poor Indian friends must make it on foot, in hunger and discouragement. They were received with a glad welcome into the household of faith at Dwight; but the Indians had new homes to build, new fields to clear, a new order to establish. And most of them had the long, terrible journey, on foot through wilderness, yet to accomplish. The Worcesters saw only the alarm and dissension that preceded the removal, and the depleted numbers and the brokenness of spirit that followed. Familiar as they were with hardships and discouragements, they found unbelievable the losses and the sufferings which their people, arrived in the West, had undergone. Among those who died en route to the new country of the Cherokees was White Path, a former chief who had headed a rebellion against the new order of things in 1828. Failing in this rebellion, he had gradually softened in his attitude and had accepted what seemed inevitable. In the removal he had headed a detachment of his people, and had done his best to make their march free of suffering; now he was dead, and without a burial place either in the old land he had left or in the new land to which he was not destined to come. They buried him by the roadside, with a box over his grave and a pole with streamers around it, so that those who came after might know where he lay. Mrs. Ross, too, died on her way to the new home that her husband had so long opposed adopting, and was buried at Little Rock, among strangers in a strange land. And Harriet Boudinot, worn with the uncertainty of life at New Echota in the troubled days preceding the removal, had died and was buried in the land that her family must soon leave.

Sickness and suffering and hardship and separation and discouragement and fear—these are words that must fill the pages of any account of the emigration of the Cherokees. However often they occur, they are inadequate. The Cherokees have left no book of lamentations; those who had been eloquent in the councils were speechless now.

A broken nation must rebuild itself, in the new country west of the Mississippi.

The Indian Press

SOME indissoluble potency strengthened the blood of Samuel and Ann Orr Worcester. Place, circumstances, state of health had no effect on such blood; it made life the same unalterable thing for them in New England, in Georgia, or in the West, among gentlemen or among savages. Such blood has given American culture its essential quality, which persists in spite of the influx of outside elements of every nationality and those repeated changes in ways of living and doing that are generally referred to as progress. For the Worcesters, their work, their ideals, and their God were the same, wherever they might live and whatever adaptations they might find necessary. Life was not an event to them; it was a current that flowed deeper than place or circumstance, and had eternity for its destination.

Now, in the summer of 1835, Worcester was thirty-seven years old. The best of his life, in physical vigor and intellectual power, was still ahead of him, and he had a work that he knew was worthy to employ that best to the end of his days. No vacillation, no uncertainty beset him. It was never to be his fate to regret his choice or to long for more favorable circumstances; what he did was appointed unto him. In that new country of the Cherokees he was to be the translator of their Scriptures, the publisher of their books, as long as he lived. And Ann was still to be the partner of his undertakings, the mother of his children, the good woman of his household, till her body wore itself out in this work. If their achievements were prodigious in an inconspicuous way, it was because they bent everything to a deep and certain purpose. Externalities must be conquered, it is true—New England common sense saw to that—but these could never be more than light deterrents which they set aside by overcoming them.

At New Echota Worcester had laid out his course and begun its accomplishments; now he was to continue and to expand what he had begun and proved himself capable of doing. The American Board were as sure of what he must do as was Worcester himself. Through translations and books issued especially for the Cherokees, he must aid in their salvation. Their civilization, their Americanization, their Christianization depended upon books. Samuel Worcester was to give them these. And since, however unwillingly , the Cherokees were to move westward across the Mississippi, their future undoubtedly lay there; The Messenger must precede them there and be prepared to meet needs when they came after him. He must go before them, and be ready with his message when they came.

The old press, now damaged and still in the hands of enemies of the Indians, would be inadequate for this larger work in the West; hence the Board sent out a new press and types from Boston, to go by water up the Arkansas to the new Indian country and to be set up there wherever Samuel thought best. It was a larger press than the first one, and more printing might be expected. In fact, it was hoped that what had begun as the Cherokee Press might be expanded, under Samuel Worcester's direction, into an Indian Press. Worcester would continue his work as translator for the Cherokees and as publisher of their books; but when the press was available it would be used in printing books for other Indian tribes. Ways of carrying out this plan were turning themselves over in Worcester's mind, while the shipments from Boston were making their slow way up the Mississippi and the Arkansas.

The Worcesters' household goods, too, must follow them by steamboat while they made their journey in their "two-seated ambulance" and then, arrived at Dwight in its new location on the Sallisaw, awaited their possessions and made their decision as to where these were to be set up.

It had been suggested that the old Osage mission at Union, now vacated, might be a suitable place for a new station. Union, about 150 miles from the old location of Dwight, on the Neosho or Grand River, had been founded in 1820 by missionaries sent out by the United Foreign Missionary Society. In spite of the savagery of the Osages, the isolation of the location from other centers of Christian influence, and the opposition of white traders who favored hunting and trapping, rather than agriculture, among the Indians, the undertaking had grown and thrived. In 1826, the American Board took over the debts and the property of the United Foreign Missionary Society, and Union became one of its stations. Its school and church and farm continued to serve the Osages until, after a succession of treaties, this tribe no longer had any claim to the land where Union stood. It had no function as a mission to the Osages, when their boundaries were forty miles away. It had been closed, therefore, until some decision could be reached as to whether it might again

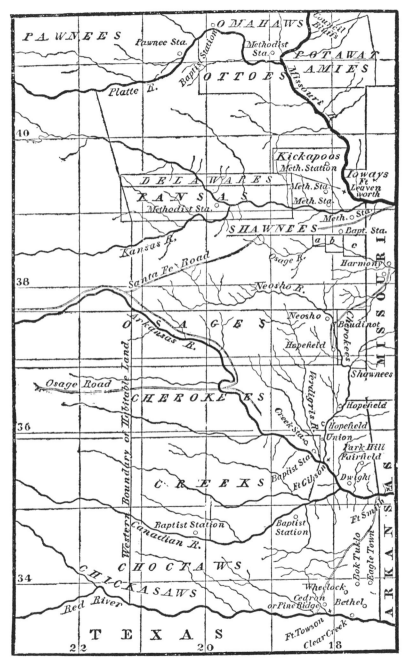

INDIAN TERRITORY WEST OF THE MISSISSIPPI

serve as a mission, perhaps to the Cherokees within whose domain it now lay.

Two days after the Worcesters' arrival at Dwight, Samuel wrote to the Board of his arrival and his progress toward settling and establishing his family. "We were obliged, or at least thought it expedient," he explained, "to take a circuitous route, through Kentucky, Illinois, & Missouri, to avoid swamps which at present are almost impassable for wagons. Mrs. Worcester was rather more unwell than usual when we set out, and, by the time we arrived at Hopkinsville, Ky., was taken with a bilious fever, which detained us one week at that place. We were hospitably entertained there in the family of the Rev. Mr. Jones, and my horse kept gratuitously by a member of the church living at a little distance from town. . . . . We had some other hindrances from high water &c., which protracted our journey. . . . . Mrs. W. arrived in better health.

"I find it to be the opinion of the missionaries now here, that Union is not the best place for the press, though they say I had better go and examine for myself. . . . . Mr. Orr has informed Mr. Hill of my goods, which I sent from Brainerd, being sunk with the steamboat which brought them up the Arkansas. I fear there is a heavy loss, particularly in printing paper and books. I expect to go tomorrow to see their state, & secure, as well as I can, what remain. My next object will be to visit Union and other places, and to fix upon a location as soon as I can obtain the requisite information. I am told there will be danger of difficulties arising, if I establish myself at any new place without the express leave of the National Council." His postscript gave important news: "Since writing the above I have learned that the printing press has arrived at Fort Gibson."

Worcester was dealing, now, with the Western Cherokees, who did not know him or his works. Was he merely another white man, come among them to choose the best site available and claim it for himself? Could even a missionary be trusted now, when their eastern brethren were struggling bitterly, as a tribe and as individuals, to retain what was their own? Their chief, John Jolly, was skeptical. But Worcester was not readily discouraged. He wrote the Board a full account of his visit to Union.

"In regard to the healthiness of the station at Union there are differences of opinion. It is not a favorable location for preaching. If a line be drawn through it, running nearly North and South, about all on the West of that line is prairie, which will not soon be inhabited. On the East Grand River separates it from almost all the Cherokee population, &, though fordable a large part of the time, it is an obstacle to attendance at preaching. East of the river is a settlement, which will probably much increase, but Union is one side from it. The place cannot be said to be favorable for exerting an influence upon the Cherokee people. The buildings are not sufficient, in their present state & form, for permanent use for the object in question, and the location is very unfavorable for building at moderate expense. The expense of fuel and of fencing timber for all purposes which would be requisite there would be very considerable. It would seem necessary to repair the mill, and keep it in operation, at least for some years, which would be a considerable incumbrance & expense to the station. It is certainly not a spot which would be chosen, if the buildings were not already there. Besides these things, there seems to be danger of a very undesirable controversy with the Cherokees, if the Board attempt to retain the place; some of them feeling as if an unwarrantable claim had been set up to the section on which the station is, as not belonging to the Cherokees, whereas, in the treaty with them, by which they obtained the country, no reservation of that section was made. You remarked, I think, in a former letter to me, that the place was held by a title independent of the Cherokees. I have looked at the treaties, such as I could find, and it seems, in the Osage treaty, to have been reserved to be disposed of by the U. S. Government & the Osages. When the country was ceded to the Cherokees, as I have remarked, the place was not reserved. All that remains, therefore, according to the treaties, is for the U. S. to pay the Board for the buildings, on condition of the amount being expended in Osage missions, & let the station revert to the Cherokee nation, to be disposed of as they see fit. At any rate the Cherokees *claim* it. And even if the Board lose the value of the buildings, I am not sure that the difference between the expense there and at another place which may be selected would not counterbalance it in a very few years. These, I believe, are the principal objections to Union as a permanent location. It certainly does not combine the advantages which you remarked should be kept in view in the selection of a place.

"I have determined, however, on setting the press up at Union for the time being, & Mr. Wheeler is now at work, making preparations for printing.

"The next week after our arrival here, the national council was in session for the purpose of supplying the place of two deceased chiefs, and considering the expediency of sending a delegation to the eastern Cherokee nation to attend to the recent propositions for a treaty. At that council the Rev. Mr. Aldrich, of the Baptist Mission, had a petition presented, for leave to continue missionary operations at the station where he was, having had some difficulty with a white person respecting the place. This application led to the adoption of a resolution by the Council, that no new missionary establishment should be erected, until the General Council should provide for it by law, & grant permission. This was the only answer Mr. Aldrich obtained. The Council had been likely to quarrel in the election of chiefs, and the old chief Jolly undertook the appointment himself, until the regular time for an election next fall. To this the Council submitted. The two new chiefs appointed were James Rogers & Jos. Vann. Rogers was understood to be opposed to missions and Jolly to be so entirely under his influence that he also might be considered as opposed, while Rogers was at his elbow. The establishment of a mission press was said to have been objected to by some of the Rogerses, and the new chief was supposed by some to be of the same mind. These things were considered by Capt. Vashon, the Cherokee Agent, as at least a temporary triumph of the antimissionary party, and I was led at first to entertain considerable apprehension that obstacles might thus be thrown in my way. I learned, however, that there were some circumstances relating to Mr. Aldrich in particular, which were urged against complying with his request, which would not stand in the way of my being permitted to establish the press. Yet the resolution adopted stands in the way of my commencing a new station until the meeting of Council in the fall. After consideration and conversation with my missionary brethren, I concluded that, if I could obtain the approbation of the chiefs, I would set up the press at Union for the time being. Without their approbation I could not, because I was informed that some had been particularly opposed to having that station occupied by the press, and if I should set it up there without the sanction of the chiefs, it might produce an excitement which would operate against obtaining leave for a new station. I have therefore visited each of the three ·chiefs individually and obtained their permission. Mr. Rogers, from whom some anticipated opposition, made no objection whatever. He and Vann also told me that they presumed [the] Council would readily grant permission to set up the press at a new station. I did not propose the question to Jolly. Thus God has given me favor in the eyes of these men, and I now see little reason to apprehend that any serious obstacles will be thrown in the way, but am led to believe that the Council will give leave to establish the press at such place as I request. In the meantime, I have a little printing which Mr. Wheeler can do, and should have plenty if Mr. Boudinott were here to revise. Perhaps Mr. Fleming will have a Creek book ready pretty soon, and probably he and the Choctaw missionaries can keep the press supplied with work, while my attention is taken up with erecting a new station . . . . .

"We shall not remove to Union for some time yet, as there is much to do in taking care of goods which have been under water, which can better be done here. I shall in the mean time, if Providence permit, spend a part of the time there, preparing the office and superintending the printing. . . .

"In a preceding paragraph I have referred to the damage done to our goods. Damage was not all—many things were stolen—such as one good feather bed, the best there was—much table linen, as many as eight blankets—1 ream

[185]

of letter paper, &c. A large part of the things stolen were of Mrs. W.'s private property. But the heaviest loss was in paper & books. How much of the paper can be made to answer for printing I have not yet ascertained. I fear not much. There were 60 reams or more."

The situation in which Worcester found himself was indeed delicate. He must lose no time in setting about his work, but he must not be too hasty or presume in any way on the tolerance of the people to whose country he had come. In international affairs, the handling of such a situation without friction is termed a master stroke of diplomacy; in an affair between some oppressed Indians and a missionary, it received no such fine terminology. But Worcester was not a man to care about fine words. The important matter, to him, was that he devised a way to make his position among the Cherokees secure, not only temporarily but permanently. He made his work seem indispensable to them. He devised a book that would seem useful to all of the Cherokees concerned, set it up and printed it himself, as material evidence to the Council of what he meant to do if he were allowed to remain. It was "merely a little book of eight pages, filled chiefly with pictures, but containing the alphabet and a little more. I had come here for the purpose of revising the forms which I supposed I should find in type, but Mr. Wheeler had been sick and they were not ready. Having two days at command, & being anxious before council to throw out something from the press to attract the attention of the people, I employed them in preparing that, & helping to print 200 copies. It pleased the Cherokees well. We shall probably print some more as it is, & after Mr. Boudinott's arrival enlarge it to something of more value."

Getting the press ready for this printing and such other

small, & not likely to increase. I think Mr. Boudinott's influence with the Council in such matters would be considerable, at least in regard to the station with which he will be connected. I think so from the manner in which he was spoken of.

Excuse me for troubling you with a few words more respecting the 5th condition on which my request was granted. I do not indulge much apprehension that it will interrupt the progress of our work, at least for a long time. The establishment is not likely to be "deemed unprofitable," while the work goes on, without occupying much land, or troubling the neighbors with many cattle. Then as to being expelled for the violation of the laws, such a thing may be, but I do not think the probability of it so great that it ought prevent the effort to do the people good. Unless the occupants of the station are very indiscreet, such a measure is not to be apprehended, i.e. unless the state of things in the nation should change much for the worse. True Mr. Aldrich, Baptist missionary, has received orders to leave the nation—but the circumstances were somewhat peculiar, so that the fact does not add to my apprehensions.

I have perhaps done with the subject as it regards the contemplated stations, but venture to add some remarks of a more general nature.

I think there is reason to doubt whether this nation will immediately or very shortly allow the addition of any missionary station except the establishment of the press.— If any are to be established, it must be on a small scale, at least as to the cultivation of land, and the holding of stock.— It is important to the prosperity of the work, that the missionaries already here confine themselves within narrow limits in these particulars.

The little book for children to which I alluded in my application to the council, is merely a little book of eight pages, filled chiefly with pictures, but containing the alphabet and a little more. I had come here for the purpose of revising two forms which I supposed I should find in type, but Mr. Wheeler had been sick, and they were not ready. Having two days at command, & being anxious before council to throw out something from the press to attract the attention of the people, & having two days at command, I employed them in preparing that, & helping to print 200 copies. It pleased the Cherokees well. We shall probably print some more as it is, &, after Mr. Boudinott's arrival enlarge it to something of more value.

Since Mr. Wheeler has recovered, we have been hindered for want of a pressman. We had intended to employ Mr Candy, but he has been, & still is unable to work. Mr. Wheeler is now at work at the press alone—of course laboring under disadvantage. He has printed a little book for Mr. Fleming, & is now printing a new edition of Scripture Extracts, & has part of the Hymnbook in type.

Mr. Wheeler wishes for particular instructions in regard to the manufacture of rollers, and the inktable &c to be used with them. He does not know what are the latest improvements, nor does he know the proportion of the materials in the composition of which the rollers are made. I wrote to Mr. Hill for a Typographia. If that contains all requisite instructions respecting the rollers, it is sufficient. Mr. Wheeler thinks it will not. If not, be so kind as to procure them from some competent person, and send them to me.

I have not heard from Mr. Boudinot since his return to the old nation from Connecticut. I presume he will do his best to come this fall, but

LETTER BY MR. WORCESTER CONCERNING THE PRESS

work as they might be able to do before permanent arrangements were made, was not an easy matter. Late in August, Samuel wrote the Board some of the details with which they might well be familiar, addressing his letter to Mr. Greene who had come out to Georgia soon after the arrival of the first press:

"DWIGHT, Aug. 26, 1835.

REV. AND DEAR SIR,

"Your letter of July 23 I had the pleasure to receive yesterday. Everything about the press came safe, except two trifling articles of iron which a common blacksmith can supply. The loss on our articles from the old nation will probably not hinder our operations, since the things from Boston came safe. Only considerable of my time is required to repair damages. I have selected from the paper about the amount of 22 reams,* which, though not uninjured, I think will answer for printing, and which is more than half the whole amount sent from Brainerd. The rest I hope to sell for *something* to be used as wrapping paper.

"I think the artist who made the alterations in the Cherokee type, which I requested last year, cannot be the same with the one who formed the original matrices, nor equally skilful in imitation. One letter, representing the syllable *mo*, will not answer at all. It is so unlike the pattern which I sent, that I am led to suppose the pattern must have been defaced, before it came into the artist's hands. We reject the new letter, and for the present supply the deficiency by altering another type, as often as the letter occurs, which is not very frequently. Be so kind as to have a new punch made,

---

* "Since writing I discover that I have yet a little more which I have not reported."

[187]

and type cast, and forwarded with our next supplies. The scheme I sent last year will be a guide as to the requisite quantity. As to the form, I must attempt a new pattern. I attach the pattern to the corner of this sheet that it may be separated if you wish. I have first made a large one, and then attempted to reduce it to about the proper size. I send both, that the large may show what the small was intended to be. . . .

"The letter C *tli* is wanting in the Cherokee fount. As it is precisely the Roman small capital we find a substitute in the English case, but as that may run out, we wish a supply to be sent for the Cherokee fount. The Arabic figures 1, 2, 3, &c., are also wanting in the Cherokee fount. We wish to have them supplied in the same proportion to the whole amount of type as is usual in English founts—or rather in a somewhat larger proportion.

"Among the articles lost by the steamboat were the bar or lever of my press for bookbinding, and the shortest of the three *dogs*. If the term *dog* is not understood, I do not know what name to give the part which is missing. I mean the irons which play in the cogs of the wheel, and act immediately upon it. Cannot those parts be supplied in Boston? If not, be so kind as to inform me soon, that I may try to have them made. The press is denominated, in the invoice, 'One (Tufts) Standing Press.'

"I have mentioned these items in my list of articles needed at our station, which I send to Mr. Hill, at the same time with this to you, but referred him to this letter for directions. The Scripture cuts you will be so kind as to have sent with the rest.

"The cards which Mr. Hitchcock has already sent it

will probably be well to have lithographed, and the experiment with them will serve as an indication respecting the expediency of adding others.

"I do not know what is to be gained by the experiment of printing Cherokee in Pickering's alphabet with the syllables divided. I have no doubt that the Cherokees could pretty readily learn to read in that manner, pronouncing *syllables* without regard to the single letters; yet it would be inferior to an alphabet strictly syllabic. So much do I regard the syllabic method of writing, where it is practicable, as superior to the other, that I have often thought very seriously of writing to some of the missionaries at the Sandwich Islands, recommending the adoption of the syllabic method for that and kindred languages; and the only hesitancy I should have about it now, would arise from the difficulty of persuading those concerned to undertake so much of a revolution, after the progress which has been made in printing and learning on the present system. If the revolution could be effected, the languages of the South Seas would require fewer characters than the Cherokee; the missionaries, being intelligent men, would of course adopt characters of a simple form, and the saving of labor and time in writing, printing and learning would be immense. I should be very glad to see Guess' alphabet improved as to the form of the letters, but much prefer it, as it is, to the Roman method. To the Choctaw and Creek languages the method, strictly speaking, is inapplicable; and in *them* I would recommend the experiment which you propose in Cherokee.

"We have put the printing office at Union in good order, and when I left there last week the *Alphabet & Select Passages of Scripture* were ready for striking

[189]

off, and I had directed Mr. Wheeler to set up the type for another edition of the *Hymn Book*. I should defer the printing of the *Hymn Book* until it could be enlarged, if Creek & Choctaw books were ready, or if Mr. Boudinot were here to revise the Cherokee manuscripts on hand; but I do not like to have the press idle, and fear an excessive pressure hereafter. The school house is our printing office.

"We expect to remove to Union for a temporary residence in October.

"What are we to do for a bookbinder? We shall presently stand greatly in need of such a man; & it is my impression that we shall have work enough in that department to keep one man pretty well employed. Can the Committee send us one? And will they think it expedient? If not, I am much at a loss what we are to do.

". . . .Excepting a slight turn of bilious fever with Mrs. Worecester, & transient intermittents with two of our children, we have been in about usual health. The other families have been well with similar exceptions.

Yours in the bonds of the Gospel,
S. A. WORCESTER"

In these days there was an overwhelming amount to accomplish, to prepare for the removal of his family to Union, to keep the press at work with suitable material for publication, and to repair the damage which their possessions had suffered from water. In August, Samuel made up the list of supplies necessary for his new station, estimating as best he could in advance what might be needed during the coming year. He urged promptness in filling and sending the list of things. "I will be much obliged to you to have the things sent as soon as possible, because the earlier they reach New Orleans, the greater the probability of our receiving them safely.

"We have to make our list somewhat longer on account of loss consequent upon the sinking of the boat containing our goods from the old nation.

"Is there not in Boston a manufacturer of a variety of articles from India rubber? If so, what would be the expense of having the bundles of printing paper covered with paper put on with paste outside the strings, and the whole varnished with Indian rubber, so as to exclude water?. . . . If such a thing could be done with little expense, it would be a valuable kind of insurance."

Samuel must also, in these busy days, prepare his formal petition to the Council, which was to meet in October. His future in the nation depended on the success of this. He addressed it to "the Honorable the Principal Chiefs of the Cherokee Nation, & the Committee & Council." Simple truth, rightly put, was the best language of diplomacy, he knew; so he wrote accordingly: "I now humbly ask the National Council, if they approve my object, to pass an act, authorizing the establishment of the press at or near the station occupied by Mr. Newton, near the Fork of Illinois. I wish the Council distinctly to understand, that the books which I wish to publish will be portions of Scripture, Hymns, & other religious books, and school books, or books containing useful information for the instruction of children and youth. I shall be careful not to intermeddle with the political affairs of the nation. I have engaged Mr. Wheeler, a citizen of the nation, to print my books, and Mr. Boudinott, a native Cherokee, who is expected from the old nation, to assist me in translating. The council, I believe, already know the character of the books which I have printed heretofore. I seek the welfare of the Cherokee people by the promotion of knowledge."

The Council granted this petition. But it was not the cause of missions that won; it was Samuel Worcester. The Council passed a law making it necessary for any future missionary establishment to be set up only by special legislation, restricting the amount of land cultivated by the mission to five acres, and limiting the cattle and swine to be held by any mission to 25 head of cattle and 60 of swine. Whoever came as a missionary, hereafter, was to "stand aloof from all political affairs of the nation, & devote his time & talents to the preparation & publication of Cherokee books, & to efforts for the literary, moral, & religious instruction of the people." Samuel Worcester asked no further privileges than these.

Now that he had official sanction for his undertaking, Samuel set about printing in earnest. There were printing methods that he did not understand, for he had been away from the sources of such knowledge for ten years now, and many improvements had been made within that time. Mr. Wheeler felt the need of "particular instructions in regard to the manufacture of rollers, and the inktable, &c. to be used with them. He does not know," Samuel explained in one letter, "what are the latest improvements, nor does he know the proportion of materials, in the composition of which the rollers are made. I wrote to Mr. Hill for a Typographia. If that contains the requisite instructions respecting the rollers, it is sufficient. Mr. Wheeler thinks it will not. If not, be so kind as to procure them from some competent person and send them to me." Binding, too was a problem. "We can *do up* little books, as we have some, but cannot *bind*, until by some means we can have a binder," another letter explained. There was indeed need of more knowledge and skillful help, with Creek and Choctaw books now to print, in addition to the Cherokee material on hand. And then, almost as if by a miracle, the problem seemed solved. Samuel wrote of their relief to Mr. Greene, "Providence threw in my way a young man by the name of Hunt, who is a printer, and whom I employed at $20.00 a month for the time being. I think it likely that if he should work long he will ask for higher wages. He has been at work upwards of seven weeks, and Mr. Wheeler calls him a good printer. He is accustomed to casting and using rollers, with which the printing is now done. He is also, he says, partially acquainted with book-binding, and when the pressure of printing business subsides, if it should do so, I shall probably employ him to bind some of the books."

While he lasted, Mr. Hunt was a boon to the press. But a settled life and the isolation of Union were unbearable to him; in a few months it was necessary to write the Board that he had gone. "His wages were $20 monthly, but we shall not be able to replace him with a printer or a binder for less than $30 and board, I think."

Meanwhile, the press had issued an astonishing amount of finished work. Except when it was stopped for a time because of lack of ink, it worked daily. The Choctaw missionaries furnished so much copy that no pause seemed possible, even for planting and harvesting and such household duties as a family in a new land must now and then demand. In Cherokee, the first few months at Union saw the second edition of the *Hymn Book*, and a volume of *Select Passages of Scripture*, each printed in editions of 500. And for distribution very early in 1836, there was a *Cherokee Almanac*. "In preparing that," Mr. Worcester explained. "I employed Mr. John Candy as translator.

[193]

The Cherokee matter on pp. 2-4 tells of the reckoning of years from the Christian era—the number of months in a year & their names, the months in each of the four seasons, the number of days in each month, the names of the days of the week, the division of days into hours, minutes, & seconds, the uses of an almanac and the manner of using it, and the visible eclipses in the present year. The matter at the head of each calendar page is religious. That on the right hand of the calendar consists of hints on agriculture, domestic economy, industry, &c, with a few of a moral character. We printed between 4 and 500. Of these I intend to send 200 to the old nation, and the rest, or as many as we can, we are trying to *sell* here. I fear our success will not be great."

To the Worcester family, Union was home even though they knew that the location was only temporary. Their household equipment was inadequate, it was true, and they found it necessary to make queer substitutions for goods they had lost when they came west; but the elements of home were in their very natures, rather than in the material possessions belonging to them, and they knew no discontent or unhappiness. Ann Eliza was ten years old now in 1836; Sarah was eight; and little Hannah was two at the beginning of the year. They helped with all the household duties that must be done with regularity from day to day or from week to week, and when they were free they roamed the beautiful prairie, making garlands of the prairie flowers that grew in bright, changing profusion around them. Brief as its history had been, Union Mission had had its share of missionary martyrs; its burial ground lay only about two hundred yards from the site of the buildings that were their home and the Indian Press. Sometimes they wandered through the long grass that grew among the graves, and read the legends on the markers. The cofounder of Union Mission, Epaphras Chapman, was buried here, and a slab of native stone marked the place where he lay. Ann Eliza and Sarah read, as if it were a story, the brief inscription that told them— daughters of a missionary as they were—far more than what the words themselves set forth:

IN

MEMORY OF

REV. EPAPHRAS CHAPMAN

WHO DIED 7 JAN., 1825;

AGED 32.

FIRST MISSIONARY TO THE

OSAGES.

"SAY AMONG THE HEATHEN THE LORD REIGNETH."

At night, when all the day's work for the family was finished and the house set in order against another day, the sponge mixed for tomorrow's baking and the sewing and mending laid aside, there were family prayers. All the household, including any visitors who might be there and any printer or carpenter or hauler employed for the time being at the mission, came into the family room for prayers. The candle shone on the page of the Bible from which Samuel read, and a holy quiet fell upon the busy household. They sang hymns—without hymn books because they all, except a tramp printer or a hauler to whom the pages of Watts and Select Hymns were not an accepted familiarity, knew every word of every stanza; and Samuel's rich, full voice led all the rest. The memory of their father, sitting near the candle with the Bible lying on the candlestand, singing the hymns they all knew and loved, was one that all his children and some of his grand-children cherished all their lives. He brought their day, however hard and long it might have been, to a quiet and holy close. They knew that after prayers, when they had gone to bed and were fast asleep, their father still sat by the candle, writing a sermon or working on a translation, or going over his accounts. But no duty kept him from this hour of praise and prayer and song with them.

In spite of their isolation at Union, the children had contacts with the outside world through reading. There were newspapers from Vermont, that far-off place where their father had lived, and from Boston and sometimes from New York; there were copies of the *Missionary Herald* in which they might read accounts of their own mission station as well as of the stations in the Sandwich Islands and in Greece and in India; there were geographies and readers and religious story-books, much worn in spite of careful handling. And, chief joy of all in the children's estimation, there was the *Youth's Companion*, their own paper because they had helped by their own efforts to pay for it, and their father had sent their subscription in to Boston. "I have received," he explained, in writing to the Board "from my two oldest children and a Cherokee girl in our family 75 cents towards a year's subscription for the *Youth's Companion*. I will supply the deficiency. Be so kind as to give the publishers my name and address as a subscriber, and pay the price for the first year."

At Union, as at New Echota, the Worcesters managed to maintain a standard of proper dress and appearance. There was something absolute about this standard; it was a part of what their Lord expected of them, and not in any sense a matter of comparison with what visitors or neighbors wore. One of Samuel's lists for Union requested

"1 woman's braid Dunstable straw bonnet—trimmed
6 yds. cap ribbon for Mrs. W.—not white
1 cloak for woman 5 ft. 8 in. high [Mrs. Worcester]
1 camlet cloak for me
1 do.   for hired man, same size as for me
1 cloth coat & vest & two prs. Pantaloons—for me
1 summer vest & Pantaloons for me—not very fine
1 Maria Monk's Disclosures—*If* it is probably true
150 reams good printing paper, of the size on which the
Missionary Herald is printed.*

* "Be so kind as to furnish us a list of the technical names of the sizes of printing paper, with the dimensions of each in inches."

The three little girls were as happy as their parents when, in March of the year 1836, their baby brother was born. He was named Leonard, for that sturdy Yankee, Samuel's father, who had preached the ordination sermons for four ministerial sons. The Indians, too, rejoiced in the fact that their Messenger now had a son. "Will it be a bow or a meal-sifter?" they had asked. "Will it be ball sticks or bread?"

"It is a bow," they smiled, when they heard of the baby's birth. "It is ball sticks." Their good white brother now had a man child.

A City Set On a Hill

THERE was no doubt now, in the summer of 1836, that the removal of the Cherokees from the east must take place. However they might contrive to delay, they must eventually come westward. Samuel Worcester awaited every communication that told him of the progress of events in Georgia, for these events concerned the people among whom he had lived and worked for nine years before he preceded them to the west. In July of that summer he wrote, "We have lately received the intelligence that Mr. Schermerhorn's treaty is ratified. I am sorry for it, because the whole transaction appears to me to have been morally wrong. At the same time it seems much to be lamented that Mr. Ross should have been so persevering, as it appears he was, in refusing any terms which there was not an absolute and manifest impossibility of obtaining. I hope all will be over-ruled for good to the Cherokees, though I have many fears, Mr. Boudinot writes to Mr. Wheeler, that Mr. Ross, as he has been informed, by letter, advised his people to submit. I hope his influence will prevent any resort to violence, against those who formed the treaty. . . . .

"Our printing has been suspended for a little while for want of ink. Our ink is now here, and I shall send it to Union as soon as practicable. High water and other

Providential occurrences have impeded the progress of my business."

In spite of such Providential occurrences, Samuel must, at whatever cost, get on with his permanent location for the mission and the Indian Press. He had ridden horseback hundreds of miles over the new country; he had studied maps and boundaries set forth in treaties; he had consulted with white men and Indians as to the most suitable place for him to choose. Now he had settled on a location at the fork of the Illlnois River as the one likely to prove most convenient and central for the complex kind of service he hoped to give the Cherokees. He must build permanent buildings here, and be ready to serve the new arrivals when they came. They would be poor, discouraged, demoralized; they would have more need of Christianity than they had ever had before.

That summer was one of unprecedented hard work, for the press must go on printing at Union under Samuel's supervision while at the same time he planned and built the necessary housing at his new location. There were, he wrote David Greene, many hindrances: "As to my preparation to remove to the Fork of Illinois, my work goes on slowly, in the midst of many difficulties of which I knew nothing at New Echota, chiefly from the difficulty of obtaining laborers, and the faithlessness of the people in the neighboring white settlements, where I have to go for help. The people generally seem to have no idea whatever that a promise binds a man unless it be for his own interest to keep it. (Of course this is not for the public.) It has come to this—that if I send to engage a man to work for me, or go myself, and he does not accompany me or my messenger to the spot, I scarcely entertain the least expectation of seeing him at all, however strongly his promise may have been expressed, and although he may be a professor of religion. A few only have shown some regard to an engagement.

"Last spring I wrote either to you or to Mr. Hill—I think to you—that I valued very highly the assistance of Mr. Gray, from Dwight, who superintended in my absence. I had scarcely written so, before he was under the necessity of going to Dwight, partly on account of feeble health, and partly for the purpose of building a mill, which work is not yet completed. Consequently I have been closely confined to the business of building. I have usually visted my family once a month, but in the last instance have been absent seven weeks. In the mean time, we have all been blest with remarkably constant health, for which I trust we are not altogether destitute of gratitude.

"My present expectation is to remove my family about the last of November or the first of December. Mr. Wheeler will perhaps remain till we can put up a printing office and have it ready, or nearly ready, to receive the press, and in the mean time go on with Choctaw printing here.

"I communicated to you, some time ago, an extract from a letter from Mr. Boudinot. Since that you have undoubtedly received intelligence of the death of his wife. In anticipation of having him for a fellow-laborer, we feel her death as a painful breach in our circle of friends and neighbors. She was a valuable woman, and to us a beloved Christian sister. To him and his family it seems that it must be an irreparable loss.—After her death Mr. B. wrote that he had some thoughts of taking some of his children to the north this fall; (He has six children, the oldest nine years of age), but from recent letters from his brothers we infer that he has given it up, and will be here as soon as he can. It is the opinion of those of my missionary brethren to whom I have named the subject, Mr. Washburn in particular, that the part he has taken in reference to the treaty should not operate against his being employed as my interpreter & translator."

News from the Board, at this time of intense effort, was less hopeful than Samuel wished it might be. The bookbinder of whom he was in great need was not to be had, and funds for the work of building and of operating the press were unexpectedly meager. Jackson's banking policies had their immediate effect on the funds of the American Board. David Greene was reluctant to write what he must write to Samuel Worcester in June, 1837. "I have made inquiry for a bookbinder, but have not yet succeeded in finding any who will go for wages, or as an assistant missionary. It seems to me that there are fewer persons following that trade who have a religious character or who can be interested in the missionary work, than any other. None of those of whom I have inquired have ventured to mention an individual well qualified whom they would recommend. Still, I hope that such a person may be found. In the meantime you must do the best you can to get your books in a form to be circulated and read. The prices of stitching and folding, including the covers, is, I am told, if the pamphlet contains one signature, 17 cts.; if two signatures, 20 cts.; if three signatures, 25 cts. The ordinary wages of a journeyman printer is about $8 per week he boarding himself; and those of a bookbinder are I believe about the same.

"I have written the missionaries of the Choctaw country respecting the amount of their printing, and I presume that they will not employ the press so much hereafter as they have done heretofore. This is important as we must curtail necessarily very much to insure the expenses of all our missions in consequence of our own diminished receipts. How far & to what straits the Lord will permit the present financial embarrassments of the country to reduce us, we cannot say. The falling off in our income is great now, & the prospect for the next twelve or eighteen months is very dark. You will of course see the importance of rendering the expenses of your station as small as practicable and as to your printing in Cherokee, I think you should proceed no faster than the exigencies of the people seem to require. We shall probably be obliged to detain at home all the missionary candidates for the next year or more. . . . . .

"This state of things, I trust, is not to be of long continuance; but coming, as it does, in connexion with powerful excitements on the theological, ecclesiastical, political, & moral subjects, it seizes & absorbs the minds of men, even Christians, to such a degree as almost to make them deaf to calls from our benevolent societies, and nearly callous to the power of religious truth. The state of our churches is most mournful & ominous. The Lord only can turn the current, & to him we must look."

Samuel's dilemma was a very real one: to prove himself useful and necessary to the Indians by operating a mission station and a press that were as yet incomplete, and at the same time to finish his buildings and operate his printing plant without the funds that he had expected to have at his disposal. Prices in the new country to which he had come were high and not stable; work that he had expected to hire done, he and his assistants must do themselves. "Mr. Wheeler seems under the necessity of devoting a little time to establishing himself here, on account of the difficulty of procuring hired help. The arrival of the emigrating Creeks has greatly enhanced the price of corn, and that, with the anticipation of the removal of the Cherokees, has put almost everybody who will work at all upon preparing or enlarging fields; and the call which was some time since made for soldiers, through fear of disturbance with the Creeks, has taken away many men from the white settlements, so that the current price for common laborers has risen to $20 a month and board; and even at that price it seems impossible to procure a single man within any reasonable distance of us." Yet economy, in itself, must not be the goal that Samuel was trying to reach. To Mr. Hill he wrote thanks "for your compliment in accompanying a remark on the necessity of economy with the expression of the belief that I have practiced it. But it was not necessary to take off the edge of the admonition by the compliment. I should very willingly have received it without, and I fear your good opinion is not altogether deserved. I am conscious, indeed, of *aiming* at a good degree of economy, but it requires *skill* as well as *will*, and of skill in economy I would not dare to boast. However, I hope your hint will help to keep the necessity of it in remembrance. But my greatest anxiety is lest the great expense which our operations necessarily involve should not be turned to good account in promoting the salvation of souls. For this we need, as we trust we have, your constant prayers."

To add to Samuel's difficulty, bank notes were likely not to be redeemable at their full value; and he, away from any financial center, could not keep himself informed as to their fluctuations. He explained this to Henry Hill: "On another page I send my quarterly account. The amount acknowledged as cash on hand is all in bills of

[203]

one bank, bills which I had on hand at the time when the news arrived of the present failure of specie payments by the banks, and I have not lately been able to dispose of them, as they are not very current here. I still hope they may avail to their full amount, but have some fear of loss." Nor was this uncertainty regarding the value of bank notes quickly ended; in 1842, Samuel was still struggling with fluctuations in their redeemable value. Yet, when one of his neighbors, white man or Indian, needed cash, he was ready to risk the acceptance of a bank note as security, and when someone must send money by mail, he managed the matter through a draft on the Board. This was part of his duty as a missionary. One of his letters to the Treasurer of the Board is an account of such transactions.

"Park Hill, Aug. 9, 1842.

Dear Sir,

"I said that I should not need to draw on you soon; and I have not needed and shall not need to on my own account. But I had forgotten that I had already promised Mr. Foreman a small draft to accomodate him in sending some money to Tennessee. I have given it accordingly—a draft for $19.00, payable to the order of Robt. H. Hodsden.

"In my last I enclosed a 10 dollar note on the United States Bank. I am sorry to have one of 50 dollars now to enclose. The history of it is this. On the 12th of May a neighbor came to me for 25 dollars, for which he offered the bill enclosed, to be redeemed in three weeks. The value of the bill, as I had seen it quoted, was so much above the sum wanted, that I supposed it sufficient security. But when I had put it in my drawer, I entirely forgot it until the last of June, when I came to balance accounts. Then I put it down in my account at $25, and sent word to the man to come and redeem it. He has made some effort to get the money, but failed, until I have told him that I will send the bill to you, and if you get more than $25 for it, will pay him the balance, and charge it to him if it falls short. Be so kind as to dispose of it as best you can, and inform me what you realize from it.

Yours most sincerely,
S. A. Worcester

"11th. I have taken out the bill. The man brought me the money this morning, having rode 30 miles by a little past nine o'clock to redeem the bill before I should send it.

"Please acknowledge in the *Herald* the sum of $7.50 received from Nelson Chamberlin of Monticello, Illinois.

Yours in haste,
S. A. W."

Small wonder, with such happenings to record in figures on a balance sheet, that his accounts frequently showed errors! He had become a sort of neighborhood banker without the protection of the hours and the regulations that a bank affords. One of his accounts for the year 1838 showed an error of $22.27 on $1181.98 as the sum handled. He was chagrined at the mistake, but finding no way to right it he sent the account in to the Treasurer, balancing it by entering the item "error, $22.27." "I believe," he remarked, "there is no kind of danger of my being appointed Treasurer of the A. B. C. F. M., or auditor of accounts. I suppose, however, that I could keep accounts somewhat more correctly, if my mind were not engrossed with other things. The last quarter I have had an unusual share of perplexities, and my accounts, too, have been more complicated than common. Somehow or other, I seem to have committed a gross blunder, and I cannot detect where." Later the deficit became a small surplus, with this explanation to account for the shift. "I afterwards found in my possession $25 which I had overlooked, which reduces the error to $2.73 and throws it into the opposite scale."

By the first day of December, 1836, the building at the fork of the Illinois had so far progressed that the Worcester family could move to their new home. The next day they finished the journey of thirty-five miles from Union. There was time, before dark came down to cover the amazing clarity of that prairie land, to set up their stove and arrange beds for the night. Then, by candlelight, Samuel led his family in their evening devotions. The house was unfinished, it was true, but it was their home, fresh and clean and new, and so close to their father's work that he might never again have to be away from them for seven long weeks at a time. Samuel's prayer was a fervently thankful one that night.

The site of the new mission was beautiful indeed. The Illinois was clear and picturesque; the prairie grass carpeted the rolling ground; trees grew in abundance to serve for lumber and for shade; the house stood on an elevation that promised healthfulness and a fine view. "Park Hill" suggested itself as a suitable name for such a place; to this day it still bears this name. For the rest of his life, Samuel Worcester was to know no other home.

Almost at once, Park Hill became the center of life in this part of the Cherokee Nation. In that new country where habitations of any kind were few and far between, the little settlement became a city set on a hill, whose light might not be hid. The needs of the people of the whole community, physical, material, intellectual, and spiritual, found some fulfillment there. One of the first achievements was the organization of a church, early in the summer of 1837. "Last Sabbath," Samuel Worcester wrote to the Board, on June 7, "we organized a church here, consisting of seven members dismissed for the purpose from Dwight, three from Fairfield, eight from churches in the old nation, and one from a church in Vermont,—19 in all. Six are whites, 10 Cherokees, 3 blacks. Of the whites, four are assistant missionaries; two, (including one of the assistant missionaries) are white men whose wives are Cherokees, and one a white woman whose husband is a Cherokee." At first they had no building, making use of "Mr. Newton's school, where public worship is held almost every Sabbath, Mr. Newton conducting the service when I am absent. We have three other places where we hold meetings, each a few miles distant from us. At each place I have for some time past ordinarily alternated with Mr. Newton. There is not usually a large assembly at either place, nor are there any circumstances of much encouragement attending our labors. At our own schoolhouse the congregation is irregular, sometimes very small, and sometimes more considerable, especially in communion seasons, which occur once in two months."

Soon, too, a postal station was established at Park Hill. Formerly, letters for the mission at Park Hill must come through Fort Gibson, seventeen miles distant. In the summer of 1838, Mr. Newton became postmaster, and mail for the mission came with less delay thereafter. "Direct your letters," the Board were advised, "to Park Hill,

Cherokee Nation, West of Arkansas, without any reference to Fort Gibson. Mr. Newton, as he may have informed you, is postmaster. I intend paying the postage on letters which I send to the Rooms (i.e., if Mr. Newton credits to the Board the avails of the office) because it will save to the Board the postmaster's percentage. Would it be well to direct other missionaries in like circumstances to do the same? When I was postmaster, I paid, for the same reason, the postage of all letters sent from my office which had to be paid from the funds of the Board."

The new mission served, too, as a dispensary and gave the sick such medical care as Samuel Worcester could offer them. In the fall of 1838, when there was some danger of an epidemic of smallpox, he wrote to have sent, "by mail, if accounted lawful, a little vaccine matter. The small pox is among the people to some extent, and much effort has been made to spread the kine pox, but with little success. We have procured matter from several places, besides using some which I had preserved, and cannot get it to take effect." Shortly before that he had written the Board that he would soon send for a list of medicines, "on Mr. Boudinot's account, which are to be paid for by subscription, and distributed gratuitously to subscribers and to the poor." The order was a long one, and included such items as "4 lb. calomel, 4 lb. aloes, 4 lb. sulphur, 4 lb. pulv. rhubarb, 6 oz. tinct. asafoetida, 20 oz. sulphate of Quinine, 1 large clyster syringe, I composition mortar—good size, 1 Eberle's Practice of Medicine, 2 good lancets." It appeared that a cure of bodies became part of a man's responsibility in a cure of souls.

At Park Hill, the standard of living for that community which it served was set. It was not an ostentatious standard, but it met all the requirements of decency and respectability. In 1838, Samuel's advance estimate of his family expenses for the coming fiscal year was five hundred dollars. "It gives me much pain," he explained, "to send so large an estimate, and I have studied much to reduce it, but do not see how it is to be done. As to family expenses they must necessarily be high, because provisions and labor are extremely high, because we have almost everything to purchase, and because heavy taxes are laid upon our hospitality. . . . . In Boston, where the system of 'division of labor' is carried out almost to perfection, *something can be done*; but here, where the same person has to *be* everything and *do* everything, it seems sometimes as if we could do but little more than take care of ourselves, even after all that is expended for our support. You will of course understand me as expressing myself rather hyperbolically, but it is too painfully near the simple truth." Always they must *be* and *do* what the standard they set for themselves required of them, and acknowledge in advance the expenditure this might require. They were a family of seven now, for their second son, John Orr, had been born to them in March, 1838. For a family of seven, with "heavy taxes laid upon their hospitality," the estimate of five hundred dollars for a year's expenditures scarcely seems extravagant. Their furnishings must not be too primitive, nor their clothes too badly cut; hence they must, in a list of supplies include, "1 doz. edged twifflers, 2 do. edged nappies—middle size, 1 cloth coat & pantaloons," and a comment must be added, "My coats have latterly been made too short in the waist—the ladies say." And sometimes, in spite of foresight, necessities were lacking. Once molasses—that item of food so dominant in the diet of Andover students that jokesters said it flowed in their veins instead of blood,—became their chief food, because "the agents at New Orleans have dealt strangely with us. I wrote for groceries for myself, Mr. Foreman, & Mr. Huss, Dr. Butler sent for his supplies, and the mission at Dwight for theirs,—and they sent us molasses alone. I presume they intended to send other things afterwards, but in the meantime the river has fallen, and will probably not rise again till fall."

Not until the winter of 1838 could Samuel and Ann replace the furnishings which they had lost on their journey to the west. Mr. Fleming, a missionary to the Creeks, resigned; and his household goods, the property of the Board, were left for Samuel to dispose of "at a fair valuation" among the missionaries of the Board who might have need of them. He wrote to the Board of his own need: "Among the articles which we lost on our removal to this country was our best bed, and also some blankets, which we have not replaced, and which we need. There are such things among Mr. Fleming's goods, and we would take them, but that we fear exceeding the amount allowed to our station for the next year. May we take them without having them reckoned as a part of that sum?"

One of the prime necessities, at Park Hill, came to be a pure and abundant water supply. This involved much labor and expense and time. And since, for a well so deep as this one must be, a pump seemed necessary, many letters to the Board were involved. At last, in 1841, something definite could be done, through the help of that Mr. Tufts in Boston who had made the press now in use at Park Hill. In November, 1841, Samuel could write, "I have at length obtained what I hope will prove permanent water, the well being 62 feet deep, from the original surface of the ground. It has been an expensive job. I have been at work at it every summer since I have been here, when

I could get help. The last 12 feet or about that has been done chiefly by blasting in solid flint-rock, where a blast made with much labor would do but little and sometimes no execution. At length, week before last, I finished digging, in a time of very low water. The next week heavy rains fell. On Tuesday and perhaps Wednesday I suppose I could have dipped up the water with a table spoon as fast as it came in. Thursday it rose 15 feet in 24 hours, and now stands 18 feet deep.

"Be so kind as to procure and forward a pump of the kind I last described, & which Mr. Tufts thought he could make. It is required to measure 66 feet 10 inches from the bottom of the spout. The pivot of the handel to be 8 inches above the spout. Of size and proportions I suppose the manufacturer can judge better than I. Let it be so small, i.e. the cylinder, as not to require great strength to work it, and work in not exceeding one foot of water— less if practicable. Perhaps, in my plan, I represented the cylinder as tapering downwards below the fixed valves, and turning thus: but let the cylinder rather retain its size, so as to stand firm in the bottom of a little basin which is cut in the rock, and let the pipe be attached to the side obliquely, in some such manner as this, with a sufficient orifice opening into it. The rods may be sent in a coil, or, if it be thought cheaper, a bundle of round iron, such as is used for making chains, say ¼ or 5-16 of an inch in diameter, sufficient to make them, may be sent, and can be welded here. Indeed the whole could be made here, except the pump itself, and the pipe; but I suppose it will be done cheaper and better in Boston."

Four years later, the first repair was needed for the pump. In a note to a letter to the Board, Samuel wrote, "My pump works finely, but the piston is getting too small. I will thank you to get directions for renewing it from the maker. It seemed to me to be made of alternate layers of leather and felt. If so, please procure some of the latter. I suppose it must be procured from the hatter. Ask the pump-maker. Can the piston be renewed as it was without a turning-lathe?"

For the stability and the progress of the Indians, Worcester judged agriculture to be essential. And every farmer, he knew, had need of an almanac. Next to the Bible, an almanac for the current year was the most essential book in any rural household. The first almanac published for the Cherokees, in 1836, was something of a makeshift, Samuel felt, for it had been printed under conditions of pressure and inconvenience and it contained no calculations made especially for that locality. Now he began to hope for something more satisfactory, and he wrote the Board of his plans. "I wish, if practicable, to prepare a Cherokee Almanac for the year 1838. I think that by having every other page English I can command sale for a considerable number of copies. I should be glad to have the calculations, as nearly as may be, adapted to this place. The latitude of Fort Gibson is said to be 35° 49′ and its longitude 18° 6′. This place is about 17 miles in a northeasterly direction from Fort Gibson. Would it be too expensive to procure the ordinary calculations from some one, adapted to this place, and forward them to me by mail? If not, I would be very much obliged to you to have it done, with as little delay as convenient. But if this be thought too costly, I will thank you to procure, or *have* procured, a copy of the Temperance or Christian Almanac, the nearest adapted

ᎯᏍᏆᎲᎯ ᎤᏃᏣᏫ

ᎤᏍᏗᏳᎸᏗ 18ᏏᏬ.

CHEROKEE ALMANAC

For the year of our Lord

1836.

Calculations copied from the Temperance Almanac as adapted
to the latitude of Charleston.

ᏒᏍᏗᏴᎳᏒᎢ	ᏈᏯ ᎫᏍᎠᏟᏆᏯ,
ᎠᏍ ᏘᎦᏪᎲᏒᎢ	ᏍᏋᏔᎵ ᏦᎡ ᎡᏘ,
ᎠᏍ ᏎᎥᏞᏢᎡᏘ	ᎣᏁᏏᎭᏎᎢᏠᎤ ᎅᎡ
ᎠᏍ ᏍᎩᎲᏒᎢ,	ᎡᎵᏍᏋᏪᎵ ᏞᏅᎯᎵ.

UNION:

MISSION PRESS: JOHN F. WHEELER, PRINTER.

ᏣᎥᏓ ᎫᎵᎦᎧᏯᏓ: ᏉᎦ ᎫᏍᏴᏬᎠ.

to this location of all that are published. Be so kind also as to inform me—for, *college-learnt* though I be, I am very ignorant on this subject—whether if I have an almanac calculated for a place in nearly the same *latitude*, the difference made by *longitude* may be considered as unimportant."

In spite of the necessity for economy on the part of the Board, Mr. Greene wrote promptly that the Prudential Committee had voted to obtain the requisite astronomical calculations. "The expense," he explained, "will probably be from $25 to $30. I have engaged a very accurate man, (so reputed), of Green Mountain nativity, to prepare the calendar, & hope to have it ready to be forwarded about the first of September. I could find no almanac calculated for a point nearer your latitude & longitude than Huntsville, Ala., which is about seven (or as the gasateer says, ten) degrees too far east, & more than one degree south, which, aside from the error in the latitude which would be considerable, would occasion, by the difference of longitude an error of near 30 minutes if the difference in longitude be 7°, and 40 minutes if the difference of long. be 10°, in the rising, coming of the meridian, and setting of the moon and sun, & in the beginning and ending of eclipses, &c. This class of errors is the only important one which occurs in a common almanac, from the circumstance of its being adapted to a wrong meridian. This can, of course, be corrected by any intelligent man who will take the pains to add four minutes to the time mentioned in the almanac for every degree which he is distant west of its meridian, and subtract four minutes for every degree which he is to the eastward of it." Late in August the calculations were sent, having been prepared "with great accuracy, by Mr. Marshall Conant. . . . a thorough scholar in such things, and accustomed to the business." They were "adapted to the lat. and long. of Fort Gibson, as a place known, and in some respects important, especially as the precise lat. and long. of your stations are not known. All the numbers represent the equated time, so that the appearances will agree with a well regulated time piece."

Samuel might, Mr. Greene anticipated, have some difficulty with the printing. "Many of the signs, phases of the moon, marks for the planets, &c I suppose that you cannot insert, as you have not the type for them, unless you have genius enough to make wooden substitutes." But before he was ready to print, Samuel must understand David Greene's explanations. It was evident that neither one of them understood, without more study, how to make the adaptations for differences in latitude and longitude. Samuel set himself to the problem with a will, and wrote his friend David Greene of his perplexities. "Doubtless at the moment of time when the sun is rising at Bourdeaux a Boston clock would say about 20 minutes past one; but would a correct Bourdeaux clock, or a correct Bourdeaux almanac, say the same? Do I misunderstand you altogether? or have you applied to the almanac what belongs only to the clock? or am I in error still?"

David Greene's reply acknowledged his mistake with a degree of merriment. "If you mean seriously to ask me the question whether I meant to say, or supposed, that the sun rose at midnight in Central Germany, I will reply very gravely that I did not mean to say nor did I suppose so; nor do I recollect ever to have heard of any such opinion having been entertained by anybody, unless it is implied in some almanac poetry, which met my eye some years since, in which a fault-finding couple are represented, among charges brought against the sun, to have

'Wondered why we need be gone
'Just as the night was coming on.'

Still, I see in my letter I made a great blunder, & not a blunder in language merely, either; my remarks about adding and subtracting four minutes for a degree are correct only when you compare the time when the heavenly bodies come to the different meridians with the time kept at one of them. It has nothing to do with the almanac, and, in the connection in which it was made, was altogether incorrect, or at least irrelevant. If haste and inconsiderateness will not excuse the blunder, you must charge it to stupidity, & let it go."

So, by diligent study and much correspondence and the help of Mr. Marshall Conant of Green Mountain, an almanac for the region of Fort Gibson was produced. By such material evidence of helpfulness, John Jolly, Principal Chief of the Western Cherokees, was convinced of the value of the mission station and won to friendliness toward it and its members. "Our almanac is popular," its publisher told the American Board soon after it appeared at the beginning of 1838; "and if we had printed earlier, and a larger edition, I am confident we should have sold at least enough to cover the expense." The next year's book met with some difficulty: "Our almanac has by no means proved a money-making affair. . . . . So far as they were spread, our almanacs for this year commanded ready sale in Arkansas, until a pictured almanac came into market and superseded it. If we had pedlars to go about and sell our almanacs in good season, we could dispose of thousands; but as it is, I despair of selling so as to cover expense, or any thing near it. Yet I think our almanac is useful, and if continued will be increasingly so, as it becomes better understood by the Cherokees. We can probably sell enough at least to pay for the calculations, if you see fit still to procure them for us, as I hope you will. Among the calculations I would be glad to have

The times of Mercury's greatest elongation

The time of the sun's entering each sign of the Zodiac

A column in calendar giving the time when the sun is on the meridian.

And in the column of the moon's rising and setting omit the word *morn* and give figures in its place."

So, by their own lives and their unflinching efforts, the Worcesters laid out for themselves and their neighbors at Park Hill a plan and a standard for living. Once in a great while, they freed themselves from their immediate duties long enough to think of their own kindred and to write a long delayed letter to some relative. Did their brothers and sisters, reading these long-delayed accounts of the Worcesters' lives at Park Hill, understand what was by faithful daily living being accomplished there? Here is such a letter, full of family details, to Ann's sister and her family in New Hampshire. Ann's part of the letter was brief, but tender. "Dear Sister," she began, "When I sit down to write to you, I feel at once discouraged, for I can seldom make a beginning; and when I recollect how few letters I receive from them, I cannot help wishing we were more fond of communicating ideas on paper."[1]One reads some bodily weariness here, and absorption in the family and the cause that demanded all of Ann's vitality from one day to the next. She left most of the news for her

1 Letter in the private collection of Mrs. N. B. Moore, Haskell, Oklahoma.

husband, whose vitality failed him less frequently than did hers.

"Park Hill, West Cherokee Nation, June 14, 1838.
Sam'l. Chandler, Esq.
Dear Brother,

"We received a letter from you dated Feb. 26th. 1835, to which we replied from Dwight, sometime in the summer following. We have not received from you any communication of later date than that, and have not even heard, from any source, whether or not you received our reply. We hope, however, that you did. Since that, we suppose you have occasionally heard from us indirectly though not frequently. I shall not have room on this sheet to give much of our history. Oct. 15th, 1835, we left Dwight, to reside at Union until I could commence a new station. The following summer and fall I was here building, and my family at Union, 35 miles distant. Dec. 1, 1836, we left Union, and the next day arrived here, and took up our abode in an unfinished house. Since that I have built a print-ing-house here, and removed the press from Union, and we have continued to do a little in publishing books in the Cherokee and Choctaw languages. We have not yet completed our establishment, but are so that we get along very comfortably. In this time two have been added to our family, Leonard, named for my father, born at Union March, 1835,[2] and John Orr, born March last. After his birth Ann was reduced very low, so that we had much apprehension for her life, and recovered but slowly; yet God has kindly spared her, and raised her nearly to her former state of health—not quite—but

2 This date is incorrect; it should be 1836.

her strength is yet increasing. Aside from this we have generally enjoyed pretty good health, Ann, however, never altogether well, but better than before we left the Cherokee Nation. It is a climate of intermittent and remittant fevers, mostly the former, which has occasionally paid us a visit, but when it is removed, after the first or second paroxysm, which has almost uniformly been the case, we regard it but a small evil. Our children are growing up healthy, and doing tolerably well as to learning. We have only to mourn that none of them yet give evidence of being reconciled to God—the one thing compared with which all our other wishes for them are nothing.

"The greatest trial we have at present is in relation to my translator, Mr. Boudinot, whom I employed in the old nation. He arrived late last fall, and resumed his labors with me here. But in the meantime, his extreme anxiety to save his people from the threatening union led him to unite with a small minority of the nation in forming a treaty with the United States: an act, in my view, entirely unjustifiable, yet, in his case, dictated by good motives. This has rendered him so unpopular in the nation, that they will hardly suffer me to continue him in my employment. A request was sent me last winter from the National Council, that I would not employ him (although the Council have authorized the establishment of the station, with the express understanding that he was to be my translator); it was an informal act, and not authoritative, and as I deemed it important to retain Mr. B., I procured a paper from the Principal Chief, authorizing me to continue him in my employment until the next fall Council. What will then be done, I know not. It is *possible* that the Council will be so offended with me as to pass an order for my removal from the nation; but as this requires the signature of the principal chief, (unless passed again by a vote of two-thirds after his veto has been given) and as he would not be likely to assent to such an act on the ground of what was done by his own authority, it is improbable. I *hope* they will not do anything further in the case, and prevailingly believe it, but it may be otherwise. We feel much interested to retain Mr. B. because there is no other to compare with him in qualifications for my work.—One of the most painful circumstances attending it is that the leader in the opposition is a distinguished member of one of our churches, and another distinguished member of my own church, and in whom I had the greatest confidence, has found it an occasion of great sin, and of keeping, for a good while, aloof from religious observances, and losing almost all religious comfort and hope. Still other circumstances I might mention. These things are an affliction to us at present, but we hope to see the clouds dispersed. In general I do not know that the cause of religion has made much sensible progress among the Cherokees since we crossed the Mississippi. One effort, however, for their good, the formation of a temperance society, requiring of its members total abstinence from all kinds of intoxicating liquor, has met with encouraging success, and the work is going forward still. I think there are about 400 members, the greater part Cherokees.

We have sympathized with you in your affliction in the death of one beloved son, and we have rejoiced exceedingly on hearing that *all* your children were believed to be heirs of the kingdom of heaven; and we think you a hundred fold happier in having one in the kingdom of God above, and the rest in the same kingdom on earth, than if all were with you here, but out of that happy kingdom. We rejoice exceedingly that you have that privilege, which so few parents possess, of looking upon your children with the belief that not one of them is any longer an enemy of God, but all heirs of unspeakable and everlasting bliss. But I cannot tell you how often our hearts have felt the wish and breathed the prayer, that, in the great day of final separation, the father may not be parted from the mother and the children.

"You inquired in your last letter, that is in the one we last received, how you should dispose of the property of ours which remained in your hands. In reply, we have requested you to deposit it in the hands of Mr. Hill, the Treasurer of the Board of Missions, to be subject to our order. As we have heard nothing on the subject, either from you or from Mr. Hill, we conclude that you have not done. If so, will you please to retain it still in your hands, until you hear from us again; and in the mean time be so kind as to write to us as soon as you can make it convenient, and let us know in what state it is, and how much of it we can at any time command.

"Give my love to Mrs. Chandler, and to your children whenever you see or write to them. I leave the remainder of the sheet for Mrs. Worcester.

Your affectionate brother,

S. A. Worcester

"July 25. Reports lately are favorable—but may be false.

"P. S. Direct letters, hereafter, to Park Hill,

Cherokee Nation,

West of Arkansas"

Morals and Theology

SAMUEL WORCESTER'S deep concern for his mission was that it keep spiritual matters foremost. Satan, he knew, had subtle, insidious ways of accomplishing diabolical ends; at a station like Park Hill, the very existence of which depended on a certain degree of success in temporal matters and a certain usefulness readily evident to the Cherokees, there was danger that the Evil One might, under the guise of this necessity to build and plant and harvest and dig wells and treat the sick, undermine the spiritual purposes for which the mission had been founded. Salvation was so complex and the way to its accomplishment so slow and devious that the end might, except by the greatest diligence, be lost in the pursuit of the means. Against so grave a danger, Samuel prayed constantly. And, being a Yankee and a Calvinist, he worked while he prayed.

One of the means by which he sought to bring spiritual matters before his people was the publication and circulation of tracts. Printed matter was rare in those years and in that remote location; any subject matter could claim the attention of readers if it were put before them in printed form. There was almost a certain guarantee that any tract put into the hands of a Cherokee reader would be read, not merely once, but again and again; if it had the added attraction of an illustration, its possibilities were beyond calculation. Such illustrations, produced from cuts "engraved on wood," were printed with many tracts from the Indian press. But here Samuel had an evil to eradicate, as he indicated in one of his early letters from Dwight. "The Scripture cuts I think will be quite important for our use, and hope they will be forwarded in due season. One thing, however, I beg leave to remark. It appears to me that it is much more than time that the custom of representing our Savior in pictures with a radiance around his head were done away. Is it not the highest excellence of every such representation, that it approach as near as possible to a correct picture of the scene represented, as it appeared in living fact? And did our Savior ever appear among the multitude with a supernatural radiance around his head? Cannot an alteration be made in those cuts in which our Savior is represented, so as to exclude this fault? It is not mine to dictate, but I suppose if I had the management, I should not hesitate to incur much more than the expense of engraving the whole series anew, rather than suffer so great a blemish to remain. I am taking it for granted that your cuts contain the fault—as I regard it—because it is common. If I find I am taking for granted what is not true, I shall be very glad."

Samuel was sure that there was no false theology, no fostering of idolatry, in the tracts he issued. Some of them were stories or extracts from the Bible; others were accounts of lives or incidents that pointed a ready moral to those who read them. By the summer of 1837, Samuel had a sizeable list:

The Worcesters made use of tracts from the American Tract Society, for their own children and for others in their mission household. One postscript added to a letter to the Board says, "My daughter Ann Eliza will pay for the following books,

"Neat morocco bound pocket Testament, pretty good paper & print, as many as can be bought for $1.50

From the American Tract Society's Children's Series

John of the Score
Bible Happiness
Mary Jones
Address to a Child
Mischief its own Punishment

Louisa's Tenderness to Little Birds
Shepherd Boy
Wishing Cap
Honesty the Best Policy
History of Thos. Frankland
Active Benevolence or Lucy Careful
Lost Opportunity or Robert Careless
Goodness of Providence Illustrated
The Vine
The Snowdrop
The African Widow"

And to one of Samuel's own lists, he asks the Board "please to add

"1 good spring lancet
1 strong shovel & tongs (Say 27 to 30 inches long)
1 Peep of Day
1 Line upon Line
1 Precept upon Precept
1 Wateringpot [a real watering pot—not a book by that title.]"

To promote temperance among his people was one of Samuel's deepest concerns. He found that, among the Indians, there was no middle ground; moderate drinking was impossible among people who had never learned self-restraint in the use of alcoholic drinks and who were plied with bad whisky constantly by unscrupulous whites. Treaties had been brought about by its potency, when diplomacy failed; deals in furs and corn and land had been put through—to the Indians' heavy loss—by means of the contents of the barrel and dipper. During the two years

[224]

between the ratification of the treaty of removal and its enforcement, no effort was made on the part of officials to restrict the distribution of whisky, for it was generally conceded that the Cherokees would be powerless if they were demoralized. And during the removal, traders profited shamelessly on the whisky they sold to the disheartened people, to whom drunkenness was at least a temporary relief from sorrow and disheartenment. West of the Mississippi, the situation was equally bad. According to the report of the acting superintendent of the Western Territory, "The Cherokees show a great degree of improvement and are still improving and bid fair at no distant day to rival their white brethren of the west, in point of wealth, civilization, moral and intellectual improvement, did there not exist one great hindrance, that of intemperance, not only a vice itself, but the prolific parent of almost every other vice. There are immense quantities of whiskey in the country, and being introduced daily, and unless the intercourse law is rigidly enforced, the evil of intemperance will spread its wide reign, and its effect will be ruinous to the morals of the natives, and dangerous to the peace of the country. The Cherokees more than any other tribe are disposed to traffic in ardent spirits; the whole extended frontier of Arkansas and Missouri is settled with this pernicious article, and unless the strong hand of Government is interposed by the aid of the military, the moral and political condition of these people will be lowered to the most degraded state."[1]

To Samuel, it was obvious that some kind of check must be devised, and he felt that it might be accomplished more effectively by moral than by military aid. Soon after he settled at Park Hill he set about forming

1 Bureau of Indian Affairs, *Annual Report*, 1837, p. 340.

a temperance society. "Such a society," he explained, "was formed several years ago, and afterwards, on account of peculiar circumstances, suffered to die down. Last fall it was thought best to renew it, which was done at the camp meeting near Dwight. Several meetings have since been held in different neighborhoods, and the whole number of names now on the Secretary's list, including whites, Cherokees, and a few blacks, young and old, is 248. One of these has been excluded, and several others are known to have violated the pledge. These names are marked as dead.—Among the signers are all your missionaries and all their children who are old enough to understand the nature of the pledge. The pledge reads thus, 'We hereby solemnly pledge ourselves, that we will never use, nor buy, nor sell, nor give, nor receive, as a drink, any whiskey, brandy, gin, rum, wine, fermented cider, strong beer, or any kind of intoxicating liquor.' "

It was never Samuel's way to leave an undertaking to its own fate. And he knew the temperance movement had too many enemies, among white men who had found it profitable to deal in whisky among the Indians, to be allowed to take its own course. To counterbalance their activities, he originated events and issued publications that would stimulate interest and a sense of unity among the advocates of temperance. He issued a temperance tract, and wrote a poem to be printed with it. Pumps or poems might be required of him without his refusal, and neither one—strange to say—would be badly done. He needed scarcely to be ashamed of his "ode" on the back of the title-page of the temperance tract, though he did explain, "The energy of the composition I cannot transfer to the translation. I give the substance of it, but it appears insipid. It is not so in the original, in the judgment of the Cherokees themselves."

"A great enemy
            And powerful,
      An enemy hard to be destroyed
            Is abroad in our country.
      Come let us unite together,
      The whole Cherokee nation as one man
      Let us now expel him
            From our country.

"The disease-maker,
      Disease-Promoter,
      The blood-thirsty creature
            Let us attack
      Of the minds of men
      The destructive enemy,
      Mischievous Alcohol,
            Let us attack.

"The money-waster,
      The hunger-promoter,
      Stands out in view,
            A great enemy.
      Come let us attack
      The destroyer of the Cherokee people!
      Let us help our children
            All as one, without delay."

Yet as much as possible, Samuel left the work of such organizations as the Temperance Society to the Cherokees themselves. The Reverend Mr. Stephen Foreman, a Cherokee who had been educated at Princeton and who had returned to his people as an ordained minister of the Presbyterian Church, became secretary of the society, and with Samuel's help at times maintained it as a large and powerful organization for many years. In 1844, in a report to the United States Agent, he gave the number of members as 2,473. "It seems evident," Samuel Worcester said that year, "that the cause is gaining ground. It is acknowledged on all hands, I believe, that there is much less whisky drinking than formerly. This, however, is not imputed wholly to the influence of the temperance society, but in no small part to the scarcity of money." Let no cause claim more than its honest share of credit!

The kind of effort that a successful meeting of the Temperance Society necessitated is evident from a letter of Samuel Worcester to David Greene.

"PARK HILL, July 18, 1844.

Rev. D. Greene,

DEAR SIR,

"I must confess I had forgotten that the time was passing by at which I ought to address to you a sort of annual letter; yet I do not know that I could have done it sooner, having had, in addition to my lameness, very much to do in preparing for a temperance meeting at Tahlequah on the 11th inst. at which an effort was made to bring together a large concourse, and which had been promised as an interesting meeting. Much of the promised interest was to depend on music, and for this we expected a considerable number and variety of musical instruments from the military band at Fort Gibson, and a choir of singers belonging to the Temperance Society there. But in the meantime the band of

[228]

music was ordered away to another post, together with the leader and other members of the choir. Our dependence there having failed, and the time being near at hand, that there might not be a total disappointment, I induced Mr. Candy with a violin, Sam'l Butler with a flute, and Mr. Newton's eldest son, who is a close neighbor, with a tenor viol, to practise some tunes by way of preparation; and they, being not very skilful, looked to me, as bad a musician as I am, for aid. Having but one book, I had tunes and songs to transcribe. For the Cherokee department I had some songs to compose, and have them printed, and teach the music. The children, too, had been encouraged that they might have a banner, and march to music as a cold water army. So finding no child's cold water song of which the music would suit a child's step, I wrote one on this sheet, and had it printed for them. And the printing of their banner fell to me also. And then Mr. Covel moved some of the neighbors to have a temperance flag, seven yards by five, and I had the letters to draw for that. And as it takes much time to do what one is unaccustomed to, all these things, with other duties, made me quite busy for a while.

"And what, you will naturally ask, was the result of the meeting? Not very great, and yet perhaps as great as, in existing circumstances, could reasonably be expected. The backwardness of the season, in consequence of long-continued rains in the spring, had rendered it an uncommonly hurrying time, and a meeting had been held in the same neighborhood a few weeks before, at which 59 names had been added to the pledge. As it was the assembly of people was estimated at from 500 to 800. I suppose there may have been 600, and 75 names were added, *some* of which might be considered as a considerable acquisition. To these may be added 14 names of children in our school, given in anticipation of the meeting, which makes 89 in all. But I suppose the principal object gained was the bringing the Society more conspicuously before the public view, and causing its influence to be more strongly felt. . . . .

"I might have mentioned, in speaking of the temperance meeting, that the principal address was made by Mr. Daniel Ross, nephew of John Ross, and brother of the appointed editor of the new paper. Daniel is a member of our church, and we hear no evil of him. His address was written—not great, but acceptable to the people. His father, who is now a member of the temperance society, thinks that Mr. John Ross can be brought in, which is quite desirable.

"Yesterday, I believe, was our hottest day this season. Thermometer 100. Today 98, as I believe it has been on several days."

Perhaps a temperature of a hundred degrees made the writing of a cold water army song a congenial occupation; at any rate Samuel succeeded in writing one, which he included in his letter to Mr. Greene. It was doggerel, to be sure, and Samuel may have preserved it as much by way of confession as by way of pride. For God required many things of his servant, including doggerel. At any rate, the children marched to Samuel's "Song of the Cold Water Army," and they sang it to the tune of "On the Road to Boston."

"Come and join our temp'rance army,
Singing, Water, sweet cold water;

'Tis a drink that will not harm you,
    Water, sweet cold water.
Water springs from hill and valley,
Dancing in the stream so gaily
And we drink cold water daily;
Water, water, sweet cold water.
Come and join our temp'rance army,
    Singing, Sweet cold water.

"Children come and join our army,
  Singing Water, sweet cold water;
  'Tis a drink that will not harm you,
    Water, sweet cold water.
Silly is the lad, though frisky,
Who has drunk his glass of whisky;
But we sing our carol briskly;
Water, sweet cold water.
Children, come and join our army,
    Singing, Sweet cold water.

"Brothers, come and join our army,
Singing, Water, sweet cold water;
  'Tis a drink that will not harm you,
    Water, sweet cold water.
See the drunkard look so sadly;
Whisky made him feel so badly;
But we drink cold water gladly;
Water, sweet cold water.
Brothers, come and join our army,
    Singing, Sweet cold water.

"Sisters, come and join our army,
  Singing, Water, sweet cold water;

'Tis a drink that will not harm you,
   Water, sweet cold water.
What though wine is bright and pleasant?
Woe and sorrow flow incessant
From the cup that cheers at present;
Not so water, sweet cold water.
Sisters, come and join our army,
   Singing, Sweet cold water.

"Come, O come and join our army,
   Singing, Water, sweet cold water;
'Tis a drink that will not harm you,
   Water, sweet cold water,
Drink that will destroy our reason,
Drink that leads to blood and treason,
Let us all abjure in season,
Singing, Water, sweet cold water,
Come, O come and join our army,
   Singing, Sweet cold water."

Until the disruptions of the Civil War broke up existing
organizations among the Cherokees, the Temperance
Society continued its meetings. And as long as Samuel
Worcester lived, he expended his efforts and energy for
their success. To this day his grandchildren, now white-
haired and rich in reminiscences of the grandfather whom
they held in deep affection, recall some of those gatherings
at Park Hill. "Grandfather had a great yellow apple tree,
of his own planting," one of them relates. "And the meetings were held at the mission in the summer time, when
the apples were ripe. They were all-day gatherings, and I
remember the crowds, who marched carrying sprays of
bloom—sunflowers perhaps—and the baskets of yellow

apples being passed about, and the singing. Grandfather loved singing, and made it a part of every gathering."

It was to advance the cause of temperance that Samuel Worcester began the use of unfermented wine in the communion service. Raisins were too great a luxury for the mission family to use as food, but they were a frequent item in Samuel's early orders from Park Hill. "The raisins charged from time to time," he explained, "are used for making communion wine. I prefer to use very little fermented wine, for the sake of members formerly addicted to intemperance."

Slavery was another issue that claimed Worcester's time and thought and prayer. Ever since missions had existed among them, the Cherokees had been slave-owners. Their system of agriculture and of household economy was based on that of the white families living in the South, and they copied the system as they saw it. As an Indian acquired property and became influential, he emulated white men of property and influence; he looked upon the black man as of an inferior race, and his government forbade intermarriage between Cherokees and negroes. In short, among the Cherokees slavery had the same status that it had among white citizens of the South. Missionaries coming among the Indians took the holding of slaves as a matter of course, and turned their attention to other matters. When they were in need of laborers, they sometimes hired slaves of slave-owners; and a few transactions are on record in which the actual ownership of slaves fell to missionaries who had the eventual freeing of the slave in view, or who saw in such ownership the improvement of the slave's situation. It was inevitable, of course, that misunderstandings regarding the missionaries' attitude toward slavery should reach the North and eventually find their way into the annual meetings of the American Board. Employment of slave labor and admission of slave-owners to churches were the two phases of the question that aroused dispute among the members of the Board. As the matter grew into a political issue in the country, the significance of every act of the missionaries in which slaves or slave-owners were involved increased. Small incidents grew, by retelling, into accounts of luxurious living at some of the Cherokee and Choctaw mission stations; and contributors to the American Board in some cases withdrew their support, in bitterness, because of such accounts. A knowledge of the hard work that entered into any day in the lives of Samuel and Ann Worcester, or of the Wrights or the Kingsburys or the Byingtons of the Choctaw Mission, would have dissipated any impression of luxurious living that might have been carried to New England. In some of the criticism leveled at the missionaries through the Board, a flavor of self-righteousness may be detected.

To the missionaries, actually in the field and numbering slaves and slave-owners alike in their congregations, slavery was not an issue to be put on a par with salvation itself. The great necessity was to live and work among the Indians, teaching and preaching and ministering as fully as they might, and to hope, by such living, eventually to bring about a better social and economic order as well as a new religious life. Before the outbreak of the Civil War, the Mission Board of the Presbyterian church took over the work of the Cherokee and the Choctaw Missions, but not until much energy had been spent and much correspondence exchanged in sectional controversy when the missionaries, and at least many members of the Board, longed to spend all on greater issues.

Samuel Worcester's position was a difficult one. He was

convinced, himself, of the wrong of slavery; the longer he lived among the Cherokees the more strongly he felt on that point. But he knew slave-owners and slaves, and had both in his churches, and the personal knowledge of these people drew him out of the classification of theorizer on the slavery question. A slave-owner could be kindly and sincere and honest, and show as great an evidence of piety as the non-slave-owner. To bring salvation was his aim, not to settle the question of slavery among the Indians. When pressed for information, however, he must write the full truth to the Board: "My views on the subject," he wrote in 1836, "are in some measure changed from what they once were. When I visited the Choctaw nation in company with Mr. Evarts, I agreed with him and with Mr. Kingsbury, in opposition to the views of some other Choctaw missionaries, in believing that slaves might with propriety be hired at the mission stations *with their own consent*. I could never, for a moment, so far as I remember my own feelings, have thought of employing them *without* their own consent, cheerfully given. For some time I employed at New Echota on such terms. I have since been convinced that even this will not bear scrutiny: 1st because, so far as example is concerned, the fact of the employment of slaves by missionaries will be known much farther than the fact of their asking the consent of the slaves. 2nd, Because hiring of slaves helps the slave-market as much as buying them—slave dealers, it is said, find it much more profitable to buy slaves for the purpose of letting them out for wages, than for that of keeping them in their own employment. 3d. Because I found by a little acquaintance in Tennessee, that many justify themselves in purchasing slaves, on the ground that those who will not buy are compelled to hire, and that, for several reasons of justice and humanity, it is better to buy than to hire. This argument can be taken from only by dispensing with the services of slaves altogether.—But my impression is that your missionaries do not all make the consent of a slave an essential prerequisite to employing him.

"Aside from these considerations, is not the present state of feeling among the friends of missions such, that a general knowledge of the fact that missionaries employ slaves, in New England, would cause an excitement unpropitious to the cause? And if so, is it right to continue a practice which it is necessary to conceal from that Christian community from whom the resources of the Board are derived?"

Unfortunately, the question could not be settled, for all, by Samuel's settlement of the question in his own mind. Organizations and individuals more and more constantly pressed the American Board for a firmer stand on the matter, and memorials against slavery and against the employment of missionaries who would admit slave-owning members to their churches poured into every annual meeting. In 1844, Samuel wrote in answer to some specific questions presented by the Board, "None of the Cherokee missionaries, I think, at present, hire slaves from their masters. But it is most true that some slaveholders are members of our church. Nor do I at present see how we can exclude them, or ever refuse to admit others, if they should give evidence of regeneration. I might possibly be led to adopt the principle that slave-holders should be excluded, if it were not for apostolic example. But I regard it as certain that the apostles did receive slave-holders to their churches, without requiring of them the emancipation of their slaves; nor have I yet obtained any light to perceive such a difference in the circumstances, as to make it appear that we are not following our own judgment, in opposition to apostolic example, if we were to exclude them." The members of the Board were convinced of the truth of this opinion regarding apostolic example. In 1845 they drew up a resolution expressing this conviction, addressed to Samuel Worcester, Cyrus Kingsbury of the Choctaw Mission, and other missionaries. It asserted that "while the strongest language of reprobation is not too strong to be applied to the system of slavery, truth and justice require this Board to say that the *relation* of a Master to one whom the constitution of society has made a slave, is not to be regarded as in all cases such a sin as to require the exclusion of the Master, without further inquiry, from Christian ordinances."

So liberal a statement as this, however, was not to settle the matter. Abolition had become a cause, and its champions were aggressive. Every new bit of evidence brought a new argument. In 1846, David was obliged to write again, explaining that "our abolitionists are threatening to pull a new string. They seem just now to have learned that some of the members of your churches & Choctaw mission churches hold slaves; & on this account they are going to show that the Board countenances slavery, or at least does not do all it can to oppose it. They would have the missionaries instructed to admit no more slaveholders to the churches. They may make some trouble in this way."

But in the East, rumors would not down. Word had come that Stephen Foreman, a Cherokee in the employ of the Board, owned a slave. The Secretary wrote, in 1851, to Worcester about this. "I am sure we shall be embarrassed if Mr. Foreman has purchased a slave, *to retain her as a slave.* I was sorry to find, in 1848, that

Mrs. Foreman was a slaveholder, but as this was an old matter, & as she held her slave as separate property, I thought we could get along with the fact. . . . . If he has not done so, will he not emancipate at once, permitting the slave to work out the purchase money? This would of course relieve the case. Providence evidently designs to keep the slavery question in a state of agitation for a long time to come; and we can hardly expect to be altogether quiet, so long as this is the case."

To Samuel and the other missionaries, it must have looked as if interfering busybodies had more to do with the agitation than Providence had. Such letters as this one of 1853, from the Secretary of the Board to Samuel, would indicate more than the hand of Providence. "I have been thinking for some time that I would have a little chat with you on the subject of slavery. The Am. Miss. Assoc. will not let us alone; & we find that their constant assaults produce some effect. We cannot enter the lists with them, for we are men of peace. And where much is said without contradiction, something will be finally believed.

"They (the Albany Convention) decided that right-fulness of suppporing missionaries among slaveholding churches did not depend upon the character of the *churches*, but upon that of the *men* sent to them. If the *men* were faithful in their exhibitions of truths, the Am. Home Soc. was justified in sustaining them. . . . . I suppose the embarrassment with you is a practical one. In the *abstract* you could assent to our principles; but when you come to *apply* them, the churches are not ready to go quite so far. Is not that the real state of the case?

"If they can be made to understand the matter, it seems to me there ought to be no difficulty. On the contrary, it places you in a more intelligible & definite status,

& one to which they cannot reasonably object. You say to the churches. 'We hold the sentiments of northern churches. We believe so and so. But we recognize your rights most fully. In the admission of church members, in cases of discipline, whatever opinions we hold or express, the *decision* is with you, & we shall never strive to defeat your right. Let us both have our liberty to think or not, as we may judge right. Perhaps we shall always be of one mind. If we are not, however, our relations need not be disturbed in the least. . . . .

"I did not write to the *Mission*, because that would look rather formal. I write to you as the oldest brother, *in trust* for all."

Year after year, the letters concerning slavery must go back and forth; every settlement of the matter must lead to its outcropping from a new source or because of new facts. Each year, Samuel longed more and more for its final settlement, that he might be free to work with things of eternal importance to his Cherokees. It was vital to him that he teach Christianity; nothing else could overshadow the importance of that purpose. And in order to teach Christianity he must work assiduously at his translations. He must make sure that he presented, in Cherokee, a theology as clear and as correct as it was presented to readers of the Bible in English. Such questions as baptism and election and grace must be considered so carefully in translating that no error of belief could creep into the minds of the Cherokees. The deepest study of Cherokee words was necessarily involved. When he came west he had high hopes that he might be more free than he had been before to devote his mind to his great work of translation; once settled, and with Elias Boudinot at hand to delve into the intricacies of language—Greek and Latin and English and Cherokee—daily with him, he believed he could accomplish his great end, the translation of the entire Bible into Cherokee. And he would work so assiduously that no erroneous theology could find its way into his work. By his correctness in every word, he would make religious truth a possible attainment for the Cherokees. But he had scarcely reached Union before a question arose as to his translation of the word *baptize*. Word had come to the Board that he had chosen the same word as that employed by the Baptists, and that the word conveyed to the minds of the Cherokees the meaning of immersion. He wrote carefully to David Greene, explaining his translation of the word. "The report respecting our translation of the word *baptize* is not correct. Your views of the proper method of translating the word accord entirely with mine. When the English translation was made, no word was found in the language to express the meaning of the word *baptize* correctly, and therefore the translators did well to form a word from the Greek to express it; just as has been done in a thousand or perhaps thousands of English words from Greek, Latin, & French. The same course we would have adopted in Cherokee, as the best, if it had been practicable. But the structure of the Cherokee language forbids it. We could adopt a *noun* from another language, as in some instances we have done; but to introduce a verb, and Cherokeeize it, is an impossibility. Where a new idea is introduced, which the language has not hitherto expressed, and which is to be expressed by a verb, the only possible course is to use an old verb with a new shade of signification, and let that signification be learned by use & explanation. This has been done in a multitude of cases, as civilization & religion have introduced new ideas, which the language had never expressed from the obvious principle that the language of a people cannot go beyond their ideas.

"But enough of this. Now for the translation. The verb by which we translate baptize signifies *to wash*, whatever the *mode* of washing. Its prevailing use, it is true, relates to washing by immersion, but by no means its exclusive use; so far from it, that there is no other Cherokee word, so far as I have been able to learn, which signifies *to wash* in a general sense, as applied to persons. One verb signifies to wash the hands,—another to wash the face—but this signifies in general *to wash* either the whole person, or any part. Your inquiry has led me to ask Cherokees to whom I have access respecting the meaning of the word, and in doing so I have learned, that the Cherokee conjurers, as they are called, have a ceremony of washing persons, in which the person *usually* goes into the water, but sometimes is only washed in some part, e.g. the hands or face; and the ceremony, however performed, is designated by the same word by which we translate baptize. Now I suppose this may be termed baptism; and we may say that the conjurers regard the *mode* of baptizing as a matter of indifference; and we are correct in using the same term in translating baptize, by which they designate their act of baptism.

"The truth is there is no ground of controversy between us and our Baptist brethren. . . . . The word we use is the same which they choose, and is *susceptible* of the signification which they would give it; and we on our part must be satisfied with it, as the greatest approximation to a correct translation of which the language is susceptible, and have no occasion to be otherwise than satisfied, since it is well understood, in its *technical* use, to designate the act of baptism, irrespective of the *mode*. The Baptists will of course put their own interpretation upon it, as they do upon the original word baptize. But they, as a denomination, are not designated by the same word by which we translate the word *baptize*, but by another Cherokee word, capable of being rendered either the *Drowners* or the *Immersers*. As applied to them, of course, it signifies the *Immersers*. This fact of itself shows, that the word we use is not understood as defining the mode of baptism.

"I have written in great haste, but hope to be understood."

This letter of explanation was thoroughly satisfactory to the members of the Board. It was another proof to them that their appointee, Samuel Austin Worcester, knew every inch of the ground on which he stood; he had not occupied it in haste or in ignorance. They thought of his great uncle, the Trinitarian theologian, Samuel Worcester, buried at Brainerd Mission where he had gone on a visit in 1821, and they held the nephew worthy of his high relationship.

Ten years later, a similar question regarding the interpretation of the word *baptize* arose. Samuel wrote the Board again, making his stand clear and definite, and satisfying the members that his ten years of residence in the West had not weakened his purpose to attain the absolute in theological truth. The occasion of this letter was a problem of publication. "A practical question arises in regard to the circulation of the Baptist translation of parts of the New Testament together with our translation of other parts. My plan has been to bind theirs in the same volume with ours, to be bought and distributed by the Cherokee Bible Society. But they have translated thus in Luke—'I indeed baptize you in water, but he shall

[242]

baptize you in the Holy Spirit and in fire.' Of course similar passages are or will be translated in a similar manner. They are also going on with the translation of scriptures at a rate altogether too rapid to be correct; though I do not know how much time Mr. Jones may spend in revising, before he suffers it to be printed. But he suffers his translator, not well versed in English, to go on at first alone. However, I had particular reference to the disputed passages relating to baptism. The Baptists already represent us as conceding, by our translation of the word baptize, that immersion was the original mode; and if we bind their books with ours, the Cherokees may consider us as assenting to the correctness of their translation. At the same time it is very desirable to circulate all the scriptures that are translated, and desirable that all should be comprehended in one volume. The Cherokee Bible Society, too, ought to be free from sectarianism. What, then on the whole, ought we to do? and what, if we could influence the Bible Society, ought that to do? Ought we to bind all together, without note or comment, and the Society to circulate them so? Or ought we to print and insert a note to this effect, that we think such passages in the Baptist translation should be *so*? Or ought we just to prepare our own, and let them prepare theirs, and the Society purchase both? Or the Society exclude the Baptist translations, and let them have their own society, if they please? The fact is that they do almost nothing in aid of the society's funds. I should be glad to know your opinion soon, as it may make a difference in the form we shall adopt in printing new editions, some of which we shall soon need.

"In the English Bible we have 'into the water' and 'out of the water' where we think it should be 'to' and 'from.'

On the other hand we have 'with water' and 'with the Holy Ghost,' and 'with fire,' where the Baptists would have it 'in.' Yet both we and they circulate the English Bible without note or comment.

"This book will be circulated. If we let them alone, they go without our sanction, but they go. The poison is diffused, and the antidote is our refusal to circulate them.

"If we bind them with ours, and circulate them without note or comment, the poison is diffused without an antidote.

"If we bind them together, and insert a note stating what is the difference of opinion between us and the Baptists, the poison is sent out accompanied with so much of an antidote as such a statement will contain."

To the very end of his life, when his energy failed him frequently and time for the completion of his translation seemed the most precious thing in life, Samuel continued this same meticulous accuracy in the choice of Cherokee words. "There is," he explained in connection with some of his Old Testament translations on which he worked until within a few days of his death, "a peculiar definiteness about the Cherokee language, which compels us to settle many questions, which the English and Creek leave ambiguous. *Definite* we must be, whether definitely *right* or definitely *wrong;* and as we *wish* to be *right,* we are obliged to spend much time in settling questions which other translators leave for the commentator."

Yet, in spite of the definite and positive aspects of Samuel Worcester's theology, and his determination that his people should have no false beliefs, he found a sweet tolerance for some of the simpler minded Indians' religious conceptions. There was the case of Jesse Barrow, that very devout and kindly Cherokee who had preached and prayed and comforted his people during their encampment and removal and had since worked among them as a native helper and evangelist. His education had been deficient and his knowledge of theology was too limited for Samuel to recommend him to the Board for ordination and appointment as a minister of the Gospel; but the very simplicity of his interpretation of religious matters had a truth and beauty of its own that Samuel did not fail to appreciate. Before his death Jesse had dictated a written message to his people, of which Samuel sent a copy to the Board:

"LITTLE VIAN, Aug. 28, 1847.

"My dearly beloved friends, fellow-members of the church, who have gone to the house of Jesus Christ in company, have been companions of each other, and worshipped our God together, I am now very weak in body, but in mind I am not weak. For I have prayed to God continually to help me, and to help all of you, my friends. I fervently thank our Savior for all the good that he has done me, preserving me from evil till the present time.

"Now I have a few words to say to you this afternoon. I present to your minds the truth that God is most merciful, if any one worship him in truth, from the very soul, and loves his fellow-men. For this is the chief commandment of our God. If you do this, you will surely obtain eternal life.

"This is a discourse from me to you; and now it is but a brief discourse from me that you can see on paper; but it may suffice to tell you in your own person what I have experienced; but I hope you will understand how much I have already seen of the power of God. When

I was about half asleep four angels of heaven came and sat, two at my head and two at my feet. I think it is a very wonderful thing which I have seen. Their bodies were very small, but they were very glorious to look upon. They said to me—one of them, who sat at my feet, on my right—we are sent from heaven, and have come here to watch over you. So they sat the whole night, and only that one spoke; and when morning came he said nothing, nor did I perceive their departure. There were lights burning the whole night, and my friends were watching with me, but they saw nothing. I alone saw what I have related. Truly wonderful are God's methods of operating upon the minds of men. I have employed a person to write this, that my brethren and friends might hear it.

"Now you that are yet procrastinating, I beseech you stop while yet the day lasts—while yet you have power to act—while yet you are taking the last step to death. I beseech you turn from your evil ways. I beseech you obey the call of Jesus Christ to you. For you cannot lengthen your lives, even a single minute. God only can continue them. And just as this day is rapidly drawing to a close, never more to be seen, so rapidly is your death approaching. Say, 'Lord remember me,' and he will save you. Knock and it shall be opened unto you.

"My friends, and all, I bid you farewell—my last farewell.

Your affectionate
JESSE BARROW"

This was scarcely the conventional form of "last words." But it is to Samuel's credit that he overlooked its unconventionality, and held it in the reverence due an honest, earnest expression of belief. When he sent Jesse's letter to the Board, he offered some comments: "The signature is literally, 'Jesse Barrow, your lover:' and so I should translate it, but for the *technical* use, in English, of the word *lover*.

"I suppose it is needless for me to make any remarks on Jesse's vision of angels. On the one hand, it is easy to regard it as a dream, resulting from his state of mind when awake.

"On the other hand, if angels are indeed 'ministering spirits put forth to minister for them who shall be heirs of salvation,' there is no absurdity in supposing that God may sometimes render them visible to the dying Christian for his consolation in his dying hour. I believe it is not very uncommon for Christians near the hour of their departure, to speak of seeing angels attending upon them, or come to conduct them away. A black man belonging to one of our churches, and esteemed decidedly pious, who died a few months ago said, as he was about to depart, 'I am going; two angels have come for me.' "

The words and the beliefs of simple people, however unorthodox, thus had their beauty and their value, in Samuel Worcester's estimation. Whatever their theological implications, they could do little harm because they were individual occurrences, and they might do much good. But the Board sent a warning of a new influence that might, he thought, be more far-reaching. "It seems also," the Secretary wrote in 1844, "that you are to have a bishop over you. The Episcopal Church, with its formality & parade, and promise of heaven to all who are authoritatively baptized and confirmed, will be just such a religion as the Rogers among the Cherokees and the Colberts among the Chickasaws will like." If there was something smug and self-righteous in the warning, writer and recipient alike were unaware of it. Romanists were idolators, in their opinion, and Episcopalians verged upon idolatry. From such heresy, they hoped the Indians might be delivered. A few months later, the Bishop came on a tour to the Indian country, riding slow river boats, making journeys on horse back, and visiting forts, Indian agencies, and missions with a friendly interest in everything.

The Bishop of Tennessee, James Hervey Otey, with N. Sayre Harris, Secretary of the Protestant Episcopal Church, visited Arkansas and the Indian tribes nearby in the spring of 1844. On Easter Sunday, while the Bishop visited the parish at Van Buren, Mr. Harris held an Easter service at Fort Gibson. He found there four companies of infantry and two of dragoons under the command of Lieutenant Colonel Loomis, "a devoted Christian." Two days later, after visiting the Seminoles to ask about opening a school among them, Mr. Harris arrived at Park Hill. In his journal he said, "Col. Loomis kindly drove eighteen miles to Park Hill, one of the stations of the A.B.C.F.M., under the charge of the Reverend Mr. Worcester, whose devotion to Indian improvement, ere yet the Cherokees left Georgia, and his patient suffering there for what he deemed truth and duty, enlisted the respect and sympathy of Christians everywhere; and yet we learned afterward that even this friend of the red men, unto bonds and imprisonment, was more than once on the eve of being expelled from the country, on the suspicion of dissatisfaction with some one of the parties into which the Cherokees are split. . . . . Mr. W. confines himself to preaching and translating. He presented a copy of the Gospels printed in Cherokee, after the alphabet of Mr. Guess. . . . .

[248]

The press at Park Hill, which we inspected, was first set up at Union in 1835, and removed to Park Hill in 1837; a number of books and pamphlets in Cherokee, Creek and Choctaw, and a small primer in them, having been printed there. . . . .

"Miss Avery instructs the day school, of about 25 scholars; Miss Thompson is also connected with the mission. . . . .

"We spent the evening very pleasantly with the missionary family; much information was gained from Mr. W. The ladies seemed very happy and very devoted to the spiritual concerns of their Indian friends."[2]

To the Worcesters, this visitor representing the Protestant Episcopal Church did not seem to be verging on idolatry. To be sure, he spoke of one of the ministers of the Gospel as a rector, and he mentioned a "cure of souls" when he meant a charge. But he had swum streams when they were too high for fording; he had eaten "Sophky" or "Tom Fuller" with the Indians; and he had found the prairie country beautiful with an appreciation common to few visitors. And like Samuel Worcester, he deplored the uncurbed distribution of whisky among the Indians. They remembered him, in spite of the reputed danger of his religious tendencies, as a gracious guest in their home.

2 *Chronicles of Oklahoma*, Vol. X, No. 2 (June, 1932), pp. 237-8.

The Lord Hath Taken Away

WHEN ANN WORCESTER left Brainerd Mission, she left behind her closest friend, Harriet Boudinot. They had a common background of New England training, a common work as assistant missionaries, and a common interest in the problems of homemaking among a people to whom their marriage had brought them. In spite of Elias Boudinot's early advocacy of the removal westward of the Cherokees, he himself did not move until he had seen the last of the emigrating bands on its way. But he meant, as soon as he had discharged his duty as a leader among his people in Georgia, to bring his family westward to join the Worcesters in their location at Park Hill and to resume his work as translator with Samuel Worcester. Ann, working busily at the innumerable tasks that are a part of making a home in a new land, thought happily of the time when Harriet would again be living nearby: they would share some of their housewifely duties; they would find time to sit together, sewing and mending and talking of memories of their childhood and hopes for their children; their children would play together and study lessons under the same teacher. Then came word, in the fall of 1836, that Harriet Boudinot had died, in August, and had been buried on the hillside near the Boudinot home at New Echota. Her busy life of childbearing and homemaking was at an end, and the headstone at her grave gave assurance of release: "We seek a rest beyond the skies."

Elias Boudinot was bewildered by his loss. He was ill from the constant strain under which the Cherokee leaders lived, and he had six small motherless children whom he loved dearly. Should he take them north, to Harriet's people, who had become reconciled to her marriage with him? Or should he, ill as he was, stay on at New Echota and attempt to rear them there, until better conditions offered? He wrote Samuel for advice, and the Worcesters, reading his letters, grieved for him in his sorrow and trouble. Whatever else was true, Samuel had need of him at Park Hill, for he must revise all of Samuel's translations and settle constantly recurring questions as to the proper choice of words in a hymn or a passage of scripture. Samuel urged him to come west as soon as he could. Then, for Elias Boudinot, the heart settled a problem that the mind had not been able to solve: he found that he loved Miss Delight Sargent, an assistant missionary who had come out to the Cherokees in 1828. It was happy news to the Worcesters, for it meant that some of the old relationship between the two families might be resumed at Park Hill, even though removal and death might lend their tinge to it. Samuel wrote, with a sense of relief and of pleasure to the Board: "Mr. Boudinot has recently informed me of his renewed determination to join me in my work, and also of a matrimonial engagement between himself and Miss Sargent. Whatever may be said of Miss Sargent's taste or judgment in forming such a connection, it is a circumstance which affords much gratification to us, healing the breach which was made in our anticipated circle of friendship by the death of Mr. Boudinot's first wife. Miss Sargent is high in our esteem."

[251]

With the coming of the Boudinots, Park Hill began to take on the aspect of something more than an isolated home. The church had been formed, and the Boudinots lent numbers to the tiny congregation meeting in the schoolhouse. There was, to be sure, some ill feeling among the Indians who had opposed removal, and a certain amount of resentment against the mission for employing him again as translator. But in the work of translation, Samuel Worcester said, "He is my right hand." Elias set about building his house, hampered by the unreliability of workmen and the scarcity of lumber, and the work proceeded slowly. He divided his time, during the day, between the work of the press and the construction of his house, but the long evenings he gave to translating. It was like the renewal of an old hope, to both him and Samuel, to know that they were making progress, verse by verse and chapter by chapter, in the Bible for the Cherokees. John Ross had built his home on the north bank of Park Hill Creek, across from the Press and Worcester's house; Stephen Foreman, the native preacher who gave promise of being more and more useful, had built his home near the Worcesters; and Archibald Campbell, a prominent member of the tribe, had a home just across the creek from that of John Ross. Indians who had been distrustful of the mission in the beginning were beginning to look to it as the center of their interests in this western country. Samuel Worcester had succeeded in making his mission station, new as it was, the principal institution in this new land. Information, money, medicine—these could be had from Samuel when they were needed. Samuel prayed that, in return, the Indians might forget their old differences over the question of removal. In the harmony of Park

Hill, he hoped, such men as Ross and Boudinot might live at peace.

But Indians' memories are long. In spite of the need, in these new circumstances, for unity among the Cherokees, the differences among factions grew. Major Ridge and his son John still headed the "Treaty Party," and Elias Boudinot was looked upon as their adherent, whether or not he devoted himself in any way to political interests. John Ross, still principal chief of the emigrant party, found himself at the head, not of a whole tribe, but of a faction known as the Ross or National Party. Those who had come westward earlier, formerly known as the Western or Arkansas Cherokees, came now to be known as the "Old Settlers." They were about half the number of the 13,000 arrivals from the east, but priority made them resent any imposition of authority over them by the newcomers. Jealousy and bitterness and misunderstanding tortured a people who had already been tortured by injustice from outside.

Some great harmonizing influence was needed, greater and more immediate than that which Park Hill could exert. David Greene, writing to Samuel, offered the explanation once customary among Christians who are baffled—that of the working of the Lord's will: "But it seems to be the Lord's will that every thing shall work against the Indians. Perhaps his purpose is to allow them to be consumed speedily. We may be sure of this, that, however wicked and oppressive is the conduct of those who manage Indian affairs, the Lord works in perfect wisdom and love." But the missionaries, alas, did not always work in this same perfect wisdom and love. Mr. Newton had been accused of self-interest in his labors among the Cherokees, and had lost their confidence to

[253]

such an extent that when he thought of leaving the mission service, he offered the only solution that seemed possible. Some of the Indians claimed the house and the school that he had occupied, and it was left to Samuel to settle the unpleasant affair as best he could, avoiding troublesome relations even at the expense of loss of mission property. David Greene, in his letter to Samuel, took a tolerant view of the Cherokees' side, however: "It seems to me that the mission has indeed but a very slender hold upon the Cherokees, when the property of the Board can be seized upon in such a manner and no redress be had. However, we must not blame the Cherokees too much. Our government have taught the lesson by a treatment of them in violation of all right, & on an incomparably larger scale."

Some of the missionaries, it appears, were far too human, too ready to take sides in a situation that required a wholly impartial attitude. Some self-interest crept into their relations with the Indians, and some personal prejudice. Even Dr. Butler, who had suffered imprisonment for the cause of the Cherokees, became indiscreet. The Board wrote to Samuel, urging him to do all in his power to preserve harmony among the missionaries and among the people whom they served: "I regret that Doct. Butler should use so unguarded language, or take any step adapted to increase or continue the prejudice of the Cherokees one against another, or against any of the missionary brethren. I have just written him on the subject, and trust that he will be more cautious in the future. A little reflection must teach him that such a course can do hurt & that only; & that the great concern and effort of all should be, on this point, to restore peace, good-will, confidence, & unanimity. . . . .

"I sincerely hope that Doct. Butler, Messrs. Butrick,

[254]

Jones, Foreman, and all others will, when they fairly get through the anxiety & toil of removal, feel the importance of exerting to the extent of their power, a softening, cooling, healing influence on the sore & troubled minds of the Cherokees; and that they will see that thinking, and much less speaking, of what bad things one or the other party may have said or done, can do no good. Especially should they refrain from thus speaking respecting their missionary brethren, as a contrary course would not only detract from the usefulness of the brother spoken against, but also from their own & that of all who bear the missionary name."

Constantly Samuel prayed for peace, but there was no peace. By the summer of 1839, when the new country of the Cherokees overflowed with arrivals from Georgia, dissension and strife dominated the minds of the men of the tribe. Misunderstandings embittered all the factions, and Samuel's steady, quiet efforts at helpfulness were a mere drop of oil that could not smooth the troubled waters of Cherokee politics. Then, on June 22, the storm broke. Three leaders of the Treaty party, Major Ridge, John Ridge, and Elias Boudinot, were assassinated. Samuel was a witness to the killing of Boudinot, and wrote of it a few days later. "Mr. Boudinot is murdered. . . . . Mr. Boudinot was yet living in my house. On Saturday morning, he went to his house, which he was building, a quarter of a mile distant. There some Cherokee men came up, inquiring for medicine, and Mr. Boudinot set out with two of them to come and get it. He had walked but a few rods, when his shriek was heard by his hired men, who ran to his help, but before they could come up the deed was done. A stab in the back with a knife, and seven gashes in the head with a hatchet, did the bloody work.

He lived a few minutes, till we had time to arrive at the spot, and see him breathe his last—his wife among the rest—but he was speechless, and insensible to surrounding objects. The murderers ran a short distance into the woods, joined a company of armed men on horseback, and made their escape."

It was as if a deed of violence had been done to Samuel himself. He bled for the bleeding Cherokees; he grieved for the children of Elias Boudinot and for Delight Boudinot; he wept at the loss of his assistant in the translation of the Scriptures. "They have cut off my right hand," he exclaimed.

Friends of John Ross placed a guard about his house, fearing violence against him; but Ross declared his innocence of knowledge of the crime and remained fearless, even of Stand Watie, Boudinot's brother, who swore vengeance against Ross and all his party. Some of the members of the Treaty party, including John Bell, Archilla Smith, and James Starr, fled to Fort Gibson for military protection. The God of peace seemed to have forsaken this people. But the Secretary of the Board had no doubt that peace would come, even though these events promised, for the Indian Press, "embarrassment for some time to come." "I am sure," he advised Samuel, "that you will do all in your power to comfort Mrs. Boudinot & Mrs. Ridge. Assure them of your sympathy & your prayers. . . . . Let us rejoice that the Lord has the hearts of all in his hand, and can hush all this violence and contention into perfect peace, whenever he shall see it best to do it."

Such violence could not continue; it spent itself with its own force in the murder of these three men whose part in the removal treaty could never be forgiven, and though the Lord did not hush the contention into perfect peace, some settlement among the rival parties now seemed possible. On July 12, a general convention of all the Cherokees was called at the new council ground on the Illinois River, and at this convention an act of union was passed, declaring the Eastern and the Arkansas Cherokees to be "one body politic, under the style and title of the Cherokee Nation." John Ross, principal chief, George Lowery, president of the council, and Going Snake, speaker of the council, signed the agreement for the eastern Cherokees: John Looney, acting principal chief, and George Guess (making his mark instead of his signature), president of the council, signed for the Arkansas or western band. Prominent members of both divisions signed their names or made their marks below those of their leaders, and when the convention adjourned there was hope of some permanent unity once more among the Cherokees. In September, Tahlequah was adopted as the national capital, and a convention made up mostly of eastern members drew up a new constitution. The Old Settlers, meeting at Fort Gibson in June, 1840, accepted the new constitution, and the reunion of the tribe was completed. Dissensions and misunderstandings were to arise, it is true, in years to come; but the tribe was essentially one, and old enmities gradually gave way in the presence of new hopes and new undertakings.

To Samuel Worcester, the union seemed like an answer to his most fervent prayers. Stephen Foreman, already settled at Park Hill, gave promise of some of the same seriousness and effort as a translator that Elias Boudinot had possessed. If Samuel's right hand had been cut off, he was to learn to work with his left.

Progress was necessarily slow. A people uprooted from their old homes and transplanted unwillingly to new ones had problems of food and shelter to solve before they could turn their minds to higher things. As late as 1842, the report of the Cherokee agent to the Bureau of Indian Affairs indicated this: "The cause of education has been neglected, and a state of feeling engendered that will take time to remove. . . . . The Cherokees are furnished by the United States with four blacksmiths and assistants, iron, and steel; also, a wheelright and wagon-maker. Independent of these, they have mechanics of different kinds in the nation. They have also a large fund for education purposes, placed by treaty under the control of the national council."

Two years later, there were noticeable signs of progress. P. M. Butler, the Cherokee agent, wrote in his report for that year that temperance was making progress among the Cherokees, and that Colonel Loomis had established a flourishing temperance society among the soldiers at Fort Gibson. This promised to further the cause of temperance among the Indians, who needed example more than words, since words had failed them in many instances in their dealings with white people. "The Cherokees," Butler reported, "are a people fond of sports and social amusements. Many of them keep up the ancient custom of annual 'ball plays' which usually take place after the crops are laid by. This is an amusement which, as a friend of their people, I would be far from discouraging or wishing discontinued, when not carried to excess. It is above all others, trying to their powers of endurance, and probably contributes largely to the development of their manly and athletic forms. . . . . Besides this sport, they pursue that of training and racing the blood horse, are fond of dancing, and have an uncommon relish for music.

"The Cherokees are exceedingly fond of reading, and have a very inquisitive mind. They seem to take great delight, too, at present, in the manual process of writing, and take every occasion to employ it in preference to oral communication, not so much among themselves, however, as with the whites and agents of the Government. Many of them possess a taste for and some acquirements in general literature. Much benefit may be expected from their printing press lately in operation. . . . . Although imaginative, they have nothing that we can call poetry; but as orators, they are conspicuous in some of the essential excellence of the art. Bold, brief, and earnest, they adapt their ideas and expressions with uniform tact to the nature of their subject and the character of their hearers, and *always stop when they have done.* . . . . In music they have a decided taste, and many of them perform well on different instruments."[1]

There was, indeed, much to encourage the Worcesters, now that the Cherokees were at peace among themselves and were removed, at least in part, from the encroachments of white intruders. Their advancement might be slow, but it was under way in spite of terrible obstacles, and it led in the right direction. Samuel and Ann had learned the lesson of patience long ago; rapidity was not the goal they sought in their efforts to enlighten the Cherokees. Such happenings as had impeded their progress were of small moment, in comparison with that eternity toward which they shaped all their efforts. To balance time and eternity in due proportions—that was their constant aim. It required reasonableness and great sanity, in home and school and church and community.

[1] Bureau of Indian Affairs, *Annual Report*, 1844, pp. 464-5.

Often, in spite of the encouragement Ann felt at the improved state of affairs among the Indians, she found herself almost too weary to rejoice greatly in it. She knew, as any number of the *Missionary Herald* proved in its notices of illnesses and deaths among mission families, that women wore out rapidly in the service to which they pledged themselves; it must be enough for them to give themselves gladly during the years allowed to them, and to make a good end when the time came. The little girls, Ann Eliza, Sarah, and Hannah were growing larger now, and they gave cheerful and efficient help in the household duties and in the entertainment of the numbers of visitors who came to Park Hill. And Miss Nancy Thompson, the assistant missionary who had been in their household much of the time for years, was equal to any responsibility that might be expected of her, whether it might be cooking in the mission kitchen or helping bind books for the press. The little boys, Leonard and John Orr, were still small, but they were sturdy and full of life, and promised already to have some of their father's energy and usefulness. They went to church services with marked regularity, wearing their palm leaf hats to the door and sitting very quietly during the sermon which their father or some other missionary whom they knew preached, powerfully and lengthily. However tired she might be at the end of the day, Ann's heart could still glow with pride in these five children of hers.

Now, in the spring of 1840, there was to be another child. Ann hoped that she might not be incapacitated long, and that she might not suffer the weakness that she had suffered after the birth of John Orr. She hoped the Lord's will might be otherwise for her in this birth; and it was. She died when the baby, Mary Eleanor, was but a few hours old. Samuel wrote to the Board "from the depths of affliction. It has pleased my Heavenly Father to give me a wife, and my children a mother, of no ordinary excellence and value. *The Lord gave and the Lord hath taken away. Blessed be the name of the Lord.*

"About one o'clock on Saturday morning, Mrs. Worcester gave birth to an infant daughter, in circumstances apparently favorable; but in a little time was seized with fainting, accompanied, soon after, with violent spasms, both which symptoms resisted every effort at relief, and a little after sunrise she fell asleep. . . . .

"The infant survives, and was baptized on the Sabbath, at the close of a funeral sermon by Dr. Butler, and before the remains of its mother were laid in the grave."

That was all Samuel could write. There were no words to say that the great love of his life was gone; that all his hard work and his devotion to translating and printing for Indians would never fill the emptiness that Ann's loss had left. For almost fifteen years, she had been his bodily and his spiritual companion. He had never known any other woman with her high bearing and her gentleness, with her intelligence and her humility. It was late summer before the consolations of the Board, written in July, reached him; but even then he was scarcely able to realize that the consoling words were written regarding a loss that was permanent. "We call such bereavements painful, and regarded as bereavements, they are so, and the heart bleeds at the separation which is effected. But still, is there not something almost indescribably pleasant in the thought that one so dear & so well prepared for the change has got safely through the world, beyond all further care or toil, or sorrow, or peril, & is perfectly blessed with the heavenly community, in the presence of the Savior?"

In less than a year, however, Samuel Worcester had married Miss Erminia Nash, who had come out to the Cherokee Mission at Creek Path in 1825, the same year as that in which Samuel had brought Ann, his bride, to Brainerd. To this day, the descendants of Samuel and Ann relate stories of the eagerness of female assistants to fill the vacant place in Samuel's household. Under the circumstances, the most persistent of them all was the one most likely to be asked to fill the place; it was not a matter of affection, for that was buried in the burying-ground at Park Hill with Ann, but of practical necessity for a sympathetic woman in the mission household. Miss Nash was prudent, sincerely pious, and of proven faithfulness. These qualities were all that Samuel could ask for, when the mission family needed a mistress and the children a responsible supervisor. Erminia lacked Ann's highest qualities; her letters, by which she must now be judged at least in part, were slightly untidy, slighty dull, and slightly self-centered. She did all in her power to be a good wife to Samuel, and she filled his needs as far as any being left on earth could do. The need for Ann herself, she could never fill.

No children were born to Samuel and Erminia. Mary Eleanor, the infant who was the price of Ann's life, was the baby of the household and the claimant of her father's deepest tenderness until his death. The residents at Park Hill feared she might not live, in that frontier community with no mother to care for her. But she grew and thrived, and she never knew any want of interest and affection. Erminia, and the whole village, substituted all they possessed in amendment to the baby for the loss of Ann Orr Worcester.

Harriet Boudinot and then Elias, John Ridge and his

father Major Ridge, and hundreds of Cherokees—including White Path and Mrs. John Ross—with whom Samuel had lived and worked as a missionary—the Lord had taken them all. The ways of God, who was all goodness, were hard to understand. And now God had taken Ann. Blessed be the name of the Lord.

No one concerned questioned the Lord's goodness, in Ann's going. Samuel must have brought all his theology into use, to write as he did of his second marriage: "While I do not by any means feel that the loss which I and my children have sustained by the removal of my first companion is now or ever can be fully repaired, yet I feel that I have much reason for gratitude that Providence has thrown in my way so excellent a woman to be a partner for me and a mother to them." The reply of the Secretary of the Board was in kind: "I have much pleasure in congratulating you on the new family connection which you have formed. May the Lord make it, as I doubt not he will, a useful & happy connection both to yourself & wife & to your children, and the means of strengthening your heart & hand in the work to which you are called. Please give my kindest regards to your wife. I have a very pleasant remembrance of the few days I spent at Creek Path, (the only place where I have seen her) in 1828. We have evidence enough of her devotedness to the missionary work among the Cherokees."

New England Schooled

THE CHILDREN were growing up. Ann Eliza was not yet fourteen when her mother died, and Sarah not yet twelve. But a single event may seem to bring a child's years to the flower of maturity; Ann Eliza, suddenly motherless and overwhelmed with a feeling of affection and sisterly pity for her smaller brothers and sisters, grew quickly out of childhood into young womanhood. Her father, looking at her with the surprise that every parent feels when he realizes that his child will not always remain a child, saw all of Ann's graces promising to repeat themselves in Ann Eliza. She had an unusual sweetness and gentleness in her manner, but she had deeper qualities than these. She learned eagerly and rapidly; she had a keen power of analyzing people; she had, in spite of her lack of experience in the world of sophisticated affairs, an ease and graciousness that sprang from complete sincerity and confidence. She disarmed people, and had her way with them without being aware of any conquest. Already, Ann Eliza had begun to indicate her unusual powers as a teacher, for she had helped in the schoolroom at times when the teacher was ill or when some additional assistance was necessary, and she had instructed classes in the Saturday and the Sabbath schools. Indian children and white children alike fell under her spell; they responded without any question to whatever she asked of them.

One of Samuel's deepest experiences of happiness was that of receiving Ann Eliza into the church. Such events, among people of his theology, were not the result of a sudden impulse; they were reasoned out, and considered long and thoroughly before they came to pass. The Worcesters, it is true, were far removed from the center of that religious controversy which made Emerson a philosopher instead of a minister; they knew nothing, at first hand, of the contentiousness that made Dr. Morse, editor of the *Panoplist*, ask, "Are you of the Bostonian religion or of the Christian religion?" Nor did they, on the other hand, comprehend that extreme liberalism of belief that made John Lowell answer, "Are you a Christian or a Calvinist?" They were happily out of the heat of this theological battle, except when the echo of it reached them in the form of a question about Samuel's translation, as compared with the Baptist Evan Jones' translation, of such a word as *baptize*. They were sure of what they believed and why they believed it. But for converts, certain steps of reasoning and certain requirements of conduct must be met. In 1842, Ann Eliza had taken these steps and met these requirements, to her father's profound gratification. His only sorrow was that Ann had not lived to share this happiness with him; but he consoled himself with the knowledge that, in that other world of rest, Ann had learned that her first-born was saved. Samuel wrote the Board of the event: "I ought before this to have informed you that, on the first Sabbath of April, I had the peculiar happiness of receiving my eldest daughter to the communion of the church. We think we have reason to believe that she has been born again, and that she bids fair to

[265]

usefulness. We are hoping to find means of sending her to New England for the improvement of her education. At the same time we received a Cherokee young lady, Betsy Turtle, who was mostly brought up at Haweis, and is now living with us as hired help. A sister of hers would also have been received, but was prevented by her husband."

Samuel voiced, in this letter, the substance of his two highest hopes for Ann Eliza: first, that she find her God, and second, that she have a part of her schooling in the New England that had nurtured Ann and him. It had, indeed, always been the Worcesters' plan to educate their children in the environment in which they themselves had grown up. No other environment and no other education seemed wholly right. They never thought of returning themselves, to stay while their children were growing up, or even to visit occasionally; and they never invented business—for the press or for the school or for the church— that provided an excuse to return. They had said good-bye in 1825, without any thought of returning. But for their children, they desired what they had forever resigned for themselves. And in 1834, the Board at its annual meeting had made the fulfillment of their desires for their children seem possible. "At this meeting the question concerning the return of the children of missionaries to this country for their education, was finally settled. The missionaries of the Board have generally been found prepared to submit, without a murmur, to the sacrifices which their employment has called them to make in their own persons; but to see their children suffer the disadvantages of an education in a heathen land, and sink below the rank they might have occupied in a Christian land,—this is a trial which they did not understand when, young and unmarried, they consecrated themselves to the work, and which it proved hard to bear. . . . . The subject was first brought up by a letter from the missionaries in Ceylon, dated October, 1822; in which they proposed that their children should be sent to the United States at the age of eight, twelve or fifteen, and educated together in a seminary established for that purpose. To this the Committee objected; and after some further correspondence, the Board resolved, at its meeting in 1825, that it could adopt no general system for the removal of the children of missionaries to this country, but would not object to their removal at the expense of friends. This was not satisfactory. . . . . The brethren in Ceylon proposed a plan, by which missionaries might send home their children, and draw at once on the Board, with suitable deduction for payment in advance, for the allowances which must otherwise be made to their children while living with their parents. A plan somewhat on this principle, was adopted, and many were sent home. Meanwhile, an excitement on this subject was rising throughout the country. Some contended, that any arrangement, by which parents were not to bring up their own children, must be at war with the designs of Providence, false in principle, and pernicious in its results; and some Christian mothers contended that women had no right to marry, with the expectation of casting their children upon others for maternal care; and the question began to be agitated whether missionaries ought not to go out unmarried. But the current of feeling was in the opposite direction. . . . . A thorough discussion produced a change of opinions, such as is seldom witnessed on such occasions. It was seen that homes in pious families, commonly of relatives, were better for children than a great boarding establishment; and that, with an appropriation, if needed, not exceeding fifty dollars a year for a boy and forty for a girl till eighteen years of age, to be charged among the expenses of the mission to which the parents belong, such homes could always be obtained. This plan was adopted with entire unanimity."[1]

Under this plan, it was arranged to send Ann Eliza to study under the supervision of her uncle, the Reverend Mr. John Worcester, who had a charge at St. Johnsbury, Vermont. Fortunately, the expenses for Ann Eliza's journey were available without any special arrangement with the Board. The money which Ann Worcester had inherited from her father's estate—referred to in one of Samuel's letters as a thousand dollars or more—had been kept during Ann's lifetime and had been looked upon as a kind of educational endowment for the children. In 1842 this fund, of which Ann's sister's husband, Samuel Chandler of Bedford, New Hampshire, had had charge, had been transferred to the Board in order that it might be available for use from time to time as educational needs arose. It was invested, and the interest from it was contributed to the Monthly Concert for Prayer for Foreign Missions, in the name of the heirs of Ann Orr Worcester and in such proportions, at Park Hill, and later at St. Johnsbury and at South Hadley in addition to Park Hill, as suited the distribution of those heirs in these places. In December, 1842, we find Samuel writing to the Board, "Also send one best *Latin Grammar* and *Latin Primer* and take pay for them from the $700 belonging to the heirs of Ann Orr Worcester."

Before she left Park Hill, Ann Eliza was already beginning to show a special aptitude for languages. It gratified her father to see repeated in his oldest child the interest

1 Tracy, *A History of the American Board of Commissioners for Foreign Missions*, pp. 244-5.

that had always been his own; he foresaw unlimited service to the Indians in this ability of Ann Eliza's. He could not know, specifically, that she was, late in her life, to be employed by the United States Bureau of Ethnology to do linguistic work in the Muskogean languages, but he could foresee great usefulness for her in her combination of knowledge of language with affection for the Indians. The other children were to follow after Ann Eliza in their study of Latin, for to Samuel it was a fundamental part of any education. His regret was that he was, in his long absence from Boston, not always informed as to the latest texts and methods. In 1845, while Ann Eliza was away at school, we find him writing the Board for more Latin books, for the use of the younger children, and making his comments on them. "I thank you for your attention to the purchase of Latin books. If Andrews is half as good at simplifying for children as he is at thorough investigation and discovery of the true principles of language, his *Lessons* will prove good. I see a second edition of Weld's *Lessons* advertised, and highly recommended by the Principal of Phillips Academy, who from the place he occupies ought to be a good judge; but if it is like the first edition, my views must change greatly before I could concur in such a recommendation."

Sometime early in 1843, Ann Eliza set out on her journey to Vermont. It was a very important undertaking for a young lady not yet seventeen, and she was anxiously awaited by the Worcesters in St. Johnsbury. On February 16, her Uncle John, who was to supervise the education of this child whom he had never seen, wrote to David Greene about her coming. John had received a letter from Samuel saying that Ann Eliza was on her way; arrangements must be made, now, to see that she was taken care of in Boston until it was possible for her to come on to Vermont. "Father has accordingly written, I suppose, to Miss Sarah Worcester at Brighton, requesting her to give her a home for a few days, which I suppose she will cheerfully do, and which will furnish Ann Eliza a very pleasant stopping place until company can be found. Mr. John Field, dealer in hides and leather, I think in Milk Street, would no doubt cheerfully convey her to Brighton, as he goes out still, I presume, every ev'g with his own horse. . . . . Please see or ask Miss Worcester, if she goes to Brighton, to see that there is no lack of mittens, clothing for this northern climate, I mean suitably provided until her arrival here, and I will be responsible, as also for her necessary expenses after her arrival in Boston." On the fifth of April, Ann Eliza was in Boston, but had not yet started on her journey to St. Johnsbury, since as yet no one had been found in whose company she might travel. "We have thought," her uncle wrote anxiously, "that if some one could be found who would have the kindness to take charge of her upon the railroad, *and see her and her baggage safely transferred to the Haverhill stage at Concord,* she would probably not meet with any difficulty afterward, and, on the whole, we think it best to refer it to her own choice, to stay at Brighton, perhaps there 3 weeks, waiting till some of the merchants shall go down from this vicinity, or to come on alone, provided such company can be found for her to Concord. I regret that she did not come on the first of this week, as the traveling must soon be very bad. N.B. Leaving Boston in the morning (earliest train) of Monday, Wednesday or Friday, she will arrive here the evening following." Eliza, born and bred in a mission among the Indians, was learning now about the

New England proprieties regarding young ladies, and about New England winters and spring thaws.

In the family of John Worcester, and among the members of the Board in Boston, Ann Eliza was accepted as readily and made a place for herself as naturally as she had at Park Hill. Her teacher, Mr. James K. Colby, found her so apt in her studies that he felt more joy than responsibility in teaching her; and David Greene saw in her all that he had hoped to see in the daughter of Samuel and Ann Worcester. When word came to the Board, then, that the health of Miss Avery, the teacher at Park Hill, had failed, the Board solved the difficulty by appointing Ann Eliza, who was to begin her work as soon as she had sufficient schooling at St. Johnsbury. In October, 1846, David Greene wrote to Samuel, "We will be ready to forward your daughter as soon as she may be ready & there may be an opportunity with suitable company. We had expected that a Mr. Strong & wife, with some female teachers, would go to the Choctaws, & one for Dwight would start about the first of November; but it is now uncertain whether Mr. Strong will be ready at that time, & possibly not at all. The female teachers are not all obtained yet, and we are not sure that we shall find them immediately. We shall probably find company in Mr. Loughbridge or somebody else, before January."

Meanwhile, Ann Eliza was making a conscientious effort to learn all that New England might offer her, to be taken back to the school that she was now appointed to teach, and to serve her generally in all her undertakings among the Indians. There was never any question in her mind about her return to them; she had no other thought than that of going on in the work that her father and mother had undertaken. In April, 1846, she wrote to

David Greene from St. Johnsbury, asking him to suggest any preparations that she ought to make, before her return to Park Hill. Especially, she asked "whether you think it would be best, or would particularly add to my usefulness, to visit schools around you, particularly a normal school, before my return." Her father wrote also to David Greene to say that, when Ann Eliza came to Boston, before setting out for the west, she was to look for some musical instrument that would be suitable for her, and to spend, if necessary, as much as fifty dollars on the purchase. "If she is disposed," Samuel suggested, "she will examine the guitar, accordion, melodeon, seraphine, and perhaps others."

Mr. Greene had already made some inquiries about instruments, at the time when he bought and shipped, at Samuel's request and expense, a tenor viol for the little boys, Leonard and John. But as to an instrument suitable for a young lady and durable enough to give service in that remote country, he wrote Samuel, "I am quite at a loss. I have inquired at a music store and of one of our musical professors, but get nothing very satisfactory. They say a guitar is the best, but that you object to. The Accordion is, with some good sounds, barren & limited in its range, and very liable to get out of order. What are called very good instruments can be purchased for $15. The Melodeon, an instrument of the same general character, is larger & has more compass, being about 20 or 24 inches long, 10 or 12 wide, & perhaps 5 high, as it lies on a table before the performer. The keys are arranged and played like those of the organ, while the pressure of the arm on the top supplies the wind. The tones very much resemble those of the accordion, and the liability to get out of tune is not very great. I am told that there is no great difficulty in repairing or tuning either. There is another instrument called the Seraphine, about 3 feet long, 18 inches wide, & 9 or 10 high, which stands or lies like a small piano. The foot of the performer works a horn which supplies the wind. This is a better instrument than the former, but is not 'portable' in the sense in which I suppose you mean. The cost is something like $50. That of the melodeon is about $30." They settled the question, when Ann Eliza reached Boston, by calling in the services of Mr. Lowell Mason; and in the end they chose a seraphine, that was packed and shipped to Park Hill. Ann Eliza's daughters, in their later lives—one of them even yet—remember their mother's playing on her seraphine and singing to its accompaniment. "Every night, until she was too frail to walk to her instrument, she played and sang. In the latter days of her life, she had a square piano," her daughter Ann Augusta recalls out of a past that began in 1851. "But I remember the seraphine, before that. Grandfather learned to play it, too, for he could not resist any musical instrument that might be at hand."

By December, 1846, the company who were to go to the Indian Missions of the southwest were gathered together, preparatory to sailing for New Orleans on the ship *Louisa*. Ann Eliza wrote to David Greene from New York, where they were to embark, a letter full of details about the journey and of the solemnity which a school girl about to undertake her first duties as a teacher would feel:

"NEW YORK, Dec. 11th, 1846.
Rev. David Greene
DEAR FRIEND,
    "I have just received yours of the 11th & in compliance with your request that I should write you from

N.Y., I sit down immediately to write as I shall not probably have another opportunity if I delay longer. But it is now 10 o'clock P.M. & I remember you did not think it well for me to sit up much later when I was with you, so I know you will excuse a short & hasty letter.

"How sad the death of Dr. Armstrong must be to you. It is felt here exceedingly. I do hope the dispensation may be blessed to the missonaries of the Board everywhere. I have not yet been in to see Mrs. Armstrong, but hope to call tomorrow.

"I met Mr. and Mrs. Loughbridge & Miss Dickinson at Northampton Monday, 7th, & went with them to South Hadley, where we spent the night. Next day went to Springfield, had the luggage marked for New York, & Mr. Loughbridge having been told wrong with reference to the cars, we sat in the Ladies' Room there for a few minutes, when we found what had happened. So we spent that night there, & next day came here. Mr. L. went to Mr. Lowrie's & we (Miss D. and I) came here where Mr. and Mrs. Merwin have been kind as could be to us. So we have been kindly provided for notwithstanding our feeling a little homesick at first, on being separated from our company and left among entire strangers. Miss D. has made up her mind to be reconciled to going by sea, & Monday at 12 o'clock we expect to sail for New Orleans. We dread the voyage, as coming through the Sound made us somewhat seasick, & so let us know what we should have to make up our minds to endure. Miss D. was told by a sister of Mr. Strong, who was in the cars with us, on her way to attend her brother's wedding, that he was to be married, & leave the latter part of next week. Such would make him follow us very soon. But even in that case we take it for granted you would think best for Miss D. to go in our company, & she prefers it to that of strangers. She has been looking to hear from you, but has not received the letter which you mention having written, in yours to me. Her mother feels rather unwilling to have her go by sea, but they have both concluded to assent cheerfully to what seems best. Whether Miss James has come today or not I do not know. I think I shall be very happy in my company, as, so far, I am much pleased with Miss D., and Mr. and Mrs. L. I shall of course be happy with, (that is, if I am not too seasick to enjoy anything.)

"I hope I may not in the confusion of preparation for the journey itself forget the weight of responsibility which rests upon me, and bring dishonor upon the cause in which I am engaged. May I not ask now & then to be remembered in your prayers, that it may be indeed for the glory of God that you with the others have seen fit to accept me as laborer in such a work. I wanted to ask when with you, but did not think of it in the right time, whether any of your children had become hopefully pious. I should be very glad to hear about it.

"I should be glad to have 2 prs. more of shoes purchased for me, to be sent on in the spring with our supplies, as I fear I may not have a sufficient supply to last until a year from next spring. Mrs. Greene will tell you where I purchased some that were just right, & the shopkeeper may remember the number. I do not, but think he sells but one number higher. And if I should have my Daguereotype taken, & left to be sent to you, could you not some time get it to

Uncle John, either by giving it to Pres. Wheeler, or to Uncle Isaac? If you could, it would be a great favor.

"Now I have written quite a long letter & must close. Please give a great deal of love to Mrs. G. & tell her I shall often think of her. I should have been very glad to call on Mrs. Evarts if I had had time, & don't know but I ought to now, on Father's account. Please give much love to all your children, to Mr. and Mrs. Anderson, & Mrs. Hill. Will it be too much to ask you now & then, when I reach the Indians, to read & answer a letter from me? If not, I should be very glad to receive letters sometimes from you, though but short ones.

Your affect. friend,

Ann Eliza"

The *Louisa* sailed for New Orleans on the sixteenth of December, with the company of missionaries and teachers bound for the Indian country aboard. Ann Eliza had added to her luggage some items ordered hurriedly by her father and including:

"1 Truss for umbilical hernia. The patient is a large woman, and the Hernia a little to the left of the navel.
1 pair silver mounted spectacles. Good glasses—focus 12 inches.
1 last Triennial Catalogue of Andover Theological Seminary."

In spite of their misgivings, the voyage must have been a fairly comfortable one, for there were no reports of ill effects from it. Judging from her father's letter, Ann Eliza made the journey more satisfactorily that did the seraph-ine: "Ann Eliza arrived safely Feb. 6. She commenced teaching March 1, and her school is pretty well filled. . . . . Our third daughter, Hannah, made a profession of religion, and was received to the church, Feb. 7th. A black man, a slave, was received at the same time. . . . .

"Our supplies arrived some weeks since, & the musical instruments with them. We like the seraphine very well, if it will only prove durable. Its tone is very pleasant, and harmonizes well with the voice. Its case is slender, and was broken some in consequence of not being packed to suit the rough handling which such things *will* have on the southwestern rivers, in spite of 'This side up with great care,' written on the lid. I could beat the Boston folks in packing such articles."

And now, with Ann Eliza returned and at work in the mission school, Sarah must be sent east. She had set her heart on going to the school founded by her mother's classmate, Mary Lyon; indeed, the renown of Mount Holyoke Female Seminary in those early days of the higher education of women made its doors the goal of many an ambitious young woman. Jokesters not in sym-pathy with Miss Lyon's religious and moral ideals in education had called her institution a "missionary rib factory," because of the number of its graduates who became the wives of foreign missionaries. But the ideals of Mount Holyoke suited the Worcesters; Samuel's mis-givings about sending Sarah there were wholly of a prac-tical nature. "Hitherto," he explained, "we have kept her back, partly through fear of consumption, to which we have thought her a little predisposed. She is *perhaps* less so now. She is past 17 years of age. She is a member of our church, pious we hope, and desirous to do good, and of tolerable capacities for acquiring knowledge; though we have not thought her quite so well fitted by nature to exert an influence as Ann Eliza. Her means, say $230, would keep her in school a little while, if there. But going and coming, at her own expense, would nearly consume the whole. If we should yield to her wishes, what would the Prudential Committee think it right to do?"

The Prudential Committee, not lacking evidence of the value of training Worcesters for their work at Park Hill, considered Sarah a safe risk. "As to your daughter," they replied, "she can come here at the expense of the Board, and receive $50 a quarter for three years, or even more if you desire it, and it shall seem at the time desirable. Therefore make your plans as you think will be most for your daughter's welfare and usefulness."

In the spring of 1847 Sarah set out from Park Hill for South Hadley, Massachusetts. Her niece, Miss Alice Robertson, has left a typescript of what she calls a "retained copy" of Sarah's account of her journey.

"The thirtieth of April arrived—the day upon which I expected to bid adieu to my prairie home, and the loved ones there to be absent perhaps for years. I had hoped that the weather would prove unfavorable and thus my departure would be delayed for one day at least, but the morning was clear and beautiful. After a sorrowful breakfast, and a tearful parting from my brothers and sisters, I mounted my horse, and in company with a lady who was to be my companion in travel, rode away. My father and mother followed in the carriage which was to convey my trunks. After riding for two miles and a half in the open prairie, we ascended a hill, from the summit of which, I beheld my father's house for the last time. Our place of destination was a mission station thirty miles distant. After a tedious journey of fourteen hours we who were on horseback arrived, after having lost our way and wandering in the woods for two hours with nothing but the light of the moon to guide us. At this station we remained for three days, during which we attended a communion service, and saw three Cherokee Indians baptized, and admitted to the church. Tuesday morning I parted from my father and mother with a heavy heart, not knowing whether I should meet them again. Another horseback ride of twentyfive miles brought us to Fort Smith which is directly across the dividing line between the Cherokee Nation and Arkansas. It was built to *protect defenseless frontiers* from the *hostile attacks* of the Indians. From this place our horses were taken back and we were left to await the arrival of a boat. Whilst we were there troops were training in preparation for the Mexican War. After a delay of one day we went on board a steamboat bound for Little Rock, where we arrived on Friday afternoon. We remained here over the Sabbath, and on that account were compelled to wait nearly a week, for the western steamboats almost invariably run upon the Sabbath. Little Rock—the capitol of Arkansas—would scarcely be called a village in New England. The inhabitants are much more intelligent than the people of Arkansas in general. The places of interest which we visited were the Arsenal, the Masonic Hall and several beautiful gardens. In one of these, a lady had just gathered a half bushel of strawberries. This was on the 5th of May. The Presbyterian, Methodist, Baptist, Episcopalians and Roman Catholics each have their respective churches in Little Rock.

"Thursday we took stage for Rock Row upon the banks of the White River. Fourteen miles of our way lay through an open prairie. The passengers were very agreeable, and on the whole we had a delightful ride. After dark we were obliged to travel in the rain for several miles. Myriads of fire flies danced among the tree tops and along the edge of the prairies gladdening us by their light, and making the darkness appear less gloomy. At ten o'clock we had eaten our supper and were on board the 'Flatchee Planter' bound for Montgomery's point, at the mouth of the White River. There we were set on shore to await the arrival of another boat. The houses at this place were few and insignificant, and from the surrounding swamps thousands of mosquitos swarmed around us, 'sounding the small horror of their bugles' horns,' so that we were compelled to make a smoke and gather round it with bushes in our hands to drive them away. We were greatly rejoiced when a boat came along about noon and bore us from their region. Our next stopping place for the Sabbath was Memphis, Tenn. This is a large and flourishing town, and is situated upon a high bluff so that the overflow of the Mississippi cannot reach it. It is a very pleasant place, and the inhabitants are kind and hospitable. We did not visit the 'Lions' of the place nor were we even told whether there were any. Monday morning found us on board the 'Belle of the West' on our way to Cincinnati. The scenery along the banks of the river was beautiful. The majestic oaks and lofty sycamores clothed with the liveliest green added new charms to all around. Everywhere rugged cliffs and precipices, hills and mountains met our eyes, and now and then a quiet village looking out from amongst the trees invited us to go on shore and pursue our journey no farther. On Tuesday we left the noble waters of the Mississippi and entered the mouth of the Ohio. On Wednesday we passed through the canal at Louisville which was the first I had ever seen. Although it was ten o'clock at night, most of the passengers were on deck to see that the boat passed through in safety. One tall portly dame leaning against the door between the gentlemen's and ladies' cabins pushed it open and fell with such force as to shake the whole boat. We all gathered round her, but finding no bones broken, enjoyed a hearty laugh at her expense. We were heartily rejoiced when we found ourselves again upon the open river for our ears had been constantly pained by oaths and curses from the men on shore.

"On Friday we arrived at Cincinnati and there we spent a pleasant Sabbath. A goodly number of ministers had gathered there to a meeting of the General Assembly, and we were permitted to hear excellent sermons delivered by able and eloquent men. Cincinnati is the largest city in the Western states, and was the largest place which I had ever seen. I found it hard to keep my eyes and hands in place and my tongue still, but I remembered that I must not do in the city as I would do on the prairie. The people in the streets gazed at me most unmercifully and I was upon the point of flying into a passion, when fortunately I remembered that I was rather tall, and thus the mystery of their extreme impoliteness was solved.

"Monday morning we left Cincinnati for Pittsburg. Our boat was small and very crowded so that the passengers in both cabins were compelled to sleep upon the floor for want of state rooms. There were a number of Baptist ministers on board who collected us together for morning and evening devotions. The accommodations of this boat were very poor, but the company was excellent. . . . .

"On Wednesday night our boat raced with another—

the Prairie Bird—during the whole night. There was great excitement among the passengers. The ladies sprang from their state-rooms and ran upon deck in their dressing gowns, begging the captain to desist, but all to no purpose. The boats came so near together that their decks rubbed several times. I slept soundly during the whole time, and of course knew nothing of the whole affair until it was all over. Then we had left the Prairie Bird far behind, but while we were at dinner, we heard her whistle of defiance as she shot proudly past us. The river was very shallow during this part of our journey. We woke one morning and found the engine puffing and blowing furiously and the boat rolling from side to side in vain efforts to push herself off from a bar of sand upon which she had struck during the night. After struggling for half an hour, she succeeded in freeing herself, and we proceeded on our journey. A boat which we passed a few hours after was less fortunate. She was lying upon a beach several yards from the water, and it seemed likely that she would be compelled to remain there for some time. The western steamboats were very different in their structure from those which travel upon Long Island Sound and the Hudson River. The three decks are entirely above the water. The lower deck is used as a storeroom, kitchen, work-room, and to accommodate those passengers who are unable to pay the full price for their passage. The middle or Promenade-Deck, leads into the gentlemen's and ladies' cabins. The staterooms are all in this part of the boat. These, too, are different from the staterooms upon the eastern boats. Each room is furnished with a wash-stand, wash-bowl, pitcher, and mirror, while there are two berths in each, one of which is sometimes wide enough to accommodate two persons. There are two doors to each room, one of which leads into the cabin, and the other to the deck. It is very pleasant to go upon the upper or hurricane deck in the evening, and see the sunset amid floods of purple and gold, whilst the trees and precipices seem all on fire, and the river dances and sparkles as if a hundred suns were floating upon its surface. But to return to my journey.

"On Friday evening we arrived at Pittsburg, and from there we went immediately to Brownsville, where we arrived early the next morning. Here we took a stage to cross the Alleghany Mountains. There were five [?] passengers besides ourselves. A Quaker and his lady, and two young ladies with their aunt and father. From the summits of the mountains we had delightful views of the surrounding country. The villages which we had left but a few hours before lay far far below us, appearing in the distance like so many little models in a toy-shop. The sides of the mountains were covered with evergreen shrubs, and early spring flowers, whilst here and there a grape vine with its clustering foliage hung over us, as if inviting us to rest beneath its refreshing shade. It was night before we descended the last mountain, and midnight came upon us before we reached our resting place for the Sabbath. We were heartily rejoiced to find when we reached Cumberland, Md., that we were to spend the Sabbath there. The young ladies in our company seemed very desirous of attracting the attention of the gentlemen. They regretted that as yet, none excepting barkeepers and clerks, had paid them any particular attention. They were on their way to Washington, with the design of spending the summer there.

"Monday morning we left Cumberland for Philadelphia in the cars. They were the first cars which I had ever seen, and I was afraid of losing my head every time that we passed through a tunnel or over a bridge. The scenery along the road was wild and beautiful. Now we passed through the very heart of a steep hill, and then shot through a tunnel cut out in the solid rock. At one moment we would find ourselves surrounded by jagged rocks, and frightful precipices, and at the next a beautiful and fertile plain would come suddenly upon our view. Beautiful torrents came tumbling and foaming down the sides of the mountains and over the rocks and cliffs, forming many a miniature waterfall. We stopped at Harper's Ferry so much celebrated for its beautiful scenery, but as I did not leave the cars I saw nothing that was worth noticing.

"We took supper in Baltimore after dark, and arrived in Philadelphia at half past three in the morning. We left the city in the cars at half past six and were soon in Newark, N.J. Here we took a boat for New York where we arrived about noon. We spent two or three days visiting the chief places of the city. I need not stop to describe the magnificent churches with their towering steeples, the busy streets, the lofty buildings, and the extensive parks with their beautiful fountains, for you have all either seen them yourselves, or read more glowing descriptions, than any which I can give. In the museum we saw all manner of beasts, birds, fishes, insects and petrefactions. At the City Hall we found the table upon which the Declaration of Independence was signed, and the original Declaration, and also Washington's writing desk.

"Friday morning we left New York to cross the Sound, on board a steamer bound for New Haven. From New Haven we went to New Britain, Conn., where we spent the next Sabbath amongst our friends. The hook and eye establishment here is well worthy of notice. It is curious to see a machine draw in a piece of wire, clip it off at the required length, flatten it, bend it into the right shape, and lay it into a box.

"On Monday we left New Britain, and went to Monson, Mass., where we spent a week in visiting. Another week was spent in like manner at Northampton, and then I came to take up my abode there, just six weeks and three days from the time I left home. A room was given me in No. 5 Fourth Story, where I passed six weeks and three days more, which seemed as many months. I thought the climate of New England was very cold, and that the hearts of its inhabitants partook of its nature, and oftentimes I wished myself at my own home in the Western Prairie. I had heard much about happy New England, but why it was so called, I could not imagine. My feelings have changed in that respect. I have found many a warm heart hidden beneath a frozen exterior, and when I am called to return to my early home it will be with feelings of sadness that I leave 'New England's happy shores.'"[2]

So it was that Sarah journeyed from Park Hill to South Hadley and established herself in Miss Lyon's school. For her mother's sake, and because she was the daughter of missionaries, she must have found a special welcome there; and by her diligence and studiousness—in spite of her tendency sometimes to "fly into a passion"—she found that initial welcome extended during her three years' stay. In her senior year Sarah's course of study included "Playfair's *Euclid* finished, Wood's *Botany* continued, Hitchcock's *Geology*, Paley's *Natural Theology*, Upham's *Mental Philosophy* in two volumes, Whatley's *Logic*, Wayland's *Moral Philosophy*, Butler's *Analogy* and Milton's *Paradise Lost*." In addition, a note accompa-

2   MS (copy) in the Alice Robertson Collection, University of Tulsa, Tulsa, Oklahoma.

nying the course of study explains that, "All the members of the school attend regularly to composition, reading and calisthenics. Instruction is given in vocal music, in linear and perspective drawing, and in French. Those who have attended to instrumental music have the use of a piano a few hours in each week."[3]

When, in 1850, Sarah returned to Park Hill, she was well prepared to teach what the Cherokees wanted their young women to learn in the Female Seminary at Park Hill. She became assistant principal, and in that office she had occasion to employ among her own pupils much of what she had learned from the lips of Mary Lyon and the assistant teachers at Mount Holyoke. She remembered, and taught, that "the young lady who will leave a spoon out of place, or drop a dipper where she may chance to use it, can hardly expect to have a great deal committed to her." Also, "The manner of sitting affects a recitation very much; leaning and lolling are very foreign to literature;" and, "It is said, and I think justly, that a lady is known by her table manners." So the standard of decorum for young ladies at Mount Holyoke became the standard for those at the Cherokee Female Seminary; Park Hill was near to South Hadley in ideals, though it was distant a month's journey geographically.

With Sarah at home again, Leonard had his turn at study in New England; before Leonard's return John, too, was sent east. And to each of the children, wherever he might be, there was a steady flow of letters from Park Hill, written in Samuel's hand with a care that was almost fastidious. He gave his children, in every letter, a sense of their special importance to him; kindliness, a fatherly

3 Beth Bradford Gilchrist, *The Life of Mary Lyon* (Boston: Houghton, Mifflin, 1910), p. 440.

interest in each child's problems, the small news of Park Hill and the large concerns of the world, filled closely written pages. Such a letter was one that Samuel wrote to John, who was in Vermont in 1855. John was sensitive, gifted in music to a marked degree, and delicate in health. This letter from his father must have heartened the discouraged, homesick boy of seventeen.

"PARK HILL, July 9, 1855.

MY DEAR SON, JOHN,

"I have received two letters from you written at St. Johnsbury. I deferred answering the first, till I should get the second.

"I am sorry that you have such a trial in regard to your health, but I hope you are better by this time. Leonard, I think, was troubled very much as you have been, before he went to Vermont, but has recovered his health there, it seems, and it was my hope that it would be so with you. I did not expect you to recover health rapidly, but I hope you will by degrees. To be sure if you cannot get so as to be able to study, it would be better that you were at home, but I still hope you will find it better for you to be where you are.

"As to your homesickness, I suppose I am the less able to sympathize with you from the fact, that I never was homesick in my life—no, not for an hour, that I have any recollection of. But if you get better in other respects, I presume your homesickness will wear away. It is a disease which I think time commonly cures. So, as to that, take courage, and expect to be well.

"As to that business of sitting an hour at a time wondering whether you can go through college or not, that is among the worst things you could set about.

[287]

Better be doing almost anything else, that is not morally wrong. If that were a question, the question whether you can go through or not, which you had now to decide, like a sum in Arithmetic, which is given you for a present task, it would then be well for you to go at it, and cipher it out. But that is among future things which you cannot cipher out; and when you have studied an hour, you are no nearer the answer than when you began. All you have to do now is, to go on while you can, and if you can,—do towards it what you can,— and leave the uncertain future for the future to decide. When I was on my way to college—I mean while I was preparing—a question arose about the *means*. Whether I could get them, or not, I could not tell. But I gave myself no trouble about it, but just concluded that I would go ahead, till I came butt up against a wall, which I could neither dig through nor climb over, and then I would stop. Just so do you. Do not look forward into the mist to try to descry whether what you see, or seem to see, is such a wall, or not, but go ahead as if there could be none, till you come right butt against it. Perhaps it will keep moving on before you, like a chased rainbow (only not so pretty); but however that may be, just let it alone, till you come to it.

"When I say, leave the future for the future to disclose, I do not mean to *deify* the *Future*. I mean that you should leave it for Him to disclose who orders the future as the present. I mean as Jesus said—'Take no thought (be not anxious) for the morrow, the morrow shall take thought for the things of itself. Sufficient for the day is the evil thereof.' Nor do I mean that you should have no desire for the future. I mean that you should 'Be careful (anxious) for nothing: but in every thing by prayer and supplication, with thanksgiving, let your requests be made unto God.' Paul says, if you do this, the consequence will be, that 'peace of God, which passeth all understanding, shall keep your heart.' Leave, then, that studying about the future, and attend to present duty.

"As to your health,—the present care of it, I will write to your Uncle Ezra, and he will let you know if he can receive you; and if he can, and if you are still not much better, and Mr. Colby thinks it best, you may go and put yourself under your Uncle's care, and return again to St. Johnsbury when he thinks it will do, if no other different arrangements can be made.

"I have been reading Sarah's letter to you, and approve what she has written respecting Mr. Colby. You have not sufficiently tried him. You looked, too, I presume, for what you had no reason to expect. You were not to look for a companion, but for a *guardian*.

"Whether your purchases were judicious or not, I cannot tell; but you should have gone to Mr. Colby for advice, and not have made the purchases yourself, nor with Leonard, unless he said so.

"Respecting Leonard's plan for you and him to board yourselves, I will write more to him, and you can read it.

"Sarah wishes you to go to Uncle Isaac. From what I have learned I think it very doubtful whether he could take you; but I cannot tell what may be hereafter.

"Your knife was found in one of your pockets. I credit you 50 cts. for it.

"Let us hear often from you.

YOUR AFFECTIONATE FATHER"[4]

4 Letter in the private collection of Mrs. N. B. Moore, Haskell, Oklahoma.

If homesickness is, as Samuel wrote his son, a disease that time commonly cures, it is also a disease to which the greatest hearts are immune. Samuel was one of these. He carried within himself all that he required for his own serenity and happiness. The assurance with which he lived sprang from sources far deeper than those of circumstances or possessions or events; it was the assurance of a perfect faith. Away from him at school, his children missed a greatness of presence which they had heretofore taken for granted, having always possessed it in their father, and they came to look in his letters for a reassurance of this presence. They learned from him, even while they were away from home to learn from others.

The Fruits of Long Labors

SOMETIMES, as he grew older, Samuel Worcester indulged himself in reminiscences. He recalled that hope of swift—it seemed to him now almost instantaneous—evangelization of the Indians that had been the expectation of the American Board; he held now, out of the wisdom of years of experience and knowledge of practical problems, a kind of tolerant amusement toward this conception of Indian Christianization. He had read the reports of the Board during its early years, and he remembered that, as early as 1816, there had been mention of efforts that had been "frustrated, or impeded, by causes utterly beyond the power of the Committee to control." Then, in those impatient years, the Board had barely begun its work ; when it set forth its aim "gradually, with the Divine blessing to *make the whole tribe English in their language, civilized in their habits, and Christian in their religion*," it had still some of the impatience of immediate accomplishment. Samuel, too, had been impatient when he first came out to the Indians; he had not dreamed, when he dreamed of saving the souls of the Indians, of the complexities involved in the undertaking. Now he knew that to evangelize the Indians meant to teach them a way of life, and that this teaching was a long, slow process. He in his own lifetime might see little more than the beginning of it. A good beginning, he had learned, was all that one generation of laborers might hope to accomplish. Whenever any substantial evidence of the good beginning presented itself, he was deeply and humbly grateful. To see the feet of the Indians set in the right direction, not to see the journey accomplished, was now his hope. Slowly, surely, patiently—only so was the work of the Lord accomplished. He could smile now, when he remembered how little the young Samuel Worcester who had set out to the Cherokees in 1825 had known of these things. Ann, he realized now, had probably understood these things better than he, because she was a woman; he felt a certain quick poignance, therefore, whenever he had some gratifying evidence of progress, in the fact that Ann was not there to share it with him. But he always checked the emotion; his heaven was one where Ann learned and rejoiced in all such events, and understood them with more than human understanding.

As years went on and the Cherokees became more accustomed to this new country of their compulsory adoption, there were more and more frequent evidences that the Cherokees were learning a way of life that could be measured by New England standards. These standards, by some leap of logic that never disturbed Samuel, remained in his mind the only ones by which to measure material or spiritual progress. There was no doubt that, for the Cherokees, no better way of life could be found; a conquered people, they could now best preserve their integrity by adopting and excelling in the way of life of their conquerors. The great admixture of white blood among them made this even more true of them than of other Indian tribes, who had intermarried less with white people.

As early as 1840, some fundamental change in the direction Samuel hoped for had begun. Mooney, writing of this new period in his *Myths of the Cherokee*, describes what was taking place. "For many years the hunter and warrior had been giving place to the farmer and mechanic, and the forced expatriation made the change complete and final. Torn from their native streams and mountains, their council fires extinguished and their town houses burned behind them, and transported bodily to a far distant country where everything was new and strange, they were obliged perforce to forego the old life and adjust themselves to changed surroundings. The ballplay was neglected and the green-corn dance proscribed, while the heroic tradition of former days became a fading memory or a tale to amuse a child. Instead of ceremonials and peace councils we hear now of railroad deals and contracts with cattle syndicates, and instead of the old warrior chiefs who made the Cherokee name a terror—Oconostota, Hanging-Maw, Doublehead, and Pathkiller—we find the destinies of the nation guided henceforth by shrewd mixed-blood politicians, bearing white men's names and speaking the white man's language, and frequently with hardly enough Indian blood to show itself in the features."[1]

To Samuel Worcester, one of the most encouraging events was the reestablishment of the Cherokee newspaper. The new journal, designed to fill the purposes filled by the *Phœnix* in the old nation, was to be called the *Cherokee Advocate*. Like the *Phœnix*, it was printed in both English and Cherokee, and was distributed without charge to those who could not read English. William P. Ross, a nephew of the Principal Chief, was the editor, and the first issue appeared on September 26, 1844. For the printing, a press had been purchased by the Cherokee nation; for this

1 Bureau of American Ethnology, *Nineteenth Annual Report*, 1897-8, Pt. I, pp. 146-7.

paper, as for the *Phœnix*, the Board had made the necessary purchases in Boston. David Greene had looked after the business for John Ross, and had written the Chief of his satisfaction with the terms he was able to make.

"Jan. 17, 1843

John Ross, Esq.
DEAR SIR,
"You have here an invoice of the several articles purchased, packed, shipped, agreeably to your request, all of which will, I trust, be satisfactory. The freight to New Orleans is paid and all the articles have been insured here.

"As to the articles sent, let me remark that we felt peculiarly favored in obtaining such a press at such a price. The maker is regarded, I believe, as the best in the country, & the one sent you, is one he made as an extra piece of work & put it in his shop as a specimen. The printers here, whom I called to examine it, say that there is not a better press in the country. In putting it up you will need a very firm flooring, level, & without any spring or settling. The press must stand perpendicular, all supports bearing equally. Some care will be necessary in this. A good printer will understand it. As to type and furniture of all sorts, let me say, that with the aid of former catalogues & schedules, we have done the best we could, in using the judgment of the type foreman & my own; & I hope that all is sent which will be required to answer your object. If anything more is needed, please inform me, & it shall be sent with as little delay as practicable. As your paper was printed formerly on many different sizes, I was at a loss what size of paper to send you; & as I did not know what number you would print, I could not accurately decide on the number of reams necessary for a two years' supply. On this invoice you have 50 reams of book paper, 25 fine & 25 not so good, but as good as is used here for common books & pamphlets, also 150 reams for the newspaper. This, though having some black specks, is a strong & good paper for the price, & better than our common newspapers are printed on. In a day or two I shall ship 50 reams more, and 200 for the newspaper, which will suffice for two years, printing 800 each week. Should more be needed, we can, if early information be given, send it the coming spring, or after the river shall rise next fall. We have purchased all at the lowest cash prices, and on better terms, I believe, than we ever made any similar purchase before.

Very respectfully yours,

DAVID GREENE"

No one in the Cherokee nation welcomed the first number of the *Cherokee Advocate* with more enthusiasm than did Samuel Worcester. He believed that the nation's progress depended largely on the intelligence of its individuals, and that intelligence, he held, must be one informed through newspapers and periodicals. During his long years of absence from New England, he had not failed to keep himself—as the Yankees expressed it—"posted up"; he read, the New York *Observer* and the Boston *Recorder* regularly, and more local papers such as the *Vermont Chronicle* and the *Puritan Recorder* whenever they were available. Now, through the *Advocate*, the Cherokees might hope to become a nation of Indians who were "posted up"; the factions that still divided them and the personal enmities that embittered them might be erased through the common information and interest that a national newspaper would promote.

It was true, in spite of their union now under one constitution, that factions still prevailed among the Cherokees and threatened to undermine their efforts toward national unity. The assassination of the Ridges and Elias Boudinot had not been the end of violence among them; the sense of loss and wrong and injury, from one side or another, still rankled in many hearts. Only time and the most intelligent leadership could eradicate this. As late as 1846 disruption through old party enmities threatened the Cherokee Nation; in March of that year the chiefs of the tribe agreed upon a fast day, appointed for the sake of prayer and meditation on the matter of national unity.

It was only natural that at times Samuel Worcester himself should come under the disapproval of one or another of the parties. Any act of friendliness toward an individual might be interpreted as partisan by the enemies of that individual. Now and then embitterment and misunderstanding threatened to result in the removal of Samuel Worcester; his very impartiality worked against him, among a people still torn by intense personal hatreds and handicapped by irrecoverable personal losses. In 1843, such a threat occurred, as Samuel explained in a postscript to a letter to the Board. "I stated in my letter to Mr. Greene last week, that an effort had been made in one branch of the National Council to procure the passage of a bill to cause my removal from this place; and that the result was an indefinite postponement. I now learn that the vote was taken directly on the bill, and it was negatived by a majority of one only. Today a bill for the same purpose was introduced into the other house, and passed by a majority of four—13 to 9. It is now again before the other house, and will probably be acted on day after to-morrow,—perhaps not so soon. I think it will be negatived again; but I am led to fear that an influence is exerted in favor of it which I did not suppose; and I may be disappointed—or if it fails this year, it may be carried another. I will seek the welfare of this people while I can, and if they will not have me, I must try to do good elsewhere. I shall probably write to Mr. Greene again next week.

"I understand it was stated in a late Van Buren paper that all the missionaries were to be removed—a false report growing out of the attempt to remove me. It is also said in a still later number, and will probably 'go the rounds' that the Grand Jury of Washington Co. have found a true bill against the murderers of Maj. Ridge and also against Mr. Ross, as accessory. I am told that it is true respecting the first but not respecting Mr. Ross."

Dissensions, misunderstandings, retaliations! Samuel knew that only time and the Lord's will could heal them. Meanwhile, the threats against him subsided as unaccountably as they had arisen, and his unrelenting work went on. And John Ross, as principal chief, went on with the same imperturbability, in spite of accusations and threats against him; he was, as his combination of Scotch and Cherokee blood might guarantee and as David Greene wrote of him, no "man of straw." As to missionaries, Samuel knew that there were some grounds for lack of confidence in them. In spite of the high standards set by the Board and the precautions taken with regard to appointments, men of mean abilities had managed to be sent out and failures in other fields had been allowed a chance to fail again in the mission field. It was in complaint against such appointments that the Superintendent of the Western Territory wrote, in 1837, to the Indian Bureau, "The time has passed when men can be picked up in New England without talent, industry, energy, or the proper spirit, and sent among these tribes to be useful. . . . . It would be better for the societies, if they are compelled to support such men, to keep them at home, and not send them out to injure the cause they cannot help."[2]

It was because of such complaints, and the grounds on which they were based, that Samuel pleaded with the Board for missionaries of the highest quality to be sent to the Cherokees. The need was not for more men, but for more good men, of the highest abilities and training. David Greene wrote him, in 1841, explaining the difficulty of obtaining such men: "Your urgent plea for additional missionaries I have taken to Andover & placed in the hands of the missionary students there, accompanied with such statements & reasonings as I was able to add. The paper has been returned without anything being said in reply. To what it may lead I cannot say. I have some reason to fear that candidates for missionary employment have their minds so dazzled with the missions of China and some of the other southern Asiatic nations that they can hardly think or feel for a few thousand of Indians in danger of being exterminated." This, to Samuel, was a bitter truth to face. And another letter, two months later, gave no more encouragement: David Greene confessed that, after a search for nearly a year, only one candidate had been found. "Your letter," he explained, "has been shown to all the candidates at Andover, & I have pressed the subject on two or three who seemed most inclined to think of it. But the millions of people in India and the

2   Bureau of Indian Affairs, *Annual Report*, 1837, p. 565.

hundreds of millions in China, & the charm that seems to hang over Greece & western Asia, appears to have so dazzled the eyes of all the candidates for the missionary work, that the poor scattered remnants of Indians are deemed hardly worthy of a thought. Going to the Indians seems hardly worth the talents of any but very inferior men. I fear there is some pride in this."

Shameful human pride! Samuel wept and prayed over the situation. Once he hoped that his brother would come out from St. Johnsbury, and his prayers for assistance seemed about to be answered in this happy manner. But his brother's wife became ill, and the change seemed inadvisable. Not until 1854 did a man appear who had such qualifications as were needed to work among the Cherokees. He was Charles C. Torrey, in charge of a pastorate at Stowe, Vermont. They were, the Board wrote, "a feeble folk," and reluctant to lose so strong and valuable a man from among them; but his mind was made up, and no false pride or fear of adverse circumstances was to keep him back. Samuel's shoulders, wearying after years of lonely work, were to be eased of some their burden at last; and he had the deep comfort of knowing that a man had come among them who could carry on what he had begun, when the last of his own strength failed him. It was not that he was an old man, or that he meant to give up easily, but that he knew—from pain and lameness and great weariness—that the years of his activity were limited. Time pressed, and results were slow. It was a sweet assurance, to know that what he failed to complete would go on.

Yet in spite of lack of adequate help for many years, there were times when Samuel felt something like suprise at what was being accomplished among the Cherokees.

As early as 1841, the National Council passed an act creating the office of superintendent of education and providing for eleven public schools; this was years earlier than the date at which Horace Mann's efforts brought about the national Bureau of Education. In 1846, the Cherokee National Council created two institutions of higher learning, the Male and Female seminaries, to be located near Tahlequah and to provide a course of study equal to that provided by eastern institutions of the same kind. Since 1835, the foundation of these institutions had been John Ross' dream; when the two schools were opened, in 1851, Samuel Worcester amd John Ross both knew that the future of the Cherokees promised well. For the fact that it promised to develop in the direction of white civilization altogether, neither of them had any regrets. Today, among men and women of Cherokee blood, may be found the third generation of graduates of these two schools. They bear themselves nobly, talk fluently, live lives of culture and usefulness. In short, they justify this bold venture in education undertaken in 1846 by the Cherokee National Council. In 1854, F. S. Lyon, principal of the Male Seminary, sent to the Bureau of Indian Affairs his annual report. The courses studied, according to this report, were grammar, geography, arithmetic, algebra, physiology, Latin, geometry, natural philosophy, Greek, trigonometry. Composition, declamation, reading, writing, and spelling all received their share of attention. The course of study for the Female Seminary was similar, according to the report of the principal, Miss Pauline Avery, but with such differences as were necessary for the the development of womanly accomplishments. The aim of both schools was to make the students "wise and good." This was an aim that no school or college has yet exceeded, whatever its methods or its course of study or its equipment.

Samuel Worecester took no credit to himself for the advancement in educational matters now indicated among the Cherokees. Yet much of the credit was due to him and his family. He had lived among them since 1825, a scholar whose ways and principles were such that the Cherokees desired to emulate them. His children had grown up among the children of the Cherokees, sitting side by side with them in the schoolroom and in the Sabbath school; and his two daughters, after their schooling in New England, were to return to teach—Ann Eliza at Park Hill and Sarah in the Female Seminary at Tahlequah—until they married. To an outsider, it was not to be wondered at that the Cherokee Nation found the white man's way of education good; they had seen its proof through a period of years in the Worcester family. But Samuel himself had neither the time nor the point of view for wonderment. His tasks were multitudinous and his time for them was never sufficient; it was only when he came to such a milestone as an annual report to the Cherokee Agent that he could see any actual achievement as the result of his constant efforts. Student by student, the children in the several schools of the mission made a goodly total; soul by soul, the members of the several churches of the mission rose to a number not too small to afford encouragement; page by page, the publications of the Indian press counted up to a creditable sum of printing.

In his report for 1845, Samuel listed in detail the amount of printing done by the mission press for that year:

"In Cherokee

Treatise on Marriage 2d ed.
   20 pp. 24 to   5,000 copies 100,000 pages in all
Miscellaneous Pieces
   24 pp. 24to   4,000 copies 96,000 pages in all
Cherokee Primer 5th ed.
   24 pp. 24to   1,000 copies 24,000 pages in all
Epistle to Timothy
   28 pp. 24to   5,000 copies 140,000 pages in all
Cherokee Hymns 7th ed.
   69 pp. 24to   5,000 copies 345,000 pages in all
Cherokee Almanac for 1845
   36 pp. 12mo   600 copies 21,600 pages in all
                 ———————   ———————

              20,600 copies 716,600 pages

In Choctaw

Child's Book on Creation 2d ed.
   14 pp. 12mo   2,000 copies 28,000 pages in all
Bible Stories
   24 pp. 12mo   2,000 copies 28,000 pages in all
Character and Works of God
   30 pp. 12mo   2,000 copies 60,000 pages in all
The New Birth
   16 pp. 12mo   2,000 copies 32,000 pages in all
Sinners in the Hands of an Angry God
   28 pp. 12mo   2,000 copies 56,000 pages in all
I Will Give Liberally
   16 pp.   2,000 copies 32,000 pages in all
The Lord's Day
   4 pp.   2,000 copies   8,000 pages in all

Salvation by Jesus Christ
and other pieces 28 pp. 2,000 copies 56,000 pages in all

16,000 copies 320,000 pages

In Creek

Muskogee Hymns
48 pp. 24to   600 copies 28,800 pages in all

Total books and pamphlets 37,200. Total pages 1,065,400"[3]

More than thirty-seven thousand books and pamphlets! More than a million pages printed, whether or not Samuel's mathematics enabled him to count them exactly! When he summarized the year's output, Samuel could see that his Indian press was accomplishing something. Always he regretted that it was not accomplishing more; but he must preach sermons, administer to the sick, visit schools and congregations, make up financial reports, give freely of his time and hospitality to Indian and white friends alike. Perhaps, after all, the press had done well in the year 1845. Yet he must not be vainglorious. More might have been done; he must always be mindful of that. So Samuel tempered the glow of his report with a final sentence of humility: "I have not the happiness to report any manifest advancement of the cause of religion, in the neighborhood of this station, within the year past; not do I perceive any material change in the state of morals."

Year after year Samuel compiled his report for the Indian Bureau when it was called for, and in the process

3 Bureau of Indian Affairs, *Annual Report*, 1845, pp. 594-5.

[303]

summarized for himself the successes and the failures at Park Hill. Even in the worst years, he could never be completely discouraged; something always afforded him hope that the cause went forward, however slowly. Sometimes he was handicapped by want of sufficient aid from his translator, Stephen Foreman; sometimes the press was idle a part of the year for want of funds from the Board. But Samuel knew how to take a long view of things; eternity lay ahead of a report of one year's efforts. His report for 1853 summarizes the work of the whole Cherokee Mission for that year. The existence of four stations besides that at Park Hill, the building of a new church at his own station, the paucity of printing done by the press for that year—all are set forth with Samuel's honest forthrightness.

"Park Hill, August 30, 1853

Sir:

"The A.B. of C. for F.M. has still under its care, in the Cherokee nation, five stations—Dwight, Lee's Creek, Fairfield, Park Hill, and Honey Creek. At the last they could support a native preacher, Rev. John Huss, who has the pastoral care of a church at the station. At each of the other stations they have an ordained missionary, with a family, and a school taught gratuitously by a female missionary, Mr. Jacob Hitchcock and his wife. At Park Hill is a printing press, employed a portion of the time in printing books in the Cherokee language.

"Not having anticipated being called upon for a report except of my own station, I am not furnished with statistics as I might otherwise have been. Statistics of some of the churches I cannot give of recent date, on account of the failure of two successive meetings of which we missionaries should have communicated intelligence to each other.

"The pastor of the church at Dwight, Rev. Worcester Willey, has been absent in New England during the past year. His return is expected in the fall. I find that I have no report of the church of later date than May, 1852. It was then reported to contain fifty members. The school at that station, under the care of Miss Jerusha Swain, has been as flourishing as could have been reasonably expected among so sparse a population, having had, I believe, an average attendance of about 20 pupils, several of whom were boarded in the neighborhood at the expense of their parents or friends.

"The station at Lee's Creek is comparatively new, and the people have not had time to learn so well as at older stations the value of the blessings offered them, or the means of securing them. Rev. Timothy E. Ranney preaches the gospel among them. The infant church contains, I suppose, not more than ten members: the precise number I do not know. The school taught by Miss Julia F. Stone has as yet, I believe, been somewhat smaller than that at Dwight; but I am told that prospects are brightening, and that there is reason to expect a flourishing school. At Fairfield, which from the time of Dr. Butler's removal to the female seminary had been destitute of a resident minister of the gospel, the Rev. Edwin Teale had been stationed within the year. I have not for some considerable time received definite information of the number of members in the church at that place. The last number reported was 74. I suppose it has diminished since. The school at that place has been much smaller than the surrounding population

[305]

would lead us to expect. There is reason also to hope for much increase. The church at Park Hill, where I am located, contained fifty members less than a year ago. Our school, during the winter term, had thirty-one scholars in all, and an average attendance of twenty. During the last term the number was 38, and the average 26. Of the whole number during the year, 23 were boarded in the neighborhood at the expense of parents or friends—a circumstance which goes to show the prevailing desire among the Cherokees for the education of their children. It may be added that, after the school was judged by the teacher sufficiently full, about 25 applicants were rejected, almost all of whom, if received, would have had to pay for their board away from their homes.

"A new house of worship is in process of erection, built by subscription, and expected to cost about $1,600 of which the principal part has been subscribed, and a considerable portion paid. The building is of brick 50 feet by 44, with a portico of 10 feet, and will seat about 400 persons.

"In printing, during the past year, we have done but little. The whole amount is

In the Cherokee Language

Paul's Epistle to Timothy 3rd ed.

    24 pp. 24to   5,000 copies 120,000 pages

Epistles to Peter, 3rd ed.

    24 pp. 24to   5,000 copies 120,000 pages

Part of *Exodus* 1st. ed.

    48 pp. 24to   5,000 copies 240,000 pages

                                            ——————

                                         480,000

Almanac for 1853
  36 pp. 12mo   1,000 copies   36,000 pages
                                             ———
                                        516,000 pages

"I am sorry that my information is so imperfect; but it was too late, after the receipt of your letter, to procure more accurate intelligence.
Very respectfully yours,
S. A. Worcester[4]

Geo. Butler, Esq.
Ch. Agent."

One of the accomplishments which gave Samuel a sense of satisfaction was the publication, in Boston, of a singing-book for the Cherokees, in 1846. Whatever the nature of the gathering, singing had always been the means of making it a success in the minds of the Cherokees and of Samuel Worcester as well. Their voices were musical; their sense of rhythm was marked; their eagerness to sing was unfailing. For a long time Samuel had wished to provide them with a songbook that would teach them some of the rudiments of music in a simple manner suited to their understanding and give them the words and the music of the songs they sang. The *Cherokee Hymn Book*, giving words alone, was inadequate. But he had no musical type, and no compositor who could make use of it. The printing of music, the Board informed him, required a particular knowledge and skill that would scarcely justify the purchase of musical type for the Indian press. For years, then,

---

4 Bureau of Indian Affairs, *Annual Report*, 1853, pp. 384-6.

Park Hill contented itself with a copy of Mason's *Choir* for musical instruction, and with the hymns available in the *Cherokee Hymn Book*. But Samuel was not satisfied. He was failing to keep pace, musically, with the advancement which the Cherokees were making in other directions; he might lose his hold on a music-loving people if he failed them in this particular interest. The solution, he felt, was to compile his own singing-book, with explanations suited to the understanding of the Cherokees, and to have it printed at Boston. He had designed a pump, and written poetry, when he needed a pump and some poems; he could compile a music book, if one· that was suited to his needs could not be had otherwise.

In January, 1846, David Greene wrote him of the progress that was being made in printing this book. "Your singing book has been some time in the printer's hands and he has set up one &, I believe, two signatures, though only one proofsheet is received. The compositor has been hindered for some ten days past by a sore finger. He is now at work again. He is a remarkably correct & careful man. Mr. Mason will not have anyone else to set his music. This attribute of his is most opportune, so far as I am concerned, as at this time my eyes are in a state not to permit me to use them on any difficult work. Between the compositor and myself & Mr. Mason for the music, I trust we shall make the book tolerably correct.

"Mr. Mason thinks that your introduction & elements, judging, as he of course, must, from the examples, &c which you give, are not sufficiently simple, & that you undertake to teach too much for such a people. He also thinks you have not had access to the latest & best methods of teaching these introductory matters. Of your tunes he says that most of those you have selected from

Northern and Eastern books are pretty good, though as he thinks not the best adapted to the Cherokees. Of about 8 or 10 of those which you have obtained from other sources, he speaks with terrible severity as being bad and incapable of being mended. He says that he cannot conscientiously touch them or have any agency in bringing them out, &c—certainly not further than to see that the printer follows the copy. I laugh at him, tell him to do the best he can, & so he is to go on. These 'horrible' ones, he says, amount to only 8 or 10. Probably they are some of which the seed was sown in some western wild, & they grew up no one can tell how, till the ears then began to relish them & habit created attachment. I will send you a signature or two of the book soon."

Much correspondence was necessary to bring the *Cherokee Hymn Book* to completion, even after it was in the hands of the printer. In February, Samuel wrote his reply to what David Greene had said regarding the book. "I presume," he admitted, "that, if I were to go over my elements of music again, with Mr. Mason at my elbow, or even with such helps as he could present me with, I could simplify somewhat more. I first wrote with the introduction to the *Choir* for a basis, and then remodelled the whole, writing anew, with the Introduction to the Boston Academy's *Collection* as a basis, varying as I thought I could best manage in Cherokee; and taking some examples from other books, & from tunes, and making some myself. I tried beginning with notes without a staff, but concluded that I could manage best by placing them upon a staff at the outset. I dispensed with the use of the letters A B C D E F G. Habit would very probably make them seem to Mr. Mason indispensable; but it was very difficult to introduce them, with Cherokees who know

[309]

nothing of reading English, and are familiar with five of the characters under entirely different names—and the chief practical inconvenience in dispensing with them consists in the want of a common name for corresponding lines or spaces in the bass & other staffs. . . . .

"But to return. Nelson Chamberlin, who has taught music among whites, and whom Mr. Willey pronounces qualified, has been teaching a Cherokee Singing School for some time, using my rules in manuscript, and says that he finds no difficulty. His scholars do not speak English, and they readily understand the rules.

"Mr. Mason thinks I undertake too much. Perhaps so. The most difficult thing I undertook was to explain the reason of the use of flats and sharps in the transposition of the scale. That can be omitted by the teacher if he sees fit. But some will seek for it, and it will direct the teacher if an explanation is asked. It made plain to Mr. Foreman, when he translated it, what he had not understood before. . . . .

"So Mr. Mason thinks my backwoods tunes 'horrible.' If he will come here, and go to some meetings with me, I think I can introduce him to some which I think he would call *more* horrible. But however that may be, I think he need not let the idea of *bringing* them into use trouble his conscience at all. It would be hard to *bring in* what is *in* already. And as to *continuing* them in use, I think the admission of them into the book will rather tend to *bring them out* of use than to *keep them in*, because they will help to introduce the book, and the book will introduce better tunes, and the better tunes will supersede the 'horrible' ones. Especially the first teachers will hardly fail to manifest their partiality for the better tunes above the *wheelbarrow* tunes, as I have heard the others called.

"The selection of eastern tunes, I have already said, was made *mostly* by Mr. Willey. If I should have occasion to publish another edition, I shall desire Mr. Mason to give me a list of such as he would judge suitable."

Before the end of the year, in spite of difficulties of printing and differences of opinion as to its contents, the *Cherokee Singing Book* was in the hands of the Cherokees. In the new house of worship at Park Hill, the congregation received instruction in singing and then, on the Sabbath during worship, lifted their voices in praise to God. The church building had cost several hundred dollars more than Samuel had estimated, and the singing book had involved far more effort than he had anticipated. But song and church edifice alike lifted themselves to the glory of God. Even the "horrible wheelbarrow" tunes that Lowell Mason had condemned carried praise heavenward from the throats of the singing Cherokees.

Earthen Vessels

THERE was small danger of asceticism, among the missionaries sent out by the American Board. Least of all, perhaps, was there this danger in Samuel Worcester's life. However much the necessity of the Gospel lay upon him, other necessities would intrude themselves; never, even for a day, was he to be altogether free to devote himself to concerns of the other world, because of the imperative necessities of this. Could asceticism claim him, when the Cherokee Agent demanded an unexpected report of him for all the schools and churches of the Cherokee mission? Could the next world absorb his thoughts, when a sick Indian besought him for bodily relief in this?

Sometimes it was his own necessities that intruded themselves. There was, for instance, the matter of an overcoat. For years he had written to the Board explaining his need of a coat that was heavy and warm and large, and each time he had been sent one that was too fine, too small, and unsuited for wear on long rides astride a horse in storms of rain and wind. The winters might be generally mild, the skies generally blue, and the sun for the most part amazingly warm in the country of the Cherokees, but a missionary must be prepared for those exceptions of cold and wind and rain that were the less endurable because of their very infrequency. Since sore throat and rheumatic pains followed undue exposure, there was nothing for him to do but to write to the Board again and again, until he had the garment he knew he must have. "I have failed," he explained, "for two successive years to get an outer garment which would answer my purpose. Year before last, I wrote for an overcoat, describing it very particularly, and it came too short, and too fine and thin—the opposite, in these respects, of what I wished. Some years ago I had sent for a cloak, and got one which suited me except as to length, which I had to have eked out. I thought to get the like last year, only longer, and wrote very specifically, but it came not long enough by a foot, and quite too light and thin. But all this will be well enough, if I can only get suited at last; for I disposed of the coat to Mr. Foreman, and the cloak can be made to serve my wife; and by having my old cloak turned, I am making it serve these two years longer. But now I want a good, warm, large, long cloak, and if you will get one made for me, I will be truly thankful. It will be so unfashionable, I suppose, that it cannot be found ready-made. I think you are near enough to my stature, and I will thank you to have one made to reach your shoes, when wrapped around you. The outside may be camlet or the like, not of fine texture, but well spun and woven—the camlet of that you sent last year was well enough—and the lining of some woolen fabric, very thick and warm. Let it have a large cape, closing well before, and lined with flannel or baize, but not so heavy as the lining of the body of the cloak."

After this plea, he was sent a coat "to his mind," and he rode the long miles to Dwight and Lee's Creek and Fort Gibson in comfort, even when snow whirled across the hills or rain darkened the dry prairie grass. He wished that all of his practical problems might be as well settled, finally, as this one had been.

But some of these problems were perennial, and never to be settled for him. Money would always be a problem: appropriations would be uncertain in amount from one year to the next; accounts would be complicated and hard to keep; cash would be subject to loss and theft. Yet a mission, in the United States and among Protestants, could not operate by the biblical injunction, "neither gold, nor silver, nor brass in your purses, nor scrip for your journey." As long as the people he dealt with were common human beings, and as long as he himself failed to master his imperfections, deplorable incidents would occur, to his grief and inconvenience. "It was for want of consideration," he confessed very humbly after one such incident, "that I have had $10.00 stolen from me. I had counted out $60.00 and laid it on the mantle-piece in piles of $10.00 each, when I was called to another room, and stepped out, not considering that I left a man alone in the room with my money. Returning in a few moments, I observed that the man had stepped out, and that one pile of money was missing. I was confident I had left six piles, but not having proof enough to convict, I said nothing about it." So, in humility, Samuel charged himself with failure to act as a careful steward of money that was the Lord's and was committed to his keeping.

Constantly, Samuel was under the obligation to send the Board information that it chose to seek from him rather than from any other missionary among the Cherokees. He was known to the Board as a man of the soundest judgment combined with a saintly tolerance and sympathy. Whether it was a political disturbance, a complaint against a teacher or a fellow-missionary, a dispute over a translation, or a need of information about polygamy or slavery or intemperance, Samuel Worcester was the man who must be consulted. How he must weigh facts, after he had gathered them, how he must sift details and eliminate prejudices, in answer to some inquiry from the Missionary Rooms! "This will be *inter nos*," the Board would explain to him, and so demand of him a currying of the whole mission territory for information.

Once there was such a request for facts about a Mr. and Mrs. Covel who had gone as teachers to the Cherokees and who had been accused of strange beliefs and conduct. Samuel wrote judiciously, "I fear Mr. Covel has not ballast enough to sail well. He says he expects to remain in the nation till the end of the 'present dispensation,' i.e. till the personal appearance of Christ to reign on the earth, which is to take place between the commencement of 1843 and the end of 1858, if I recollect rightly. He quotes Professor Bush as a preacher of the second advent, in the sense of 'The Literalist.' Can that be so?"

The reply of the Board was scarcely the sort to simplify matters for Samuel, while the Covels remained as fellow-workers: "I am sorry that Mr. Covell does not promise fairer for usefulness; & still more sorry that he should have entertained such opinions as you mention about the end of the world, & not told us of them, when he knew that we feared he was liable to some such freakishness and doubted about sending him on that account. He is mistaken about Prof. Bush. He does not, as I understand him, believe in the personal reign of Christ on earth—does believe in substantially our millenium, though he thinks the period pointed out in Daniel & the Revelation is not it, &c. You and the Cherokees must make the best you can of him. He has no claim on very much forbearance, if he has deceived us on such points."

Later, when the Board proposed reëstablishing the Osage Mission, Samuel was consulted in advance as to the man who should have charge of it. He made plain, in his reply, what he considered were some essentials in a missionary and a missionary's wife. "Mr. Redfield would not do. He travels and allows his team to be driven on the Sabbath, is too worldly-minded, and has been too much in the habit of treating the Osages as a little below the human race, to do very much good among them. Nor is his wife better adapted to the work. . . . . Mr. R.'s wife is a Missouri woman, young, I suppose, compared with himself, and not of superior early advantages. She may be such as would be a valuable helper in missionary work, but I should want to hear more about her, before making the experiment. I do not know whether she is pious or not.

"It is a general objection to all these men that they have, I suppose, possessions not far from the borders of the Osage nation, which would be likely to occupy a share of their attention. And, as Mr. Wheeler says, they don't appear like *real Yankees*, and Osage missionaries ought to be real Yankees."

Whether we follow Samuel's logic or not, we can agree with his conclusion; Mr. Redfield would not have done. It is not recorded that the Worcester children, making their first religious inquiries, asked whether God was a Yankee; but it is to be suspected that they knew He was. As to Samuel, he had seen those virtues that he held most important in missionaries best represented in Yankees; he was demanding, for the Osages as well as for the Cherokees, the best he knew.

Strange characters, more than once, attempted to throw in their lot with that of the Cherokee Mission; strange waves of what, to Calvinists of New England descent, seemed fanaticism and heresy, swept over the surface that should have been calm. All Samuel's anxiety and caution could not always protect the mission from imposters, and when Mrs. Chamberlin arrived, in 1853, he was greatly disturbed for the welfare of Fairfield and Park Hill. "Mrs. Chamberlin, widow of Rev. William Chamberlin, former missionary with us," he said in one of his letters after her arrival, "is making a long visit to her son, near Fairfield station, who is as yet a member of this church and holds the office of Deacon. Unhappily, Mrs. C. has become a subject of the spirit-rapping delusion, and imagines herself to have received various communications from her deceased husband, and her father the Rev. Ard Hoyt, also formerly of the mission. She has been spending a month or more with our nearest neighbor, Mrs. Hoyt, who is her sister-in-law. Mrs. Hoyt and two daughters are also members of our church. Mrs. C. has been telling wonders to them, and to some others. I have trembled for them, but I suppose she has not yet convinced them that her necromancy is real, and good, and right. Whether or not she has in some measure influenced the mind of her son and daughter-in-law (who, by the way, is still another daughter of Mrs. Hoyt's and belongs also to our church,) I am not sure. I presented, last Sunday, a resolution to the church for adoption, to the effect that we would regard any member of the church, who should either pretend to act as a medium, or through any such pretended medium pretend to consult with the dead, as guilty of a disciplinable offence. The consideration of it is to be resumed next Friday night. I hoped that we should

[317]

anticipate any occasion for putting such a resolution in practice; but it is reported that a female member of the church has already become a medium. I hope it will prove a false report."

Weeks later, Mrs. Chamberlin was still a menace, as well as a financial burden. "I believe I sent you a resolution adopted by our church on the subject of modern necromancy," Samuel continued in his account of the difficulties which she caused. "Last Sabbath I preached on the same subject. As I had given notice several weeks beforehand, of my purpose to do so, curiosity brought the people together so that our house [you know it is small] was filled to overflowing, and they listened very patiently to a discourse about an hour and a half long. I hope it will have an influence in fortifying the minds of the people against imposters, if any of that class should undertake to perform their miracles among us, as it is not unlikely they may do. They have been some time at Van Buren, doing wonders. Mrs. Chamberlin has not done much. She has tried in vain to move tables, as she used to do at Alton. She has written a little, imputing it to the spirit of her husband, but not much. The last communication to her, I understand, was that he would make no more communications to her, until the offence was past; which last expression she says she did not understand until I conversed with her, and then concluded that that must be the 'offence' perhaps.

"When Mrs. Chamberlin came to visit her sister-in-law, Mrs. Hoyt, with an adopted daughter, she sent her horses to me, with a request that I would keep them for her. Her son had proposed to send for her horses, but she said they would want to ride about some, and she would not hesitate to ask Mr. Worcester to keep them a little while,—an old brother missionary so. I did not quite convince myself of the duty of saying nay, and so she staid a month or more, and I fed her horses.

"I have an ox wagon, which cost fifty dollars, and my neighbors use it perhaps nearly as much as I (My wife and others think more than I), and sometimes money has to be paid for repairing it; and will, more and more, as it grows older, and when it is gone, and I have paid perhaps $80 including repairs, my neighbors will not *dream* that they are thirty or forty dollars in my debt on that account.

"I have also felt necessitated to purchase a small horse wagon, which with alteration has cost more than fifty dollars and within a year I must have a new harness for it; and that will go in the same way, and nobody will owe me anything for the use of it. In such ways as that a very large draft is made upon us in the course of a year,—the rule, 'Give to him that asketh thee, and from him that would borrow of thee turn not thou away,' proving, so far as cash is concerned, a very costly one to me."

What pettiness threatened to undermine a great undertaking! What a multitude of providential hindrances stood in the way of the translation of the Scriptures! How faulty were they all,—these earthly vessels that contained the excellence of God!

Samuel made no exception of himself, when he thought of the faults of these, the earthly vessels of the Lord. For however he prodded his weary body to accomplish what his mind desired of it, there were times when it failed to respond. Sometimes, now in his later years, his hand—that had written firmly and finely the family letters, the official letters, the copy for the press, the reports for the Board and the Government, the sermons and the proclamations, and the medical prescriptions that were asked of him—grew stiff and swollen; sometimes he resorted to a pencil when a pen seemed unmanageable, and sometimes he could not write at all. Early in 1855 he was bitten by a dog that was undoubtedly mad; animals bitten by the creature died, and those who knew and loved Samuel had grave fears for him. He grew very ill, and was afflicted with lameness long after the first effects of the bite had disappeared. Inflammatory rheumatism followed this, and Samuel found himself unable to write even the official letters due to the Board. His family wrote for him, as best they could, and the Board replied with admonitions for patience under his affliction. Dr. Pomeroy, someone from the Board wrote, was absent from the Mission Rooms because of inflammatory rheumatism; it was as difficult for the Board as for Samuel to carry on the usual correspondence. The substitute secretary did what he could in Dr. Pomeroy's absence, for "it is about as necessary that we have one Secretary at the Mission House as that one Indian should be sober in a frolic." Then, Samuel and the Board members must realize alike that "we have no immunity by reason of any sacredness of function. No. God would teach us all to be ever looking away to the 'other country'." Samuel felt the reproof that was meant only to lighten his sufferings, and prayed for humility under this chastening. In time he threw off his affliction, and by prodding his limbs and straining his eyes succeeded in accomplishing almost as much as he had done in his most vigorous days. But he had been warned that the time of his labors was short; if he gave the Cherokees their Bible, he must be diligent without ceasing.

Some of his interruptions were happy ones, to offset those that arose from trouble with fellow-missionaries or from illness. The distractions that his family responsibilities offered were always sweet; no duty came between him and quick response to any need of his family. Erminia had developed asthma, and what Samuel diagnosed as "dropsy of the pericardium—all is not right about the heart." He nursed her through her attacks and rejoiced greatly when she improved; and when she was well he had time for all her interests in the house, the community, the school. And for his children, growing older now and showing in their several ways a maturity and a sense of judgment that never ceases to be a surprise to a loving parent, he had an affection that increased and quickened as the years went on. Long after the days of childhood were past, he felt the wonder of parenthood; its richness grew with each enlargement of their interests and activities. John, still in Vermont, had overcome his illness and his homesickness; he was reported to his father as having grown "quite tall and quite musical"; the sensitiveness that had seemed too deep had found a happy outlet in music, to his father's mingled joy and apprehension. For music, much as he loved it, was but a means to an end in Samuel's estimation, and young people must beware of the temptation to make it an end in itself. "If you do take lessons," he wrote warningly to John, "you will have to take great care lest your musical skill should lead to the consumption of too much time in attention to it; and especially lest it should lead you into too much company, cause you to be injured by flattery, and lead you to be little else than a musician. . . . . The care must be—and that care must be great—lest that which should be only secondary and subsidiary, interfere with, or even supersede, that which is primary."[1]

And Samuel's two oldest daughters, rich now in mature graces that still, somehow, took him by surprise, were both engaged to be married. Sarah, teaching at the Female Seminary, was to marry Daniel Dwight Hitchcock as soon as their plans allowed, and so would remain among the Cherokees. Ann Eliza, teaching in the school at Park Hill, would soon leave to marry William S. Robertson and live at Tullahassee among the Creeks to whom William was a missionary. Something very tender and affectionate, the special tenderness of a father for his first-born child, marked Samuel's letter to the Board regarding Ann Eliza's coming marriage. "Do you allow your missionaries to run away, without special leave, before their stipulated time of service is expired, and join another mission? If not, please make haste and give leave to my daughter Ann Eliza, to join the Creek Mission under the General Assembly's Board, for she is expecting to go about the middle of April anyhow; and besides *I* have given her leave, so that, if the Committee don't give it, the blame will be on my shoulders. . . . . One W. S. Robertson, of the above mission, principal of the school at Tullahasse, has obtained from her the promise of herself. . . . . Ann Eliza, however, at first insisted on remaining to teach our school another term, and I suppose would have done so still, but for my advice. Since she resumed her school after the last vacation, she had been sinking under the labor of it, until, before her contract with Mr. R. was closed, I had insisted on her suspending the school for a season. . . . . In a different sphere I

1 Unpublished letter in the Alice Robertson Collection, University of Tulsa, Tulsa, Oklahoma.

hope she may have strength enough to do much good; but the school I do not think she could have safely resumed, at least without a long interval of rest."

Later there was word that Ann Eliza had a daughter; then, in 1854, that a second daughter had been born to her, and that Sarah, married now to Mr. Hitchcock, had a daughter too. In 1856, it was the youngest of the Worcester children, Mary Eleanor, that claimed her father's special attention. She was in very frail health, and Samuel's concern for her was so deep that he was ready to undertake what he had never considered before, —a visit to New England. "It seems just now desirable," he wrote to S. B. Treat, "very much so, to get our youngest daughter, Mary, to New England this coming summer, if we find a good place for her, and if circumstances allow. Her state of health is such, that we cannot trust her without special company; and I do not know that we can find any body to go, unless I go myself. If it should seem practicable—which is very doubtful—and important, may I go?" They wrote him from the Mission Rooms to "come by all means—it is time you made a visit to New England."

But it was not a visit to New England that Samuel sought; it was his youngest child's health. That he must have found, by making the journey, for Mary grew strong and well, married and had children of her own, and lived until 1919, telling from her rich memories fascinating stories of her father Samuel Worcester's life and work among the Indians. Samuel worked incessantly, in preparation for his absence in New England. Knowing that his days were numbered and that the great task appointed to him was far from complete, he felt himself under a stern necessity to lose no time from his translating and printing. Stephen Foreman would preach for him, being paid two dollars each Sunday, while he was away, and would go on with the translations. The press would be occupied with printing the Gospel of Matthew in Creek while he was absent, and then would be free for more printing in Cherokee upon his return. His people and his work must suffer no loss at all, because of his visit to New England.

He had been too busy to think of the changes that were taking place during the long years of his life among the Cherokees. Now, in Vermont once more after an absence of more than thirty years, he found the small changes that had been recorded in letters to him, one by one, had heaped themselves into an overwhelming total. His father was dead and buried at Peacham; the college at Burlington and the seminary at Andover had grown and changed surprisingly; his brothers—young men when he left them —were grey and stooped now. They had never seen these Indians whom he loved and about whom he talked incessantly; the work that had become nearest to him by years of effort lay outside their range of vision; the multiplicity of duties that urged him at Park Hill was foreign to the lives of his kinsmen here. His brothers saw a far-away look in Samuel's eyes; it was the look of a man whose work is calling him. As soon as he had satisfied himself of Mary's welfare, he hurried home again. December, 1856, saw him at Park Hill once more. His report to the Government, for the year ending with the summer of 1857, scarcely indicated his absence from the press. "Since my return," he stated, "we have printed as follows:

Cherokee Almanac, in English
   and Cherokee, 36 pp. 12mo   1000 copies   36,000 pages

Genesis, concluding part, Cherokee

  56 pp. 24to   5000 copies 280,000 pages

First part, *African Servant*, Cherokee

  16 pp. 24to   5000 copies 80,000 pages

Beginning of *Mark*, Cherokee

  24 pp. 24to   1000 copies 24,000 pages

                                              420,000 pages

"There continues to be an earnest desire for more Cherokee books, particularly for more of the scriptures; and we are progressing as fast as possible with the work of translation."[2]

Back in Burlington, Vermont, the university that was his alma mater sought to honor this son who had gone to the Cherokees. They conferred the degree of Doctor of Divinity on him, in recognition of his work as a scholar in linguistics. He found himself referred to by the Board, and addressed in letters, as Dr. Worcester. The honor embarrassed him. They could not know, he thought, how little of the scholar's life was possible for a missionary. Building churches, painting banners, devising pumps, composing jingles, making accounts balance—these things had no relation to scholarship. Samuel took time for a brief letter of deprecation of this honor to which he could lay no honest claim.

"PARK HILL, Sept. 1, 1857

Rev. S. B. Treat,

DEAR SIR,

"I am informed that the 'University of Vermont,' hard pushed, it would seem, for timber to make doc-

2 Bureau of Indian Affairs, *Annual Report*, 1857, p. 215.

tors of, have dubbed me **D.D.** Please omit that mark in the publications of the Board, and in superscribing and addressing letters to me.

Yours truly,

S. A. WORCESTER"

Thus having put aside the honor paid him as a linguistic scholar, he hurried on with his translations.

And There Was Light

YEARS did not curb the multiplicity of Samuel Worcester's interests, or diminish the keenness of his undertakings. He found no need to leave Park Hill for any renewal or enrichment; he stood fixed there, in the center of an ever widening circle of life's fullnesses. What had begun as an isolated, struggling mission among a transplanted and unhappy people had become an institution scarcely able to fill all the demands upon its church and school and press; what had been a doubtful venture, even in the small world it was meant to serve, now drew that small world to its doors and had its share of importance in the larger world outside.

The Male and Female seminaries were now both flourishing schools with suitable buildings, teachers of the highest qualifications that New England could send out, and the best blood of the Cherokee Nation in attendance. Their public examinations, conducted at the end of each school year, were great events that gave large audiences proof of the students' attainments in classrooms, in music, and in decorum. A copy of the program for the public examination which closed the year 1855 at the Female Seminary remains. This is probably the principal's copy, hastily written out for her own use in conducting the exercises; but it affords the reader today, as the exercises themselves afforded the attending audience on that August day, evidence of what Samuel Worcester had been able to achieve in the seminaries under his supervision:[1]

"CHEROKEE FEMALE SEMINARY
Order of exercises
for
Examination day—Aug. 1, 1855
Devotions—7¼—7½
h m—h m

Geography. . . . . .7-30—7-50. . . . . .Miss Raymond
Latin. . . . . .7-50—8-15. . . . . . .   "   Avery
Arithmetic. . . . . .8-15—9-00. . . . . . .   "   Ross
Rhetoric. . . . . .9-00—9-30. . . . . . .   "   Raymond
Geometry
   Star of Twilight. . . .9 ½—10¼ 'Abou Ben Adem [*sic*]
Miss Avery
Physiology. . . . . .10¼—11¼. . . . . . .   "   Ross
Recess 11-50
Algebra. . . . . .11-50—12-20. . . . . .   "   Raymond
Intellectual
   Philosophy. . . . . . .12-20—1 . . . . . .   "   Avery
Dinner 1—1½
Nat. Theology. . . . . . . .1 ½—2 ¼ 'Merry goes the time'
Miss Raymond
Evidences of
   Christianity. . . . . . . .2 ¼—3   Music. .   "   Avery
We plough the fertile meadow
Paper—& Marks—3¾
Singing—'I'm going home'."

Through his children, too, Samuel now saw his own undertakings enlarged and strengthened. Ann Eliza,

1   MS in the Alice Robertson Collection, University of Tulsa, Tulsa, Oklahoma.

living happily with her husband and her little girls in the Creek Mission at Tullahassee, seemed to have some of her father's fine power of adaptability. Even the hindrance of frail health in the early years of her married life she turned to advantage, for the time she must spend resting on her lounge she devoted to studying and translating Creek. She had a gift for languages and a gift for people; when she spoke their words affection warmed her voice, and the Creeks called her their mother. There remains among her papers a copy of an article, written for children, about the Muskogees; simple as it is, it illustrates her gentle skill as a teacher and her knowledge of Indian languages.

"THE MUSKOKEES

"I wonder how many of you in studying U. S. History have noticed the name Muskokee, (spelt in different ways,) as belonging to a body of warlike Indians in the South. They sometimes made trouble for the people of the U.S., but much more frequently fought on their side.

"Hon. Wm. P. Ross of the Cherokee Nation made an address on our 'examination day,' at Tullahassee nearly ten years ago, in which he talked to the Creeks assembled there about their past history, from which I will quote a little. He says, 'the existence of the Muskokees dates from unknown generations before the record of man. Whence they came meets with no response from the uncertain voice of tradition. They lived and fought and died beneath the genial skies which overhang the Alabama Chatta-hoochee and the Altamaha, before the adventurous prow of Columbus sought these western shores. For more than three centuries and a half have their euphonious words and warlike deeds helped to swell the records of the New World.'

"Then he goes on to speak of their driving the Spaniards away from Florida in 1512 & 1528, and later and farther west of their defeating Hernando de Soto, (helped by other Indians,) after long fighting, in which 'thousands of the simple and unarmed natives' had been driven before him.

"He speaks of the welcome a Muskokee chief gave to Gen'l Oglethorpe, in 1733, when he began the city of Savannah.

"I think those of you who study U.S.History will be interested in looking for mention of the Muskokees. There are six different languages spoken among them, for they are a confederacy, that is five tribes have been added to the Muskokees, and are now called by their name. But all of these, except one, use the Muskokee language also, so that, when I am translating for them, I may have the pleasure of knowing that the book can be read by them all except the Yoochees, whose language is so different from the Muskokee that but few of them learn that. They did not join the Muskokees of their own accord, but were conquered by them many years ago. They have the same rights as others, but are somewhat kept back by their hard language (or rather, I should say, by its being different from others). How I wish they had a good missionary to translate books for them, and tell them about Jesus in their own tongue!

"The Seminoles, too, once belonged to the Creeks, and speak their language; so, when I translate, I am working for them as well as for the Creeks. (The Creeks call themselves Muskokees, and it is said that the white people named them Creeks, because they found so many of them living along the creeks and rivers in the South.) Seminole means *wild*, and the Creeks named them so, because they wandered away from them.

"Now, you will not wonder so much that Mr. Ross speaking of the Muskokee warriors could say, 'Their bones are at Talladega, Tolossehatche,' (Chicken creek), 'Emak-fau and Tohopke,' (A fort). 'Ay, not only there, but scattered from the Gulf to the Ohio, from the Neuse to the source of the Arkansas.'

"I should love to stand before you with a large map of the United States, and point out to you names of towns and rivers which came from the Muskokees. Natches, Mississippi, is named from one of the bands that joined the Creeks, and Alabama from another. Coosa River has the name which the Cherokees give the Creeks, Chatta-hoochee means *a rock written upon*, and Withlakoochee, *a little river*. And so I might go on, showing you from these names how large a country was once theirs. Now look on the map of the United States at the Indian Territory, and measure with your eye about one twelfth of it, and you will see what a small country they now have, and I am sure you will not wonder that it makes me feel very badly to hear even good white people insisting on having it cut up into sections, so as to let the white people have a part of it. This would take them again from the homes they have chosen, and break them all up again. Like all the other Indians, and just as you would be, they were entirely unwilling to give up their dear southern home, but, on the promise that, if they would, this country should be theirs forever, they came. But oh how many of them died in consequence! I was a little girl then, but I remember how I pitied them, when I heard of their suf-ferings. They were just becoming fairly settled and pros-

[331]

perous once more, when the Civil War, which began in 1861, drove them hither and thither, and for five years they were homeless again, and their graves are scattered from southern Kansas to Texas. On their return they again had to build new homes, or rebuild the old ones.

"And now don't you think, as I do, that they ought to be allowed to hold their little country in peace, and so missionaries be able to go on with preaching, translating, and mission and boarding schools among them until they become a christian people.?"[2]

In William Schenk Robertson, Ann Eliza's husband, Samuel Worcester found a man after his own heart. They were both men of wide and varied abilities, on whom the avowal of Christianity had laid an unlimited responsibility, and to whom it brought a correspondingly wide range of satisfactions. To them both, agriculture was a concern that had some close, if unexplainable, relation to religion; they found nothing incongruous in the compilation for the Indians of an almanac offering agricultural advice and Christian precepts on the same page. Both men found a delight in William's friendship with the entomologist Asa Fitch, dating from earlier days when William and Asa had hunted insects together; and they held it a privilege now to gather specimens from this territory "west of Arkansas" to send to the entomologist in New York. By such links they bound themselves to the great world of progress outside the Indian country. There was reward for all the labor of catching and mounting and sending off specimens, in Asa's rare letters to William; such letters declared an indebtedness to Park Hill and Tullahassee, and joined these remote Indian missions with great ventures in science and culture.

2   MS in the Alice Robertson Collection, University of Tulsa, Tulsa, Oklahoma.

"Scarcely a day passes," Asa wrote on April 25, 1857, in a hand as fine as engraving, "but what I write in my Manuscripts 'Tullehassie W. Ark.; from W. S. Robertson' and sometimes write that item half a dozen times a day. Nearly half the American species in my collection have been gathered by you. And I verily believe with the exception of Mrs. R. you are present *in my mind* more than in that of any other person living. And yet more than a year has slipped by since I wrote you. . . . . But however much I neglect others, I ought not to neglect you. You are my *right hand man;* I owe more to you than any body, yes, than to *every body* else who have gathered insects for me. All that others have sent me does not equal in amount & value what I have received from you. You have been the making of me, as the saying is:—at least, take away what you have sent me, and half the material which I have to work upon would be gone. So, though I do neglect you, I cannot forget you; I cannot take in hand half a dozen specimens without finding one or more of them registered 'Tullehassie.'. . . .

"The box you speak of having sent last fall, has been received I presume; for I find specimens registered from you last year—one of them a grasshopper, ticketed 'Park Hill, July 11, very numerous and destructive' and a fly 'Swamp horse fly.'. . . . I have also a pile of letters with quills, &c, from you—several of them received since I wrote to you. It is not in my power to find leisure to open these & pin & put away the specimens—though I know I shall find many valuable specimens among them. But they are all safely preserved, with the accompanying letters; and I hope in a year or two to have an assistant, to do up all this back work that is accumulating more & more on my hands—and perform the drudgery that I cannot and ought not to waste my time upon. So keep on sending me all you can. It will all be safely preserved, & will some time be overhauled, and everything put in order, for me to study out. . . . In this way, I anticipate that everything you send me, will be preserved, and will continue to be doing good service to science, for many years after we are laid in our graves, as we shall be, ere many years. . . . .

"But I have written double the amount I thought of doing when I began this. I must bring it to a close. I shall by the first opportunity, send to the Mission Rooms at New York, for you, one of my Paris boxes, for you to fill with Lepidoptera—especially the small butterflies and moths—as I have had fewer of these from you than of other insects—and there must be a great many new & interesting kinds around you. I am studying these insects pretty thoroughly, & want a full supply of the Southern species. They get broken & spoiled, worse than any other insects, by the pins falling down in the box; but the box I will send, being lined with cork, will hold every pin securely. I will send with it pins & other conveniencies for you; and also my *Second Report*. A few days ago, I was looking at a little yellow butterfly from you, smaller than your little finger nail. Lo—it belongs to a new genus, formed by Boisduval, for a Mexican species in his collection. This will be a second species in the same genus. I would not part with that little butterfly for a dollar."[3]

Was there something about a missionary's faith, that could turn even a Park Hill grasshopper, ticketed "very numerous and destructive," to good account? At any rate

3 Unpublished letter in the Alice Robertson Collection, University of Tulsa, Tulsa, Oklahoma.

it became a bit of valuable information for the first American economic entomologist, Asa Fitch.

But while Samuel Worcester might glorify a grasshopper, he could never be accused of glorifying any of his own children unduly. Their faults were undiminished when seen through their father's eyes. Ann Eliza might be the mother of three children and a valued teacher and translator among the Creeks, but she drew her father's reproof in 1856, for her failure to date her letters carefully. Samuel wrote her a letter concerning that fault of carelessness into which she had lately fallen, making no allowance for Ann Eliza's ill health and implying that any letter worth writing is worth writing properly. "Then today," the reproof continued, "I was filing a few letters. I file by date. But I took up another from you, and found no date to file by. But enough of this. I guess you will hereafter make it a point to date your letters."[4]

He had written with similar frankness and fatherly precision to John, in 1855. "In one of your letters you said you were 'afraid?' you should never be a Methodist. I suppose you alluded to the doctrine of perfection. The nearer you attain to perfection, if we know of it, the more we shall rejoice. If you should *quite* attain it, and we know it, we should indeed rejoice over you with exceeding great joy. But, having no hope that you will ever make that attainment, we hope you will never *imagine* that you have made it; but will always be able to see enough of your own sinfulness, to keep you ever humble before God, and ever striving to attain what is yet before you. But, my dear Son, let not the fact that you have not attained what 'no mere man, since the fall,' ever did attain, keep you from

4 Letter in the Alice Robertson Collection, University of Tulsa, Tulsa, Oklahoma.

[335]

enjoying the consolations of religion, or from performing the duties of a Christian."[5]

In the same letter, Samuel added a postscript containing family news. Black Sukey, the cook, was ill, and therefore Mary—who was with her sister Ann Eliza at Tullahassee attending the school there—had been called home to Park Hill to do what she could in the kitchen, "till we can contrive some other way. The school at Tullahassee began day before yesterday. Yesterday was National Temperance Meeting, and Mary played the melodeon. Made out well enough to do." He might have boasted, if he had been a vain and overproud father, that he had a daughter of fifteen who could meet an emergency in the mission kitchen and play the melodeon for a great temperance gathering, all in the same day. But he indulged in no boasting. To him, Park Hill was as a light that shone in the darkness, and he was the keeper of that light. He must keep it trimmed and burning, at all costs. His own family knew his responsibility, and respected him for measuring them by a standard as high and uncompromising as that by which he measured his own efforts.

Early in their lives, the grandchildren came to understand their grandfather's position at Park Hill and to mingle their respect for him—his learning, his authority among the Cherokees, his grace of manner and mind—with great affection. A visit to grandfather's was a happy event to anticipate and a memory to cherish ever afterward. Miss Alice Robertson, even late in her life, had vivid memories of the Robertson children's visits to Park Hill and left an account of some of her recollections.

"In going from Tullahassee to grandfather's mission at Park Hill we usually had to cross the Verdigris, and

5 Letter in the Alice Robertson Collection, University of Tulsa, Tulsa, Oklahoma.

then the Grand, and sometimes by a ferry which took us from what was called the 'Point' on the Arkansas, so that other rivers were crossed, the Arkansas, Verdigris and Grand. Usually, however, we crossed on one of the fords. Rock formations made the water shallow, the Verdigris being a deep and narrow stream, running through a thin formation from the Grand. The waters of the Verdigris were usually turbid, while the Grand, except at flood tide, was clear as crystal, running from many bubbling springs in the lime-stone region, and filtering over pebbly bottoms. It was never safe to attempt to ford the Grand or Illinois without knowing absolutely the ford, because what looked like three feet was likely to be thirty. When I was but six years old, in our trips to grandfather's we had a balky horse, and just in the deepest part of the ford in the Grand he decided to go no farther. The water was running into the wagon, we could not help getting wet, though there was no danger of our being washed away; some men came on horse-back and attempted all sorts of measures to make the balky horse move, one tied a knot in his tail and twisted it. Another prodded him behind his ears, but he just got more stubborn, until finally they took him out and put another horse in, and led him gloriously triumphant up the bank. It spoiled our day, because instead of stopping on the Bayou Manard where we used to eat our luncheon—and we always counted so on feeding crumbs to the little fishes that came in great numbers to be fed—we had to eat our luncheon jolting along in the wagon and could not dip our cups in the spring for a cool drink.

"The early missionaries, of necessity, great scholars though they might be, indulged daily in manual labor. My grandfather used to milk the cows. I remember him bringing brimming buckets of milk which he carried over his shoulder, on what was called a yoke, and there were two pet cats to keep the mice out of the house and the barn, they used to follow the path down to the milk lot and come rubbing against grandfather's trousers, and mewing happily, to the stone steps. Grandfather had chiselled two shallow receptacles, and the frothing milk was poured out for the cats. And that was always one of the features of going to grandpa's—to see the cats fed.

"And then there was a mocking bird, and when there was family prayer in the morning and grandfather led the singing and my aunt played the little melodian, he used to chime in and try to follow the music of the hymn.

"A very wonderful thing in going to grandfather's in the Tullahassee summer vacation was the seeing, on Sundays, the Murrill coach, as it was drawn up with its liveried coachman and footman to the plain little mission church. Mr. Murrill was a Louisiana sugar planter who had married Miss ——— Ross, and so had, under the old-time laws, the rights to a home in the Cherokee Nation. The house on the Murrill place stands yet, and while it shows the ravages of time, and much weather beaten, since statehood it has passed from one owner to another until now it is being restored to its former glory by its most recent purchaser. I remember spending the night there as a little girl, and having to climb up the steps to the great four-poster [by the ladder] that even grown folks had to use, and which was big enough for several people to sleep in comfortably. There was wonderful mahogany furniture, each [piece] of which was later carried back to Louisiana, some every year. The Murrill place was kept always as though its owner lived there, the manager-overseer having a sufficient number of slaves under his control to tend the farm, the orchard, to look after all the details of a comfortable planter's home, so when they came up in summer time, the smoke house was well filled with wonderful cured meats, hams, etc. Chicken and turkeys abounded, and there was abundance of wild game also in the nearby mountains.

"I particularly remember the occasion of a double funeral, two [members] of my grandfather's church, a young Ross and a daughter of the Rev. Stephen Foreman, a Cherokee minister and my grandfather's assistant, died at the same time, and the family services were conducted at the same time, but they were buried at different places. On the box of the coach was the negro coachman, with high cocked hat and uniform. The dress of the planter himself was the old southern style, while Mrs. Murrill,— I was six years old but I remember perfectly well,—wore a voluminous flounced silk, with the mantle heavily bedecked with spangles which glittered in the sunlight with every movement. I thought Mr. Murrill must be the richest man in all the world."[6]

This was Park Hill, seen through the eyes of a little girl. For a Louisiana planter, for an entomologist in New York, even for a mocking bird that chose to make its home in the trees outside the mission house, it shed its particular light, continuous and clear.

6 Unpublished typescript in the Alice Robertson Collection, University of Tulsa, Tulsa, Oklahoma.

The Messenger Goes Home

SCARCELY any time remained. And of that precious little, much must be given to other matters than the translating and printing of the Scriptures. Once it was a charge of abolitionism that was brought against Samuel Worcester, but he made short work of it and sent Mr. Treat word of the accusation, explaining, "There has been no excitement, that I have heard of, nor have I recently said anything in my preaching on the subject of slavery." He inclosed the Cherokee Agent's letter to him, and his reply.

"Tahlequah, C. N., June 30, 1858
"Sir—You have been reported to me as an abolitionist, teaching and preaching in opposition to the institution of slavery in this Nation.
"You will please attend immediately to the truth or falsehood of this charge.
Very respectfully,
George Butler,
U. S. Indian Agent"

"Park Hill, July 2, 1858
George Butler, Esq.,
Cherokee Agent,

SIR:

"I have received your note of day before yesterday, calling upon me to answer to charges presented to you against me. I plead not guilty.

Yours respectfully,

S. A. WORCESTER"

Perhaps the very simplicity of Samuel's denial was the convincing evidence that Mr. Butler needed. At any rate, nothing came of this threatened difficulty. Indeed, Stand Watie, whose sympathies were with the slaveholders, came to him soon afterward with a list of petitioners who asked for a missionary at Honey Creek; Watie and his fellows, it was obvious, had no fear of Samuel's partisanship. Samuel was greatly moved by this desire for a missionary in a new section of the Cherokee Nation; it was an encouragement that he had scarcely hoped for, in these times of disturbance and misunderstanding. The peace of the whole nation seemed threatened over the question of slavery; there were some who declared that the issue would never be settled without a war. At such a time, it was good to know that Stand Watie and his friends could turn their thoughts to the need in their community of a missionary.

Other difficulties were less readily solved than that of Mr. Butler's charge. Stephen Foreman had been called to Texas, where his wife had gone with their daughter, a consumptive. Nothing final could be written and made ready for printing, while he was away. Mr. Torrey had learned the language with a rapidity that gratified Samuel, but he had other mission duties besides that of translating, and he could not give that final approval to every passage that a native scholar could give. Whether or not he had

[341]

any claim to honors from the University of Vermont, Samuel Worcester maintained this uncompromising standard for all his translation of the Scriptures.

Another handicap was the sudden lack of funds that confronted them. The slavery question absorbed the minds and the interests of people throughout the country; they scented war, and held back what they had formerly given to missions. For the year 1858, only three hundred dollars were available for printing and binding at the Indian Press. Samuel was bewildered by the blow that this announcement brought. In March he could still see no way to surmount his difficulty. "We are now printing 1 Corinthians. 2 Corinthians is also ready for the press, and we are in the 8th Chapter of Romans. But suddenly our work is suspended.

"How we shall get along in regard to the curtailment of our appropriations for translating and printing I do not know. When all are urging us forward in the work of giving the scriptures to the Cherokees, it will be hard to stop for want of funds. In regard to translating, *if it is only for one year*, I can, *perhaps*, keep along, because I am considerably in advance with Mr. Foreman; but I do not see how we can curtail printing expenses, without stopping short, when the appropriation is exhausted. If I could canvas the whole Cherokee Nation, preaching on the subject at every preaching place of every denomination, and could take up collections for the purchase of Cherokee books, I could probably get enough. But that I cannot do."

But before more funds for printing were needed, Samuel was ill. By the fall of 1858 he was obliged to spend much time in bed, and to do his writing with a pencil, lying down, because of what he called "local rheumatism."

Carbuncles appeared on his back, till he could lie only on his face or his sides, and lameness in his hips gave him great pain. In such a reclining position he could scarcely work by candlelight; and the short winter days gave few hours of good daylight. But Stephen Foreman returned, and they worked together whenever Samuel could command the strength for it. Even in his pain, it gratified him to feel that they were making progress with a manuscript that would be ready to print when more funds were available.

In March, 1859, when spring had begun to brighten the hills and the prairie flowers were patches of color in the wild grass, Samuel had hoped to improve. There was warmth in the air, and the sunshine of the Southwest—of a burning brightness that no native of Vermont has ever seen in his own state—sent down strong arms of light. But they had no power to lift Samuel Worcester from his bed, or pour strength into his aching bones. Never before had spring failed to renew his vitality. He knew, because his mind grew clearer as his body weakened, that "this present sickness is my last."

And his work was not yet done. "We have now only the principal part of the *Epistle to the Hebrews*, the *Epistle of Jude*, & two thirds of the *Book of Revelation* lacking, to complete the N. Testament. I had much set my heart on the completion of this work; but God is wise. To Him I would humbly submit the case, chiefly praying, that at whatever time, & through whatever suffering he shall see fit to call me away, I may be enabled by his grace, to bear all without murmuring, & to honor Him, whether in life or in death."

On the fourth of April, he wrote his last letter to the Board. His hand was very unsteady now, and his penmanship was scarcely legible; but he must write, for the sake of Stand Watie and his friends, to urge the Board to send a missionary to Honey Creek. He believed, personally, in the abolition of slavery; but he prayed that no such issue as that of slave-owning would prevent the sending of a missionary to a community that petitioned for one.

After that, Samuel had no more strength for letter-writing. He concentrated all the force that was left to him on the unfinished work that he was leaving behind, and laid plans for its completion under Mr. Torrey. He remembered where everything was in the printing shop, and under his direction Mr. Torrey packed boxes that were to go to the New York Bible Society, arranged manuscripts for the next printing, made notes on the translations that he and Stephen Foreman were to complete. The last days were strangely busy ones, for a man whose body awaited its release. Sometimes he must rest for a long time, before he could command enough strength to explain a new point or give a further direction. But at last it was all done. Mr. Torrey knew, as well as he, the state of every manuscript and the plans for the rest of the translating and the printing. There was nothing more to do now, but to thank them all—he told them they had been inexpressibly kind —and then to go. *Thessalonians*, *Titus*, *Philemon*, and part of *Hebrews* had been finished in spite of pain and weariness and the inconvenience of lying on his face much of the time; now this young Torrey, fresh from Andover and with strength and intelligence given him for the task, must go on with what was still to be done.

On the twentieth of April, early in the morning, word went about among the Cherokees that their Messenger had gone home. He had left them the Heaven-Book in their own tongue, they said.

They buried him in the burial ground at Park Hill, where Ann had lain without him nineteen years. And they wrote a few words on his stone, telling in the inadequate way of words what he had done for them: "For 34 years a Missionary of the American Board of Commissioners for Foreign Missions among the Cherokees. To his work they owe their Bible and their Hymn Book."

The Cherokees have long since forgotten the theology that Samuel taught them with thoroughness and persistence, as the only final truth. Indeed, they probably never grasped it, with their Indian consciousness. But they remember something more vital than a system of theology. Even now, to the third and fourth generation, they remember that a good man came among them, and cast his lot with theirs. When they were sick, he was their physician; when they were in trouble, he suffered imprisonment for them; when they were exiled, he shared their banishment. Words, of which he was so great a master, were not needed for the lesson he taught them. They learned a way of life from him, and they have not forgotten it.

Index

Sanford, Col. 131, 132.
Sargeant, John, 154.
Sargent, Delight, 251, 256.
Sawyer, Sophia: 118-119, 122, 136, 153; letter of, 119-121.
Schermerhorn, J. F., 169, 170, 172, 198.
Sequoyah, *see* Guess, George.
Slavery, 233-239, 340-341.

T

Tahlequah, 228, 257, 301, 340.
Temperance, 85-87, 212, 226-233, 336.
Thompson, John, 130, 136, 163.
Thompson, Nancy, 53, 249, 260.
Tollunteeskee, 72.
Torrey, Charles C., 299, 341-344.
Treat, S. B., 323, 325.
Tullahassee, 322, 329, 332, 333, 336, 338.

U

Underwood, Judge, 154, 156.
Union Mission, 180, 182-185, 189, 193, 194-197, 206, 217.

V

Vann, John, 75, 121, 146, 162, 174, 184, 185.

W

Watie, Stand, 174, 256, 344.
Wheeler, John: 64-65, 128, 137, 183, 185, 186, 190-193, 198, 200, 202; account by, 80-83.
White Path, 38, 177.
Wirt, William, 154, 158.
Womankiller, speech of, 111-112.

Wool, General, 171, 173.
Worcester, Ann Eliza: 67-68, 121, 137, 158, 222, 264, 271, 301, 323, 335, 336; letters of, 272, 273-275; account by, 329-332.
Worcester, Ann Orr: 15, 21, 51-55, 58, 60, 115-117, 131-132, 146-147, 260-261, 268; letter of, 151-153, 216.
Worcester, Hannah, 175, 194.
Worcester, Isaac, 156, 276, 289.
Worcester, Jerusha, 131, 136-137.
Worcester, John, 268, 269, 271, 276.
Worcester, John Orr, 209, 217, 260, 272, 287-289, 321-322, 335.
Worcester, Leonard, 197, 217, 260, 272, 289.
Worcester, Mary Eleanor, 260, 323, 336.
Worcester, Samuel, 19, 29, 242.
Worcester, Samuel Austin, letters of, 22-25, 26-27, 28, 44-48, 51-52, 53-54, 60-66, 84-86, 92-93, 93-94, 94-95, 98-103, 121, 123, 124, 125, 126, 126-127, 128, 132-136, 138, 148-151, 155-156, 181-182, 182-186, 187-190, 191, 191-192, 192-193, 193-194, 196, 197, 198-199, 199-201, 203-204, 204-205, 205-206, 207, 207-208, 209-210, 210-212, 212-213, 214, 215-216, 217-220, 222, 223-224, 226-227, 228-230, 233, 235-237, 240-242, 242-244, 247, 251, 265-266, 272, 276, 276-277, 287-289, 300-303, 304-307, 314, 315-316, 317, 318-319, 322-326, 335, 336, 340-341, 342.
Worcester, Sarah: 118, 137, 159, 194, 195, 264, 277, 286, 322, 323; account by, 278-285.
Worthy, Thomas, letter of, 142-143.
Wright, Alfred, 33, 234.

Y

Youth's Companion, 119, 136, 156, 196.
Yanugunski, 38.

UNIVERSITY OF OKLAHOMA PRESS : NORMAN, OKLAHOMA